Tatum's Town

Tatum's Town

The Story of Jazz in Toledo, Ohio
1915-1985

By Bob Dietsche

Bobson Press
Brooklyn, NY

Publisher's Cataloging-in-Publication
(Provided by Quality Books, Inc.)

Dietsche, Robert, author.
   Tatum's town : the story of jazz in Toledo, Ohio, 1915-1985 / by Bob Dietsche. -- First edition.
   pages cm
   Includes bibliographical references and index.
   LCCN 2017903934
   ISBN 978-0-692-76513-5

   1. Jazz--Ohio--Toledo--History and criticism.
2. Jazz musicians--Ohio--Toledo. 3. Nightclubs--Ohio--Toledo. I. Title.

ML3508.8.T65D54 2017   781.6509771'13
                           QBI17-900038

Bobson Press
111 Butler Street,
Brooklyn, NY 11231

© 2016 Robert Dietsche
All rights reserved.
First edition 2017
Printed in the United States of America

Cover Design by Don Dietsche
Book Design and layout by Anuprita Deshpande

DEDICATION
For El Myers

Contents

Foreword		xi
Acknowledgments		xiii
Who's Who in *Tatum's Town*		xv
Introduction: Great Moments in Toledo Jazz		xxi

Chapter 1	Mount Tatum	1
Chapter 2	Badman's Territory	11
Chapter 3	Speed Webb and the Territory Bands	15
Chapter 4	Appointment in Toledo	21
Chapter 5	House Busters	27
Chapter 6	Jon Hendricks – A Lyricist Supreme	31
Chapter 7	Jack Runyan – Thanks for the Memories	35
Chapter 8	Centennial Terrace – "Some Enchanted Evening"	41
Chapter 9	Arv Garrison – Parker's Guitar	53
Chapter 10	Buddy and El	65
Chapter 11	Jazz Goes to High School (DeVilbiss)	75
Chapter 12	Jazz Goes to College	85
Chapter 13	The Case Against Jazz	91
Chapter 14	The Willard-Dempsey Fight	97
Chapter 15	Jimmy Harrison – "The Toledo Terror"	99
Chapter 16	Action at the Green Mill	105
Chapter 17	Cakewalkin' at Tony Packo's	111
Chapter 18	The Joy of Sax	113
Chapter 19	Candy Johnson – Both Sides of the Street	121
Chapter 20	Claude, Cliff, the Detroit Connection	127
Chapter 21	The Man Behind the Mast	137
Chapter 22	Gene Parker – The Head Master	145
Chapter 23	Jack Walter in the Land of the Giants	149
Chapter 24	Fred & Preston – Last of the Lounge Players	155
Chapter 25	Horatio Hornblower	161
Chapter 26	Jimmy Cook – "Nobody's Better"	165
Chapter 27	Rusty's Jazz Café – "She Coulda Been Mayor"	171

Afterword		179
Endnotes		180
Bibliography		187
Index		190

"Do not tell me only ... of the magnitude of your industry and commerce; of the beneficence of your institutions, your freedom, your equality; of the great and growing number of your churches and schools, libraries and newspapers; tell me also if your civilization—which is the grand name you give to all this development—tell me if your civilization is interesting."

Matthew Arnold

Foreword

What defines Toledo? What gives it confidence and character? What tells its story in a way that makes its citizens proud, self-assured, and happy to be living here? Toledo may lack a great landscape. People don't move here for the mountain air. Toledo may be a blue-collar town with not much urbane, cosmopolitan sophistication. Yet, it still has a stellar cultural landscape. Bob Dietsche tells us about Toledo in ways never told before. He tells the story of a town's association with jazz music—not something you see, but you hear. But Dietsche will not only help you hear it, he will make you see it.

Dietsche, a DeVilbiss High School graduate, has been a Northwest Coast resident most of his adult life. He spent his formative years in Toledo and returned many times researching Toledo's music history. A jazz historian, columnist, and critic, he authored a book on Portland, Oregon jazz and has written a number of articles over the years on Portland and Toledo's jazz history. Curiously, both cities, so unlike in many ways, are not so unlike when it comes to jazz. As Dietsche has pointed out in his book *Jump Town: The Golden Years of Portland Jazz, 1942-1957*, "Inland seaports with great railroads make for great jazz...."

Dietsche is a graduate of the University of Oregon with a Master's Degree in Liberal Studies from Reed College. He taught English and composition in high school and college, taught jazz history at area community colleges, and hosted jazz radio shows. He plays piano, instructs, and, as one Oregonian music critic stated, he is "one of the most knowledgeable people on the subject of jazz." Well-known to Portland music enthusiasts and artists, Dietsche owned and operated the famed Django Record Company in downtown Portland from 1977 to 1999, a legendary used-record store.

Dietsche knows jazz. He discovered jazz as a teenager listening to Windsor's CKLW radio, watching the Disney film *Make Mine Music*, and attending live concerts at Toledo's Sports Arena. He writes about the money and time spent as a young man at Seligman's Record Bar, a West Toledo hangout for record buffs, with the largest collection of 45s east of the Mississippi River. At age 17 he attended the performances of Les Brown and Woody Herman at Centennial Terrace, an event he recalls as the most exciting music experience of his lifetime. His high school and college years were spent listening to jazz. He writes about Toledo jazz greats at DeVilbiss High School while he was there: Arv Garrison, Charlie Mewhort, and Bob White, as well the young jazz fans like Fred Lutz, who later became a well-known *Toledo Blade* movie and book critic. As a college student, he attended concerts at the Toledo Museum of Art's Peristyle to hear jazz greats Stan Kenton, Don Shirley, Duke Ellington, and the Dave Brubeck Quartet. These experiences and the early exposure to jazz shaped him, to be sure. They also helped meld jazz and Toledo for Dietsche. Dietsche knows Toledo. *Tatum's Town* tells the story of the saloons, the after-hours joints, the speakeasies, the dive bars, the honky-tonks, the classy nightclubs, cocktail lounges, and supper clubs that today are mostly long gone. The jazz venues, known at one time to almost every Toledoan, now largely forgotten, are summoned back. He remembers summer evenings sixty years ago at the famed outdoor ballroom, Centennial Terrace, near Sylvania, Ohio, dancing with the big bands of the early '50s. He recalls Toledo's great hot spots: the Trianon Ballroom on Madison Avenue, the city's most famous dance club, the Aku-Aku, perhaps the town's last nightclub, the Chateau La France, a three-story mansion, Kin Wa Low's, a hugely popular downtown Chinese restaurant and cabaret, Tony Packo's Cakewalkin' Jass Band, Murphy's and Fifi's jazz clubs, and the legendary and nationally known Rusty's Jazz Café, once the third oldest jazz club in the country.

Great jazz was not always played in great places. In Toledo it began and thrived in more dangerous, dimmer, and not-so-lofty quarters. Jazz was born here in the tenderloin in the city's brothels, gaming halls, and juke joints where there were copious amounts of alcohol, drugs, and bar girls. Dietsche tells us the lost history of the seedy underside of the town, with stories about places long gone, like Chicken Charlie's, the Waiters and Bellman's Club, the Tabernilla, Herman's, the Dixie Villa, and the Dixon Hotel. He describes how the Willard-Dempsey fight in Toledo in 1919 attracted jazz musicians who, over time, filled the music halls and gin joints with great jazz talent. He tells the story of Toledo's bad guys who ran the town and brutalized Toledo in the 1930s.

Dietsche knows music. He knows how it is played and why. *Tatum's Town* is not only a history lesson, but also a lesson in understanding an art form. Toledo's jazz greats are all here to teach us. Interviews he conducted with numerous Toledoans tell Toledo's jazz story in fascinating detail. The stories and anecdotes of Toledoans such as Art Tatum, Jack Runyan, Johnny Knorr, Candy Johnson, El Myers, Buddy Sullivan, Gene Parker, Bill Takas, John Mast, and Jimmy Harrison give us a history of music we want to listen to. There is here an element of surprise. Toledo has, as Dietsche teaches us, an incredible music history, sometimes hidden away, but not yet forgotten.

Toledo is Art Tatum's town. The greatest jazz piano player of all time was born here and played here. We have something to memorialize, to take enormous pride in, and to celebrate. *Tatum's Town* spreads the word.

James C. Marshall
2014

Acknowledgments

To Fred Lutz, Lee Raymond, Jay Hoffman, Nick Ceroli, Steve Calvert, Dick Querl, and Bernie Kehoe for turning my ears in the right direction.

To Mrs. Perkins at DeVilbiss High School for showing how a sentence works and to Don Black and Morrison Van Cleve for providing some self esteem.

To Tom Josephson for his vivid memories of DeVilbiss and to Joan Culp Theilman for conversations 35 years ago that sparked an idea for a book.

I was lucky to have had such teachers as Norman Stone, Ray Krebsbaugh and Pete Exline at Eastern Washington, Herb Nelson at Oregon State, Kester Svendsen at the University of Oregon and Charles Svittofsky, David Tyack, and Kenneth Hanson at the Reed College.

To Mary Kennington Lang, Dave Frishberg, Phil Stanford, and the late Jack Berry for convincing me I had something to say.

To Leo Ostransky, Joe Mosbrook, and the team of Bjorn and Gallert for books I could have not done without.

To the Toledo-Lucas County Public Library's local history department and especially Jim Marshall whose contributions were indispensible.

To Toledo's history detectives, Bonnie and Ken Dickson, whose delving and gleaning produced Chapter 18.

To Gene Confer for ten years of piano therapy.

To Marge Jay whose help on Jack Runyan was indispensible.

To JDD who made me get an education.

To my editor, Donna (Eagle Eye) Christian who can spot lint on a bowling ball, a big thank you.

To my love, Susan, without whom this book would still be in pieces of scrap paper.

Who's Who in *Tatum's Town*

Abrams, Eddie, "The Detroit Funnel" (1926-1997): the house pianist at Rusty's Jazz Café and patient mentor to the young at jazz

Austin, Cuba (1906-1961): innovative show drummer with the McKinney's Cotton Pickers, in Toledo off and on in 1925 and 1926

Austin, Harold "Dean" (1929-2000): a most melodic drummer who became the third horn in some small combos

Barefield, Eddie (1909-1991): Swing era star, saxophonist, and arranger who came to Toledo to arrange for Frank Terry and the Chicago Nightingales

Berry, Andrae "Fifi" (1943-living): the glamorous owner of Fifi's, a New York styled supper club and piano playhouse

Black, Claude (1933-2013): Detroit born supreme pianist and alter ego of bassist Cliff Murphy

Buckner, Milt (1915-1977): two-fisted pianist, organist, and co-inventor of the Block Chord style

Casa Loma Orchestra: best white big band of the early 1930s with a zealous following in Toledo

Celeste, Tony (-living): drummer and leader of the band at the Aku-Aku

Chittison, Herman (1908-1967): dazzling pianist who on a good day could give Tatum a tussle

Clark, Algeria Junius "June" (1900-1963): excellent cornetist in the manner of King Oliver and the "Toledo Terror's" best friend

Cook, James Willis "Jimmy" (1930-2008): a Chet Baker devotee and the best jazz trumpet player in Toledo for forty years

Coyle, Bill (-living): a fine bassist and Toledo's foremost authority on the subject of Stan Kenton

Cowell, Stanley (1941-living): award-winning, Toledo born piano player best known for his work with the Heath Brothers before becoming a professor in Rutgers University music department

Cummerow, William Otto "Bill" (1916-1990): pianist, an Art Tatum follower who discovered the great Arv Garrison at a high school talent show and later became Arv's piano player

Edgerton, Art J. (1924-2000): a highly respected pianist and close follower of Art Tatum whom he portrayed in a film about the master

Ellington, Edward Kennedy "Duke" (1899-1974): frequent visitor to Toledo after his first visit at Luna Pier in 1930

Garrison, Arvin "Arv" (1923-1960): the most highly acclaimed guitarist to come out of Toledo, made important recordings with Charlie Parker

Garry, Vivian (also Vivien) (birth name: Mildred Vivien Craven) (1921-2008): Arv's wife and leader of the fabulously successful Vivian Garry Trio

Goldkette, Jean (1893-1962): Detroit based leader of an orchestra some think was the best white unit of its time, starring Bix Beiderbecke

Gottron, James P. "Jim" (1935-living): Toledo's keyboard surgeon and cocktail pianist with a touch of Hank Jones

Harrison, James Henry "Jimmy" (1900-1931): the most influential black trombone player of the early '20s; known as the "Toledo Terror"

Heitger, Raymond A. "Ray" (1943-living): clarinet leader of the "Cakewalkin' Jass Band" the most popular, most enduring band in Toledo's history

Hendricks, Jon (1921-living): the John Dryden of Jazz and one of the two or three best living lyricists in the whole wide world

Herman, Woodrow Charles "Woody" (1913-1987): band leader with a huge following in Toledo, including his oldest fan

Holden, Jean: An excellent vocal coach and dynamic song stylist with a trace of Nancy Wilson

Howard, Bart (ca. 1880-????): Toledo-born, Black, popular barrelhouse piano stylist, spent more time in Detroit

Jackson, Ozie "Jack" (1914-1996): house pianist at the Hawley Café, backing up crowd-pleaser guitarist Neil DeBoe

Jaffe, Harold (1921-1991): the history of jazz in Toledo would be very different without the unwavering support of this benevolent jeweler

Johnson, Floyd "Candy" (1922-1981): big toned tenor saxophonist and the only Toledoan to win a membership to the great Count Basie Orchestra

Johnson, James P. (1894-1955): the real beginning of piano jazz who along with Fats Waller inspired the young Art Tatum

Jones, Samuel M. "Golden Rule" (1846-1904): Toledo's turn of the century Progressive mayor with an aversion to throwing people in jail

Kenton, Stan (1911-1979): leader of the jazz orchestra with the most impact on Toledo

Keys, Preston (1940-living): soft-spoken Bill Evans disciple and the last of the lounge pianists

Kieswetter, Mark (ca. 1954-living): Top-notch pianist and excellent storyteller, left Toledo in 2004

Kinney, Brad (1937-living): DeVilbiss High School trombone whiz kid and most likely to succeed

Knorr, Johnny (1921-2011): the Glenn Miller of the Midwest, keeper of the big band flame

Kopp, Fred (1932-2010): house pianist at Fifi's, a man of a thousand tunes, sharp ears, and a devoted following

Lee, Delbert C. (1906-1996): top tenor in Toledo in the 1930s but escaped to Cleveland before he could make a single record

Lee, Lewis C. "Swing" (1923-1988): a colorful house drummer at the Indiana Tavern, home of the Friday night blood-and-thunder drum battles

Licavoli, Thomas "Yonnie" (1904-1973): the Al Capone of Detroit, a vice lord with a preference for jazz music

Lindsey, Harold (1928-2012): the Gene Ammons of Toledo with a sound that could warm up an auditorium faster than central heating

McKellar, Phil (-1983): CKLW broadcaster was voted the jazz disc jock of the year in 1955

McGowan, Russ (1902-1996): altoist, trumpeter, and eyewitness to history

Marterie, Ralph (1914-1978): the beefy band leader of the first big band to fully incorporate the elements of rhythm and blues

Mast, John (1933-2014): classically trained piano prodigy and accompanist to some of the biggest names in music: Dick Haymes, Carmen McCrae

Melle, David "Dave" (1941-2008): deeply missed arranger, most likely the best that Toledo ever had

Mewhort, Charles Alan "Charlie" "Chazz" (1942-2005): likable Kenton aficionado and a big band drummer of note

Mole, Irving Milfred "Miff" (1898-1961): Glen Miller's idol and the most technically equipped trombonist of the 1920s

Monroe, Margaret "Rusty" (1918-2008): Owner of Rusty's Jazz Café

Murphy, Cliff (1932-living): a name synonymous with Toledo jazz, club owner, and leading bass player for more than fifty years

Myers, Elvin F. "El" (1925-2008): Toledo's "Gentleman of Jazz" and leader of the #1 small combo of the '80s

Nesbitt, John (ca. 1900-1935): arranger, trumpet player, and brains behind the first version of the McKinney's Cotton Pickers

O'Connell, Helen (1920-1993): poll-winning big band singer of the 1940s, raised in Toledo

O'Neal, Johnny (1956-living): heir apparent to Claude Black's piano stool, played Art Tatum in the movie about Ray Charles

Parker, Gene (1944-living): saxophone colossus and leading jazz educator in Toledo

Payne, Harold F. (1905-1993): banjoist turned businessman and Tatum's long time friend

Rhodes, Todd (1900-1965): charter member of the McKinney's Cotton Pickers before reinventing himself as Todd Rhodes and His Toddlers

Riggs, James Garland "Jim" (1941-living): the man to hear on alto saxophone before he became a professor at the esteemed North Texas State University

Rothman, Seymour (1914-2013): *The Blade's* matchless storyteller with the uncommon capacity to make the usual unusual

Runyan, Jack Pearson (1925-1995): leader of a well-rehearsed big band stocked with outstanding soloists

Russell, Joan (1933-2011): the heart and business acumen behind the success of Digby's and Murphy's jazz clubs

Russo, Frank (1937-living): flugalhornist with a soft attack reminiscent of Miles Davis

Russo, Mary Ann (1933-2008): "Toledo's First Lady of Song"

Rusty's Jazz Café: internationally renowned jazz club owned and operated by a shrewd, strong willed, big hearted business woman named Rusty Monroe

Sawicki, Henry J. "Jerry" (1930-2011): real estate magnate and the best baritone saxophonist Toledo's ever had

Seligman Brothers: owners of Seligman's Record Bar, one of the best record stores in America featuring an enlightened selection that attracted collectors from everywhere

Senior, Milton Penn "Milt" (1900-1943): founder of the McKinney's Cotton Pickers and truly one of the pioneers of Toledo jazz

Stewart, Sammy (1891-1960): the flashy leader of the Knights of Syncopation, spent an entire year at the Secor Hotel

Stewart, William W. "Doc" (1893-1976) **and Ella P.** (1893-1987): jazz beneficiaries whose small hotel above their pharmacy housed hundreds of Black entertainers at a time when housing was scarce for Blacks

Strawbridge, John E. "Bud" (1928-2007): the most in-demand, most versatile big band trumpet player in recent memory

Sullivan, Buddy (ca. 1923-living): Stan Getz's protégé, who along with Harold Lindsey set the pace for tenor saxophone in the 1950s and '60s

Szor, Samuel "Sam" (1930-2014): Toledo's music man and MC at the Arv Garrison Memorial Concert, Toledo's first Jazz Festival

Takas, William J. "Bill" (1932-1998): inventive Woodward High School graduate left Toledo to become one of New York City's most successful bassists

Tatum, Arthur, Jr. "Art" (1909-1956): Toledo's greatest gift to the world of art and entertainment

Teagarden, Weldon Leo "Jack" (1905-1964): Jimmy Harrison's Texas counterpart

Terry, J. Frank (ca. 1888-????): his Chicago Nightingales were the best band in town for ten years

Thacher, Addison Q. (1876-1963): junk dealer and sports promoter turned Mayor, who did more for the advancement of jazz than he ever knew when he convinced city officials to bring the heavy weight boxing championship of the world to Toledo in 1919

Walter, Jack V. (1931-2010): fine saxophonist and member of the Scott High Five with John Mast, Dean Austin, Don Arnold, and Dave Seaman

Webb, Lawrence Arthur "Speed" (1906-1994): leader of the best territory band out of Indiana and some say as good as Count Basie

White, Bob (-living): excellent show drummer and one of the reasons the Runyan Band was so good; still sitting in after all these years

Whyte, Zach (1898-1967): leader of a Cincinnati territory band and prep school for future jazz stars

Williams, Francis (1910- 1983): trumpeter, boyhood pal of Art Tatum, only Toledoan to earn a chair in the Duke Ellington Orchestra

Wilson, Theodore Shaw "Teddy" (1912-1986): the dominant pianist of the swing era, spent two years in Toledo studying at the University of Tatum

Wooding, James D. "Dewey" (1898-1970): Tatum's piano stand-in at the Chateau La France

Introduction
Great Moments in Toledo Jazz

For her size and weight, Toledo, Ohio, has had more than her share of great moments in jazz. What a scholar wouldn't give for a front row seat at the Armory on May 26, 1929 to see Bix Beiderbecke, the crystal-toned baby-faced genius of the jazz age and its most important white soloist. Or to be present at Herman's on Lafayette Street (a block away from where the Spaghetti Warehouse is located today) in 1920 when the "Toledo Terror," Jimmy Harrison, met the grandfather of jazz piano, James P. Johnson. Or for a tape recorder and a ringside seat at the Green Mill in 1926 for an evening with the McKinney's Cotton Pickers, one of the three top big bands of the 1920s.

Jazz people in Toledo still talk about seeing trumpeter Jimmy Cook and saxophonist Buddy Sullivan at Rusty's Jazz Café in 1985. And no one who was there that night could ever forget Zoot Sims' last stand with the Toledo Jazz Orchestra at the Clarion Hotel on Secor Road.

Students of jazz piano might fantasize about being at the Chateau La France in the summer of 1930. To get there from downtown, you drove way out to Dorr Street, past the city limits; just before you got to the Inverness County Club, you turned off onto a narrow dirt road as if you were headed for a chicken ranch instead of Toledo's state-of-the-art speakeasy.[1] It was a three-story mansion, wide as a barn with fronted columns and pyramid shaped windows. To the side and back of the house was a water plant where the original owners, the de Bouchet family, manufactured LaFrance bottled water, a kind of predecessor of Perrier. Chet Marks, a racketeer with lots of connections, bought the house in 1927 and turned it into the place to be.[2]

There was a sliding peephole in the middle of a fortified front door where someone with the measuring eyes of a pawnbroker screened various guests. Not many were turned away. Inside were expensive draperies, thick imported rugs and fine furniture.[3] You could find gambling on the second floor and love for sale on the third. The crowd at Chateau La France was a cross section of Toledo's night people: rounders, call girls, playboys, ex-Mud Hens, gangsters in suit coats packing heat and driving armored Packards with sixteen cylinders and eight seats.[4] Mitch Woodbury, a columnist at the *Toledo Blade*, was a regular.

In the dining room, Black waiters in white waistcoats wearing Paris garters zoomed in and out of the kitchen carrying eight-course dinners and steaming pots of black coffee—all for two dollars and fifty cents. The bootleg Canadian Bourbon was extra.[5] Sitting at the piano, one eyelid at half mast, his head turned upward, a glass of beer and a pack of Luckies within reach, was Art Tatum, a legally blind, 21-year-old native Toledoan who would become the "greatest piano player of them all." Some would say he was Toledo's greatest gift to the world of art and entertainment.

Chapter 1
Mount Tatum

In an interview many years ago, Oscar Peterson, billed as the heir apparent to Art Tatum, compared Tatum to the world's best golfer at that time, Ben Hogan. "Art's even bigger than Hogan, because after all, Hogan got beat. Nobody has ever beaten Tatum and I don't think anyone ever will."[1] In a poll taken decades after his death, Art Tatum was still the number one jazz pianist among his peers. Not that there haven't been contenders: Lennie Tristano and Bud Powell in the forties; Phineas Newborn and Dick Hyman in the fifties. One of his first challengers was Herman Chittison who played in Toledo occasionally with Zach Whyte and his Chocolate Beau Brummels. Chittison was put in his place at a jam session in Harlem one night. Les Paul was on guitar and witnessed the whole thing. Tatum listened for a while to Herman playing "China Boy" on a beat-up piano. He could hear that the keys B Flat, C and G were sticking. Tatum solved this sticky problem, according to Les Paul. "When Tatum went to the piano, he was as magnificent as ever. When he made a run, coming down with his left hand, he pulled the keys that were stuck with his right hand in time to play them again. And when he began a run with his right hand, he pulled the keys up with his left hand."[2]

Tatum's left hand was a wondrous thing. Jazz singer Anita O'Day celebrated it in her version of Cole Porter's "You're the Top" when she compared her lover to "Goodman's swing band and Tatum's left hand."[3] Tatum's left and right hands were completely independent of each other, as if his nervous system was split right down the middle. That's why people hearing him for the first time thought they were hearing two pianos and why he had no trouble playing two tunes at once.

So, how did he get so good? His sister Arlene said he would practice scales, classical exercises and piano concertos for eight to ten hours each day plus taking lessons from Overton Rainey who disliked jazz but could never get Tatum to refrain from tapping his foot when he played.[4] Arlene said he was listening to piano rolls by Fats Waller and James P. Johnson while manipulating carefully selected Brazil nuts between his fingers so as to extend his reach on the piano. Arlene added that if Art Tatum had not been blind, he would have divided his time between the athletic fields and the piano following the footsteps of his brother Karl who was an all-star football player for Scott

Chateau La France
Courtesy of George Presser

High School. "Art was crazy about sports," she said. "He kept statistics on everything and read the sports page cover to cover, memorized it, in Braille."[5]

Russ McGowan, who was five years older than Art Tatum, said he took Tatum to his first recital. "There was plenty of inspiration around Toledo for young Tatum. Johnny Waters was number one. He played in an older style than Art, more stride. He could play 'The Pearls' better than Jelly Roll Morton could, who wrote the tune. But the whores and bad liquor got to him. Then there was Dewey Wooding. He couldn't read but he played pretty nice chords, minor sevenths, flatted ninths. Dan Fry was from Springfield. He was playing with Cecil Scott and his brother. He was very good. Then there was a Jewish kid who really could play, but he moved to New York when he was pretty young. I know that Tatum heard Bart Howard."[6] Howard was born in Toledo but divided his time between Detroit and Toledo. He was a barrelhouse piano player, a very small man with small hands; in order to get more reach, he had the skin between the thumb and index finger of each hand cut by a doctor. He always played with a cigar firmly clasped between his teeth like Willie "The Lion" Smith.[7]

Harry Gregory, Art Tatum's long-time friend and chaperon said, "Locally, there was a devout following. One was Herman Easterly," said Gregory. He spent his whole life, or most of it anyway, trying to play like Tatum. I used to see him standing on a corner waiting for a bus working his fingers in kind of a manual patomime of a Tatum lick he was trying to learn. Eddie Holland was also very taken by Tatum and played a little bit like him at times. Jack Jackson wasn't really a jazz player but a very, very good player. Mozart Perry, a very close friend of Art's, practically lived in Art's house.[8] Art Edgerton was another close friend of Tatum. He portrayed him in the movie, *Not With Empty Hands*. Edgerton was one of the six piano players chosen to pay tribute to Art Tatum at the Toledo Museum of Art in 1989. He said he played "Wrap Your Troubles in Dreams" because it was the first song he ever heard Art play. "The simple melody was embellished with such fullness," said Dave Yonke of *The Blade*, "it was hard to believe that one pianist was turning out all those notes."[9]

Bill Cummerow, Arv Garrison's piano player, was also blind and said that he tried everything to be like Tatum. "I studied with the same teacher, I tapped my foot just like Art did much to the teacher's chagrin. I liked Fats Waller like Art. I even started to put beer at the end of the piano. I have the same sized hands, I think, as Tatum had. You know, I finally figured out that Tatum's brain and motor system were going about three times faster than mine and that was the difference."[10]

Johnny O'Neal, an expatriate from Detroit to be discussed later, played Art Tatum in the film about Ray Charles. Stanley Cowell, whose family has long-time roots in Toledo, came into his own after leaving Toledo and credited Tatum for his inspiration. Cowell is probably best known as the keyboard player with the award-winning jazz group, the Heath Brothers. As of this writing, he teaches at Rutgers University. Cowell's first meeting with Tatum made an indelible impression on his life.

"Art came to town to visit his sister. My father knew him and knew his father, saw him and invited him to our house. My father insisted that he play and I don't think he really wanted to. He had a way of choosing titles that reflected the way he felt so he played 'You Took Advantage of Me,' and he played the hell out of it. He played it so strongly and powerfully that my mother left the room and went into the kitchen, kind of shaken, seemingly upset. I asked her what was wrong and she said, 'Oh that man plays too much piano.'"[11]

At fourteen, Cowell was a soloist with the Toledo Symphony. Later he would sneak up to Detroit as much as possible to hear those Detroit piano players. "This was one of my important influences, places like Klines. That is where I saw Yusef Lateef and met Barry Harris and Terry Pollard."

CHATEAU LA FRANCE

Announces

THE SUMMER SEASON

TOLEDO'S ONLY NIGHT CLUB

catering to those who enjoy an informal though exclusive place to dine and dance.

PHONE FOREST 3143
For Reservations

Art Tatum
Courtesy of Unwin Paperbacks

Cowell also remembered a lot of local piano players who had a part in his development: Mozart Perry, John Mast, Claude Black, and Eddie Abrams, "a pianist from Detroit who moved to Toledo who allowed his house to become a place for guys to play and have sessions," said Cowell.[12] Cowell's dazzling rendition of "You Took Advantage of Me" from his solo album *Stanley Cowell Live at the Cafe des Cobain* is a lasting tribute to Art Tatum.

Harry Gregory
Courtesy of Rusty Monroe

A British journalist who came to Toledo thirty years ago to write a biography of Art Tatum was unpleasantly surprised to find that his hometown had failed to recognize the giant in their midst. A fact, he said, that will "eternally embarrass the city." He went on to say that if Tatum had been born in London, there would be a bust of him in the London Museum and he was not kidding. Today there are all kinds of festivals and events honoring Art Tatum in Toledo. But in 1952, four years before he died, you could have taken a poll outside of Grace E. Smith's busy cafeteria and be lucky to find one out of thirty who had even heard of Art Tatum. Three events brought Tatum's name to a wider audience. One was a live broadcast done from the London House in Chicago with radio personality Dave Garroway. More importantly were two appearances on *Tonight Starring Steve Allen*. During one of the performances, the television camera zoomed in for a tight close-up of Tatum's hands while he was executing one of those finger twisting quick-as-a-wink passages, prompting Steve Allen to say later that "trying to take in an Art Tatum solo is like trying to appreciate a Rembrandt painting while riding by on a high speed bicycle."[13] The third event that spread the prodigious talent of Art Tatum was a marathon piano recital under the supervision of jazz impresario, Norman Granz. Granz sat Tatum down at a Steinway "for the most rigorous recording project in all of jazz history," said John S. Wilson of *The New York Times*, "A dozen albums, over 140 songs. Picking favorites is like picking a kitty from a newborn litter."[14]

Both Harold Gregory and Harold Payne said that Tatum would play any place that had a piano, no matter the condition: brothels, blind pigs, churches. One of his first jobs was at the Hotel Secor where he was paid in "all he could eat" from the kitchen. Gregory said that he had a devout following in Cleveland, Ohio, where he often played at Val's in the Alley, a small one room shack with no ventilation and only one door. There was sawdust on the floor and orange crates served as chairs. There was an old upright piano that was way past its prime. There was always a line to get inside where "the decor was smoke piled up like concrete blocks as the place never closed and each layer would build up to the ceiling that nobody ever saw," said a Cleveland journalist. Another writer described it this way, "when Tatum and company really got going, the place would get louder and louder and throb and expand like in the cartoons."[15]

In Toledo he preferred to play at the Waiters and Bellman's Club on Indiana Avenue, or Chicken Charlie's at 616 Lafayette Street, originally called Nobles after its owner, Noble Boyd; but it eventually was known as Chicken Charlie's. Like the Waiters and Bellman's Club, any musician coming to town ended up there. It was a meeting place for everybody.

Mozart Perry
Courtesy of El Myers

Chicken Charlie's was about thirty yards long and ten yards wide with a stage just short of accommodating a fifteen piece band. Russ McGowan said it could be a pretty rough place. "I was playing trumpet there one night when the band leader suddenly yelled out, 'Swing those whores, swing 'em wide,' and somebody from the crowd yelled back, 'We ain't no whores,' and our leader yells, 'Yes you are or you wouldn't be here.'"[16] Tatum sat in at Chicken Charlie's one night when the McKinney's Cotton Pickers were there and June Cole who was on tuba remembers that even at fifteen, "he was already fully developed."

What must be the strangest place Tatum ever played was The Jail located near Jefferson Avenue and Superior Street in downtown Toledo. The maître d' was dressed in sheriff's garb and wielded a billy club. He escorted the clientele (or prisoners) to two rows of individual cells with hard wooden tables and chairs. Waitresses in convict stripes and pillbox hats brought the succulent fried chicken and cheese bread on cardboard plates. The coffee came in tin cups. No silverware was allowed.[17] Gregory said that Tatum loved playing rent parties. Rent parties were very popular during the Depression. They were neighborhood benefits to raise money for families who needed financial help at a time when landlords gouged tenants. Prerequisites were a roomy apartment, plenty of refreshments, and a piano. Admission was 25-50 cents. "Tatum was treated like a king when he walked in," said Gregory. "There would be mountains of homemade cakes, biscuits, whole chickens, and pitchers of home brew. He'd sit down after a few other players had played. He'd go into 'Tea for Two,' Chopin, Liszt, Bach, and his favorite tune, 'Tiger Rag' which he played three times faster than Jelly Roll Morton."[18] Bud Osborn captured Tatum's many venues in this excerpt from his prize-winning poem for *The Blade* on July 18, 1977: "... maneuvering ivories in any alley honky-tonk on any after-hours off-key tub, in any plush & dim-lit club on any perfect steinway."[19]

In his book, *Jazz Masters of the Thirties*, cornetist Rex Stewart told about hearing Art Tatum for the first time after a call from Milt Senior about this teenage sensation. Milt Senior was a great musician who, unlike so many others, did not hype. His word was the truth. So when the Fletcer Henderson Band came to Toledo, Coleman Hawkins, Fletcher and I found him in a back-alley joint. We kept asking how this blind kid could get so much music out of a scarred, chipped upright piano covered with cigarette burns and make it sound like a Steinway. Coleman Hawkins changed his slap-sticking tenor style after hearing Tatum and began to think much more harmonically. Tatum invited Fletcher to sit in on piano. Henderson, realizing that talent like this comes once in lifetime, respectfully refused.[20]

When Count Basie came through Toledo with the Benny Moten Band about 1930, he was in for a big surprise. "We stopped off there," said Basie, "where we could get cigarettes, sandwiches, and candy. They had a good piano in there and that's the part I'll never forget. Because I made the mistake of sitting down at the piano and that's when I got a personal introduction to the keyboard monster named Art Tatum. I don't know why I sat down at the piano. It was just sitting there. So I went over there and started playing. That was just asking for trouble in Toledo. And that is exactly what I got because some people went out and found Art. Turned out it was his hangout. He was off somewhere waiting for someone like me to come in and start messing with the piano.

"Showing off because there were a couple of good looking girls in the place. Well, they brought Art in and I can still see him and the way he had of walking on his toes with his head kind of tilting. He proceeded to show me how the tune that I was playing should be played. I'm pretty sure that I'd already heard tales about Art. But when I went to that piano, I didn't have any idea the place was his stomping grounds. 'I could've told you that,' one of the girls said at

ANNOUNCING NEW MANAGEMENT
of Toledo's Only Downtown Black and Tan Night Club

Golden Pheasant CAFE
616 LAFAYETTE STREET

CHICKEN CHARLEY
Now Back at the Old Stand
Serving Those Famous Chicken Dinners at 50c

Featuring JOE STANLEY,
Gypsy Baritone
and DEWEY WOODY'S
Golden Pheasant Serenaders

DRAUGHT BEER 5c
Private Rooms for Parties
ADams 6537

513 Jefferson Ave.

It's Not a **CRIME** *to Eat at The Jail*

Wonderful Food is being served daily at

THE JAIL
513 Jefferson Ave.

A new type of restaurant combining novelty, intertainment and the finest of foods

Chicken is our specialty. And How!

It's our earnest hope to see you in

the **JAIL**
513 Jefferson Ave.

We notice that the Chateau La France (out Dorr Street) has decided not to be quite so exclusive as was first planned. At any rate they have let down the bars to *hoi polloi*. They are serving an excellent dinner for only $2.50 a plate and there's dancing and music.

the bar. I said, 'Why didn't you, baby, why didn't you?'"[21]

Rex Stewart and others tried to convince Tatum that he was more than ready to take on New York. Tatum disagreed. He was becoming the talk of the town. He had close friends and relatives in Toledo, and there was his disability to consider. Plus, he could work anywhere he wanted to and on his terms, which meant no contract, no union, a pitcher of Buckeye beer, and no loud talking when he would go into one those classical interludes of Chopin, Liszt and Bach.[22] In 1928, the *Toledo Blade* announced that "Toledo's famous blind pianist Art Tatum will sprinkle Ellen Kaye's shopping talks on WSPD radio with sparkling syncopations on the piano."[23]

Art Tatum left for New York in 1932 when Adelaide Hall, a former vocalist with Duke Ellington came to town. She was looking for a pianist to replace Joe Turner, not to be confused with

the Kansas City blues shouter. Hall was staying with Doc and Ella Stewart in a room over their pharmacy and it was Ella Stewart who suggested Art Tatum. After a swift audition, Hall took Tatum to New York and within a couple of weeks, he made a recording of "Tiger Rag" that would be close to what he must have sounded like at the Chateau La France. In New York, Tatum played at recording sessions, jam sessions, rent parties, concert halls, and some after-hours clubs in Harlem, where Dan Morgenstern, noted jazz writer, thinks Tatum was at his best. On some nights Jerry Newman, a young fan, would follow Tatum around with his recording gear, recording his performances at Clark's Uptown and Ruben's. An album of Newman's recordings was released thirty years ago called *God is in the House* featuring Tatum singing "Toledo Blues," which ends with the lines:

I'm gonna sing this verse and I don't care to sing no more.
I'm gonna sing this verse and I don't care to sing no more.
To tell you the truth, folks, my drinks are coming too damn slow.[24]

Art Tatum's importance transcends the jazz piano. He influenced a number of instrumentalists and sowed the seeds of bebop. Art Tatum also worked at Jimmy's Chicken Shack in Harlem, a fashionable club whose clientele included Joe Louis, Ethel Waters and other celebrities. Charlie Parker was the dishwasher, the only non-musical job he ever had. Parker, his hands, face, and hair splattered with grease, heard the quotations, the dive bomber runs, the arpeggios played with the finesse of a Horowitz, and wondered if he could play his alto saxophone with the speed and accuracy of Art Tatum.[25]

Arlene Tatum with friends
Courtesy of Rusty Monroe

Don Byas, one of the three or four most important tenor saxophonists of the 1930s and '40s, was very influenced by Art Tatum when he heard him on 52nd Street at the Onyx Club. Byas was so taken with Tatum that he went out and bought all of Tatum's records, went home and memorized his solos. He wrote some of them down.[26] A good example of Tatum's influence on Don Byas are his recordings of "Indiana" and "How High the Moon."

After Art Tatum died, his sister Arlene lived all alone in that canary yellow house on City Park Avenue. She didn't own one Art Tatum record or anything to play them on, for that matter. The only traces of her brother's presence were two dust-covered ESKY trophies for being selected by the writers of *Esquire* magazine as the number one jazz pianist and the faint outline on the wall where the famous Tatum piano used to be. What happened? She explained it this way. "I called up to get Art's piano tuned and two guys showed up who started to rave about the piano and said that they could make it look almost new if they could take it down to their shop. Well, they came back with a truck, hauled it off, and I never saw it again."[2] There is not much of Art Tatum on film. The best documentary on his life is John Cleveland's *The Tatum Legacy* produced by WGTE and the Library. It is available at the Toledo-Lucas County Public Library and should be required viewing for all high school students in Toledo.

Chapter 2
Bad Man's Territory

Tatum left Toledo during the reign of Yonnie Licavoli, the Al Capone of Detroit and just as brutal. Prohibition and the police were closing in on Licavoli. He needed to get out of town. So he sent his brother, Pete Licavoli, to check out the scene in Toledo, Ohio, just sixty miles south. The man in the know was Jake "Firetop" Sulkin, a red-haired, freckle-faced fixer with a short fuse and quick fists. He was fond of saying, "In Toledo, Ohio, honesty is stupidity."[1]

In was an easy sell for Sulkin, who saw nothing but privilege and power for himself. He could point out the easy access from Point Place to the many distilleries in Windsor, Ontario, making Toledo a smuggler's paradise. Firetop knew all the important people in the city and their soft spots. Blackmail and bribery were his specialties.[2] City Hall and the police could be bought off easily; and in Toledo, the police didn't hassle the criminals the way they did in Detroit or Chicago. It was a wide open city. What Sulkin probably did not know, was that it had been that way for decades, all the way back to the beginning of the twentieth century when Samuel "Golden Rule" Jones was mayor—or anti-mayor. Toledo has had some colorful mayors during its history, (Carty Finkbeiner is most recent) but you cannot run them in competition with Jones who was mayor from 1897 to 1904 when he died in office.

It was theater of the absurd. He turned Toledo into a sanctuary; make that a Utopia for criminals. All kinds of ne'er-do-wells flocked to Toledo: forgers, hit men, thieves.[3] Why? The simple answer is that gambling, alcoholism, prostitution, and various other crimes were the fault of economic inequality and society should be responsible. "Golden Rule" Jones was a progressive humanist just this side of "whoopee." He didn't believe in political parties, throwing people in jail, or that government should make a profit. Perhaps you are asking what "Golden Rule" was smoking. His high was the life of Jesus Christ, especially the "do unto others" part, which he believed should be applied to every area of human activity.

One of the first things he did was take the billy clubs away from the police force and exchange them for walking sticks. He had the City Council repeal the Sunday laws, making it permissive again to drink and gamble on Sundays.[4] After all, he reasoned, if the rich could play

Northwood Villa
Courtesy of the author

the stock market, the poor ought to be able to gamble. When a committee wanted to know what Jones was going to do about the growing number of prostitutes, his answer was, "You go and select two of the worst women you can find and I'll agree to take them into my home and provide for them until they can find some other home and some other way of making a living. And then you, each of you, take one girl into your home under the same conditions, and together we'll try to find homes for the rest."[5]

Dance halls, gaming halls, pool halls and taverns proliferated. In 1908 taverns were everywhere.[6] They all played ragtime, a pre-jazz syncopated music composed for the piano. For the first two decades of the twentieth century there were hundreds of itinerant players roaming from city to city, from St. Louis, the center of ragtime, to Toledo and all points everywhere. If the spirit of a city (especially a jazz city) rests in its early history, as some wise person once said, Toledo would be the perfect model.

Like an invading army, Licavoli and his hefty entourage marched into the city one day and for two and a half years, Toledo, Ohio, was under occupation. With Firetop Sulkin running interference and Wop English, an ex-pug, as enforcer, Licavoli consumed everything he came across: nightclubs like the Tabernilla, distilleries, all kinds of gambling, slot machines, the numbers, all the booze in town, dry cleaners, prostitution, and Luna Pier. Plus he had the protection racket all sewed up. Resist, and you might find yourself in a cement suit at the bottom of the Maumee River or, as in the case of Chet Marks and Jimmy Hayes, a bullet in the back of your head.[7]

The King Cobra of the Toledo underworld was no Rudolph Valentino. He had a long face, a crooked nose, and a receding chin, but one launched look from those narrow eyes sent the chill of death at its target. It is not certain how Licavoli felt about jazz, except it was the best music for drinking and dancing at his many enterprises. Some in Toledo saw him as an antihero. To some it was even a status symbol to know him, according to Seymour Rothman of *The Blade*.

The Villa, Mid-1920s
Courtesy of Anwgelo Tsipis

He employed hundreds of people in one of the worst times in Toledo history, and many of those were jazz musicians. As Jon Hendricks once said, "Gangsters did more for jazz than the gentry ever thought of doing." Frazier Reams, the Eliot Ness of Toledo, put an end to the conquest of Licavoli, Sulkin and Company. For more on Licavoli, consult Ken Dickson's book, *Nothing Personal, Just Business*.

When Licavoli arrived, Toledo was suffering from an urban form of Lou Gehrig's disease. The Depression had hit Toledo hard and early, and by 1930 almost half the city was unemployed. Its infrastructure was breaking down. There were potholes and crumbling sidewalks everywhere. Police and fire departments were shutting down. Banks were closing.[8] Proof was a walk downtown. Foreclosure and for-sale signs were everywhere, and there was hardly any construction except for the completion of the Ohio Bank Building. Battalions of hobos wandered the streets, fresh off of the freight cars, beleaguered hollow men who used to be somebody. Now in threadbare food-splattered suits, crumpled caps and outworn shoes, they were standing in soup kitchen lines or fighting over garbage cans.[9]

By 1932 some had moved to the West Side. Joanna Shank, whose father and uncle helped prevent the Mud Hens from leaving town, was seven years old and lived in an apartment on the corner of Upton Avenue and Bancroft Street. She said, "We used to set plates of food on the porch and by morning they would be gone."[10] Skilled jazz musicians and casino owners were pretty much Depression-proof, if not bulletproof as in the case of Jimmy Hayes. Hayes was a former gambling king in Toledo before he met his untimely death.[11] His pride and joy was his deluxe roadhouse casino on the Dixie Highway, otherwise known as "booze alley." It was called the Dixie Villa back in the days of Licavoli. The building is still there, now called Angelo's Northwood Villa, and is still doing business after ninety years, offering some of the best dining in the area. Much of the credit for maintaining the reputation and tradition of the Dixie Villa

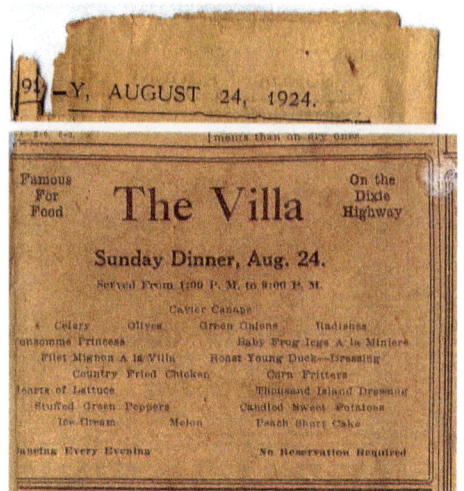

goes to the DoKurno family who owned it for years.[12] The current owner is Angelo Tsipis who loves to give guided tours back to those lawless days in the early '30s. The outside has changed considerably, the inside very little since Licavoli and Sulkin ran the place. Much of the décor, like the crystal chandeliers, is still intact. Tsipis likes to point out the reflecting mirrors that hid the roulette wheels and crap tables, the concave ceiling light which was a surveillance window at one time, and the hidden passageways which were quick getaways for the Purple Gang on nights when the roadhouse was crowded with criminals, thrill seekers and hot jazz.[13]

Chapter 3
Speed Webb and the Territory Bands

Most of the music at the Villa was provided by the territory bands. There were a number of ways for jazz musicians to make a living in the 1930s: pit bands, nightclubs, hotels, circuses, minstrel shows, or cruises on Lake Erie. Many musicians joined territory bands, a byproduct of the ballroom dance mania that was sweeping the country.[1] By 1930, they were all over the United States, some with their own regional sound. They ranged in quality from Triple A to the sandlot variety with self-taught musicians playing beat-up instruments in mismatched uniforms.[2] They were a farm system for the big names like Jimmie Lunceford and Cab Callaway. Many of the future stars of jazz were buried in these road bands. They were traveling music schools for the young at jazz who learned how to read and write music on the job. Almost every city of any size had a dance hall. Some of them even had their own band.[3]

The dancers' choice at the Villa was the Hoosier Melody Lads. In 1927 they left for Hollywood to back up some silent films. When they returned, Speed Webb, a certified mortician out of Peru, Indiana, completely reformed the band and put together a unit that must have been decreed in heaven with Roy Eldridge on trumpet, Teddy Wilson on piano, and Vic Dickenson on trombone. He changed the name to The Speed Webb Orchestra. Teddy Wilson said that it was as good as Count Basie. They went into a studio a couple of times to record, but nothing was ever issued, enhancing their reputation even more. What an indelible impression this band must have made when they played at Forest Park for the summer of 1929.[4]

There was a time when all amusement parks, especially lakeside parks, had ballrooms like the ones at Luna Pier, Willow Beach, and Forest Park, eight miles out Woodville Road, where the Speed Webb Band shared the Pavilion with Toledo's own Frank Terry and the Chicago Nightingales. Roy Eldridge came to Toledo many times after his days with Speed Webb. He was in town with Gene Krupa and Artie Shaw, but mostly with Jazz at the Philharmonic at the Paramount Theater or at the Sports Arena. Onstage he always seemed to be bursting to let loose and when he did, it was like the sudden release of a pent-up fire hose. Once in England he ripped the seat of his pants apart when he spread his legs trying to hit a note he'd never hit before.[5] Roy Eldridge is the main link between Louis Armstrong and Dizzy Gillespie. Gillespie confessed at first he tried to play like Roy but discovered no one could imitate him.[6]

In an interview one time Eldridge was asked why he chose the trumpet over the saxophone that his brother Joe was playing. "Tell you what I like about the trumpet," said Roy. "I love to hear a note cracking. A real snap. It's like a whip when it happens. It hits hard and it's really clean, round, and cracked."[7] Roy was intense. His signature song was "Rockin' Chair." His own favorite was "Dale's Wail," a quartet session done in 1953 with Oscar Peterson on organ. "It was one of those nights," said Roy, "when everything you try comes out perfect. It comes out of nowhere and later when I am off the stand, maybe at home, I try to figure out why it happens only a couple of times a year."[8]

> New Year's Eve Reservations Now
>
> # THE VILLA
>
> "Road House DeLuxe"---On Detroit-Toledo Dixie
>
> THE HOOSIER MELODY LADS
> 8—Dusky Monarchs of Mirth & Music—8
>
> FROG, FISH OR CHICKEN DINNER, $2.00
>
> Daily from 4 to 9, Cabaret 9

At one time Roy Eldridge could play higher, faster, louder, and softer than just about anyone. He figured he was unbeatable in any kind of cutting session. But one night at his favorite club in Toledo, the Waiters and Bellman's Club, he was in for a surprise. Jon Hendricks was playing drums in a sextet when a local trumpeter took advantage of Roy having a bad night. "He was furious," said Hendricks. "He was so competitive. The next day, he left the band he was with, got a ride all the way back to Toledo just so he could kick ass. And he did."[9]

The other time it happened was when he challenged Jabbo Smith. At one time Jabbo Smith was the second best trumpet player next to Louis Armstrong. There are some authorities who think that Jabbo was superior rhythmically and harmonically. Roy Eldridge admitted that he was given a trumpet lesson that night, one that he said stayed with him the rest of his life. "He wore me out before that night was through. He knew a lot of music, and he knew changes."[10]

Jabbo Smith was in Toledo frequently in the 1930s. Jabbo, who got his name from the Native American in the W.S. Hart cowboy movies of the 1920s, was a character so eccentric that people still talked about him fifty years after he left Toledo. They remembered the time he played at an outdoor dance concert stripped to the waist and when he got so high he was arrested walking down Jefferson Street in his socks and underwear while playing "America the Beautiful."[11]

"When I was young," said Roy, "I used to go out looking for every jam session going. I used to stand outside on the sidewalk smoking, listening to the band inside, sort of summing up the opposition. Eventually I would walk in and try to cut everybody. All my life I've loved a battle and if they didn't like the look of me and wouldn't invite me up to the bandstand, I'd get my trumpet out by the side of the bandstand and blow it in from there." John Chilton, noted jazz historian and author of the only book on the McKinney's Cotton Pickers, said this about Roy, "He thrived on ambush. Jamming was not simply an ego exercise. It was a tough apprenticeship that would take him to the top of his profession. Roy felt that he learned something from every encounter and that early each day he would get out his trumpet and begin an idea that began to germinate during a previous night's skirmish."[12]

Vic Dickinson supplied his trombone stories with sound effects, everything from farm animals to bumblebees to yelping buckaroos. He was called the "Fats Waller of the jazz trombone" but the comic, Jonathan Winters, would be more accurate. After 1929 he was in Toledo often with the Zach Whyte Band and the Claude Hopkins Band. In 1946 he made four records with Toledo's Arv Garrison.[13] Two of Vic's recordings got the attention of other trombone players. One was his record with Lester Young on the Aladdin Label called "Lester Blows Again," and the other one was his solo on "Let Me See" from 1940 with Count Basie. This piece of musical poetry was immortalized in 1960 when Toledo's Jon Hendricks, as part of Lambert, Hendricks & Ross, put words to it.[14]

Teddy Wilson and his brother, Gus, were playing with the local bands in Detroit when they joined Speed Webb. They were from Tuskegee where their father was an English professor and their mother a teacher of music. They decided on Detroit after a couple of visits to their aunt's house. Both were well educated with an extensive classical background. Their exposure to jazz came from their father's record collection, where Teddy and Gus first heard Fats Waller's "Handful of Keys," "Singing the Blues" by Bix Beiderbecke, and Earl "Father" Hines, whose trumpet-styled right hand impressed young Teddy.[15]

Gus Wilson did most of the arranging for the Speed Webb Band, much of which was based on the recordings by Red Nichols and his Five Pennies. He left the Webb Band after awhile, went to the Southwest and ended up playing with Alphonse Trent.[16] Teddy Wilson stayed in Toledo playing at the Tabernilla with the Milt Senior Sextet while attending the University of Tatum, following Art everywhere, cherry-picking what he could digest and what he could handle technically. "Before either of us had been to New York," said Teddy, "I followed him to every blind pig in Toledo, all the rent parties, where he usually played on some old upright church piano. Sometimes the sessions would last until early morning or till late afternoon. I just watched and listened to everything he did."[17]

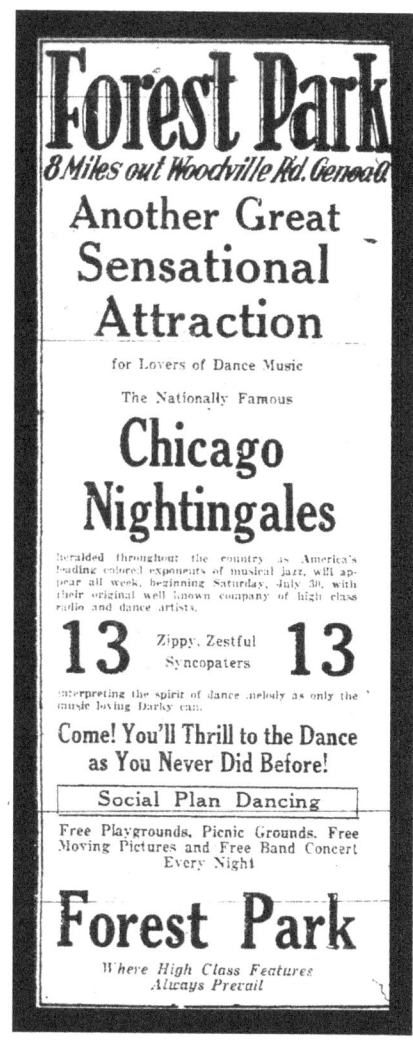

Wilson arrived with kind of a short-hand version of Tatum: fewer notes, more space, relaxed. As someone said, "He let the piano breathe a little bit." He stayed in Toledo for about two years

Young Roy Eldridge
Courtesy of Unwin Paperbacks

before moving to Chicago. There he sat in at the Grand Terrace with Earl Hines before joining Benny Goodman in the first interracial small combo in jazz.

Teddy Wilson took the piano out of the Hot and into the Cool. He was one of the first to show how the piano could function in a jazz ensemble. He was the first one to popularize playing ballads on the piano. His recordings with Billie Holiday in the mid-1930s advanced the art of accompanying vocalists. From 1935 until 1942, thanks in large part to his exposure with Benny Goodman, Teddy Wilson was the King of Swing Piano, with hundreds of disciples. Tatum was impossible, but piano players and fans could understand the succinct, polished statements of Teddy Wilson that were perfectly suited for the three-minute recording limitation of the 78 RPM. Teddy Wilson was the beginning of the light, lyrical school of jazz piano, a style that extends to Nat Cole, Al Haig, Bengt Hallberg, Hank Jones, and to Toledo through the playing of Tommy Flanagan.

He dignified jazz like Duke Ellington and Stan Kenton, even the way he sat at the piano—perfectly erect, motionless, as if he was sitting for a portrait. There were no histrionics, no head bobbing, torso writhing, no hand lifting ala Liberace. Today you can wait years to hear any Teddy Wilson on the radio. Today's jazz fans consider him quaint but obsolete like manual typewriters. But there was a time when the sound of Wilson was everywhere. When Sam plays "As Time Goes By" in the epic film *Casablanca*, you're hearing Teddy Wilson.

His discography goes into the hundreds, but you cannot do better than Teddy Wilson's performance with Benny Goodman at Carnegie Hall in 1938, the night he and Lionel Hampton broke the color barrier. Teddy Wilson and a gathering heavy with talent played "China Boy," "Dizzy Spells," and Teddy's tour de force "I Got Rhythm."[18]

Jabbo Smith
Courtesy of Herwin Records

Chapter 4
Appointment in Toledo

The number one band in Ohio next to the McKinney's Cotton Pickers was Zach Whyte and his Chocolate Beau Brummels out of Cincinnati. Unlike most territory bands they made records; they were on the radio; they had a booking agent, plus a very impressive roster starring Vic Dickinson who joined after the Speed Webb Band folded.[1] Al Sears was on tenor, and Tatum's rival, Herman Chittison on piano. When they came to Luna Pier late in the summer of 1934, the great Dick Wilson was playing tenor saxophone. Leonard Feather, jazz writer, called him "one of the precursors of bebop."[2] Sitting next to him was the top saxophonist in Toledo in the 1930s, Delbert Lee. His cousin said that when Lee finally returned to Toledo after the Whyte Band, he was an accomplished musician, good enough to sit in for Hershel Evans when Count Basie came to town. Later he played with Andy Kirk and his Clouds of Joy band. He and trombonist Frank Lightfoot had a luncheonette on Indiana Avenue before Delbert moved to Cleveland.[3]

Zach Whyte graduated two of the best arrangers in all of jazz, Tadd Dameron and the more famous Sy Oliver. Sy Oliver became the highest paid arranger/composer of the swing era, a man who could claim full responsibility for the overwhelming success of the Jimmie Lunceford and Tommy Dorsey Bands, with such evergreens as "Tain't What Ya Do" and "Opus # 1."

Sy Oliver was in Toledo with the Whyte Band when he ran into his former employer, Cliff Barnett, leader of the Royal Serenaders. Barnett, who was in town putting together a new band, was a highly educated musician, with degrees in harmony and theory. Most of the Zach Whyte Band repertoire was based either on stock arrangements, the blues, or heads, that is, tunes made up on the spot. What was needed to get this band up off its feet was fresh material. What this band needed, thought Oliver, was an arranger. And

LUNA PIER
Lakeside, Mich.

CLOSING DANCES OF THE SEASON
Tonight and Tomorrow Night
Featuring
ZACK WHYTE
and His
14 Chocolate Beau Brummels
DANCING, 9 TO 1 A. M.

> **WALKATHON MARATHON**
> Now in Progress
> **COLISEUM THEATER**
> Ashland at Bancroft
> 312 HOURS ON FLOOR AT 8 P. M.
> MATINEE TILL 6 P. M. 25¢
> 5 — MASTER OF CEREMONIES — 5
> 24 Hours — Continuous Show — 24 Hours

he wanted Barnett to show him how. Barnett agreed, and for a whole weekend in Toledo, Sy Oliver took a crash course in arranging and composing, so that he could take a sheet of manuscript paper with the melody line, the chords and lyrics and interpret it for fifteen sidemen. "He sat me down," said Oliver, "and explained major and minor chords and all about open and augmented chords and how to use scales against certain chords. Things you should have learned in the fifth grade, and how to do all this on the piano. Well, after that it was just experimenting over and over again until I had the right formula, until I knew the right key for a song, the right tempo, where the solos go, what kind of backgrounds to use." Oliver arrived with a bouncy two-beat style that was all his own.[4]

Vic Dickinson said that, "the Zach Whyte Band survived the Depression by playing many dance marathons,"[5] otherwise known as "legalized death marches." In Toledo, these spectacles took place in the appropriately named Coliseum. At any one time there may have been thirty or forty walk-a-thons, as they were called, all over the country. The patrons, some of whom would have been court side at a beheading, bet good money to see what couple would still be moving after days, sometimes weeks of agony. The key word here is moving. Refs in striped blouses, roller skates, and whistles would descend upon a couple for a ten count and a disqualification if one or both of the victims happened to fall asleep from exhaustion. After every eight hours of dancing they were given two and a half hours to rest. There were nurses' aides, massage therapists and, in some cases, physicians on hand.[6] Two bands alternated every two hours, a break that could not come fast enough from the monotony of playing "Melancholy Baby" at the speed of a snail. The greed, exploitation, and treating the contestants like cattle are all part of Sid Pollack's 1969 award winning film *They Shoot Horses Don't They?* Gig Young won best supporting actor. A pictorial essay in *Life* magazine exposing in detail some of the horrors of dance marathons caused the Federal Government to finally put a stop to it, labeling it cruel and unusual punishment.[7]

Frank Terry and his Chicago Nightingales were Toledo, Ohio's territory band. They arrived in

1928 and stayed for more than a decade. Some great musicians passed through the band in that time: Bert Cobb who played tuba with King Oliver, Ben Thigpen, the drummer who went on to fame with Andy Kirk, a trumpet player named Henry "High Note" Devore, and the great Emmet Berry from Cleveland, Ohio.[8]

Terry's most valuable acquisition was Eddie Barefield, a name you'd find on any "who's who" of the swing era. He played saxophone, clarinet, and was an excellent arranger and musical director for Ella Fitzgerald. Later he became the musical director for the Broadway production of *A Streetcar Named Desire*, starring Marlon Brando.[9] The eminent jazz historian, Gunther Schuller, compared Barefield's solo on "Moonglow" with Lionel Hampton's Orchestra to some of the things that Eric Dolphy and Charlie Mingus would be doing twenty-five years later.[10]

Barefield came to town in 1930 and stayed for more than a year.

"I got a letter from Frank Terry and his Chicago Nightingales asking me to join his band in Toledo as arranger and lead saxophone player at the Recreation Ballroom," said Barefield.[11] In the summer, the Terry Band would play at Willow Beach or Forest Park. Most of the winter, they would have long engagements at the Recreation Music Box on Superior Street. Harold Payne said, "That was the only place that had the latest jazz and blues phonograph records. Jimmy Wade's Alabamians liked to play there when he came on his annual visit to Toledo. And it was a favorite hangout for Jabbo Smith when he was in town."[12]

Barefield said that he lived across the street from Art Tatum. "He was just a kid. One Monday night some man brought Art in to play at the Rec Room and Frank Terry said to me, 'I want you to listen to this piano player,' and I said, 'I've heard all the piano players around here, Earl Hines, everybody.' Well, I was just going out the door for a drink that I badly needed at intermission, when suddenly I heard

Eddie Barefield
Courtesy of Eddie Barefield

a crescendo on the piano that stopped me in my tracks and as I turned around Art went into 'Tiger Rag.' I never got out for that drink as I was too amazed at his style and technique.

"He and I got pretty well acquainted and I used to play with him at a little club called Nobles, later called Chicken Charlie's, where he was working. That is how I really learned about music:

Francis Williams with Savoy Sultans
Courtesy of Black and Blue Records

how to play fast, how to go through all the keys, and all that. Art was one of the little gang of musicians that included me and Teddy Wilson who went around drinking and enjoying ourselves after work."[13]

Francis Williams, a Toledoan, played trumpet with Frank Terry before he joined Duke Ellington in late 1945. Williams and Art Tatum were the same age. They played every day at the church across the street from Art's house. "One day Art said to me, 'I got a new piano roll today, Francis.' 'Well I'll come over' I said, and I'd come over and he'd put a piano roll on the machine and he'd turn it on and then when he finished, he played it by ear, and it was like a one-man-band. He'd say, 'This is the intro, now listen for the reeds, and this is the brass.' One of the reasons I gave up the piano and took up the trumpet was, I concluded, that after hearing Art, there was no way I would ever play the piano like that."[14]

Francis Williams was with Ellington for about seven years. In all that time, he got few solos. He may have felt outranked sitting next to trumpet stars Cat Anderson, Ray Nance, and Shorty

Baker. Williams is heard to his best advantage on an album called *Gettin' in the Groove* with Panama Francis and his Savoy Sultans. The album never did much in the United States, but the writers of *Jazz Journal*[15] in Great Britain voted it one of the top recordings of 1979. Williams gets even more solo space on an Illinois Jacquet album called *Jacquet Street* done in Paris on the Black and Blue label with Milt Buckner on piano and organ.

The first territory band to call Toledo its temporary home was Sammy Stewart and his Knights of Syncopation. They were a ten piece group originally from Columbus. In 1922, the Secor Hotel booked them; and evidently, they must have been well received because they stayed for a whole year.[16] It was a change for the Secor Hotel whose policy was to hire all-white high-society bands like Frederick Seymour or Jack Frost and his Eskimos. It might have been the first time the Upper Crust had ever heard anything close to this new thing called jazz when Sammy Stewart would throw in "My Baby Rocks Me with One Steady Roll" along with "Nutcracker Suite" and songs of WWI.

The Secor was Toledo's grand hotel, nine floors high, the first fire-proof hotel in America.[17] It

The Secor Hotel Lobby – Like stepping into Shangri-la
Courtesy of *Toledo Times*

was a hotel for big shots. The stately lobby could boast of imported marble floors, ceilings and pillars, plus Oriental rugs, a bar, a barbershop, and pool tables. There were three dining rooms with mirrored doors, serving "cuisine with a conscience." It also had two ballrooms and a hundred and ten service departments. It was, as the management liked to say, "for discriminating tourists."[18] President Harding stayed there, so did many celebrities; and when the Detroit Redwings won the Stanley Cup, they stayed there. It was absolutely the best job anywhere for an all-Black territory band.

Sammy Stewart has the dubious distinction of being the only bandleader to dismiss Louis Armstrong when he auditioned for the band. Sammy thought he didn't play sweet enough. Stewart was a flashy dresser who wore a velvet cap and fur coat and was openly gay at a time when being homosexual, particularly a Black homosexual, was akin to leprosy.[19] When the Knights of Syncopation left Toledo, they went to Detroit for a while and finally to Chicago where they were an immediate success and eventually became part of the Chicago big band establishment.[20]

Sammy Stewart with later edition of his Knights of Syncopation
Courtesy of the author

Chapter 5
House Busters

There have been at least two times in the musical history of Toledo, Ohio, when the audience came close to losing it, when it became so overwhelmed by a performance that even after several encores and standing ovations, they were still shouting and chanting for more, on the verge of storming the stage. It's called "bringing down the house." It happened in 1923 when *Shuffle Along* came to Toledo on Easter weekend.[1] People were lucky to get a seat. The *Toledo Blade* announced a month before that the tickets were going fast. There was so much demand that the company added aother day. *Shuffle Along* was the most important musical event of 1923 in Toledo. It played an entire year in New York, four months in Boston, four months in Chicago and all over the South. The columnist Heywood Broun wrote, " . . . there is every indication that there is nothing in the world which they would rather do. They are all terribly glad to be up on the stage singing and dancing."[2] Years later *Newsweek* called it a "thermo-nuclear fusion of opera, jazz, dancing, and comedy."[3]

This Noble Sisson and Eubie Blake production was the proto-type for all musicals to come and brought jazz dancing to Broadway. It required white chorus girls to learn Black steps for the *Ziegfeld's Follies*.[4] The huge cast had many stars, Ethel Waters for one. But the biggest attraction was Josephine Baker, a sepia Twyla Tharp with a $250,000 wardrobe and more moves than Red Grange. In public she flaunted her Blackness like a female Muhammed Ali and raised the eyebrows of polite society before moving to France.[5]

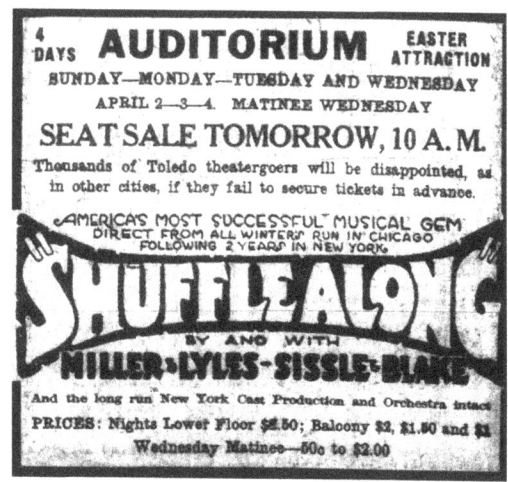

Here's what the *Toledo Blade* had to say about the performance, "*Shuffle Along* . . . swept into Toledo Sunday night with its jazzy ... melodies, its merry comedians, its fine musicians and singers, its brilliant dancers ... and aroused to enthusiasm an audience that filled every seat in the Auditorium Theater. No advance praise ... was too fulsome. *Shuffle Along* is all that ... and more. ... [T]he whole show moved with a snap and swing that never slackened through almost three hours of entertainment. ... The Sunday night audience expressed enthusiastic approval of 'Wild About Harry' [which 25 years later became President Truman's campaign song] ... [and] 'Love Will Find A Way.'"[6]

The *Blade* went on to say that a dinner dance given for the King and Queen of England gave jazz its first formal recognition in that country by selecting for the musical program a number of songs from *Shuffle Along*.[7] *Shuffle Along* played to racially mixed audiences throughout the United States, helping to break down the color line and open the door to integration. It convinced many that there was something worthwhile to this new music called jazz.

Another time when the audience went a little crazy was ten years later when the Casa Loma Band, under the temporary direction of Henry Biagini, came to Willow Beach for the week of the Fourth of July. It was a vacation from the nine months of college dances. Opening night at the Green and White Dance Pavilion at Willow Beach was another great moment in Toledo jazz.[8] In 1933, the Casa Loma Band was the best. They were the model for the swing era and copied by all of their colleagues, including Benny Goodman and Jimmie Lunceford. The Casa Loma Band's records sold well; and they were on the radio once a week, required listening for swing enthusiasts and many band leaders. One leader recalled, "We used to time our breaks on the jobs so we could catch at least part of the program."[9] The Casa Loma Band was known for their precise ensemble pas-

sages, but they had excellent soloists: in Clarence Hutchenrider the clarinetist; trombonist, Murray McEachren who came later; and the great Sonny Dunham who had a huge hit on "Memories of You."

World famous drummer Buddy Rich said that the most valuable sideman was the band's drummer, Tony Briglia. "He was a bitch. Listen how he holds this headlong express from jumping the tracks on those killer dillers like 'Casa Loma Stomp.'"[10] Part of their appeal was the way the band looked, black tie and tails, spit-shined shoes, and platinum cufflinks.[11] "Like waiters at Sardis," someone said. But this great orchestra which had dominated the early part of the thirties would never have reached its heights without the banjo strumming genius from Texas named Gene Gifford.

Gifford gave the band an identity and a purpose which was to write jazz instrumentals like "No Name Jive" and romantic ballads like "Smoke Rings." Gifford slowed down the tempo on ballads, from the businessman bounce of the 1920s. Gifford joined when the band was known as the Orange Blossoms (dreadful name) before they became the Casa Loma Orchestra led by a handsome former pole-vaulter named Glen Gray. Gifford was an admirer of John Nesbitt of the McKinney's Cotton Pickers and borrowed some of his mannerisms.[12] And like Nesbitt, Gifford demanded long hours of rehearsal to handle the technical difficulties of these arrangements. The most in-tune, most precise, most technically equipped band of its time[13] played Luna Pier in 1934, and the Trianon Ballroom on Madison Avenue, June 6th, 1935, a couple of months before the rise of Benny Goodman.

Chapter 6
Jon Hendricks - A Lyricist Supreme

The boy who turned into one of the world's great living lyricists was always on hand when a famous big band came to the Trianon Ballroom. "I used to climb up the drainpipe which led to a glass roof," said Jon Hendricks. "You could look down on the bandstand. I wanted to play drums and I remember watching Ben Thigpen from the roof. He went on to star with Andy Kirk and his Clouds of Joy. Times were tough for our family of 17. Instead of mice, we had kids. During the depression all we had to eat for supper often was bread and bacon fat with some syrup on it."[1]

To help out, Jon devised various ways of supplementing the family income. He had a shoe-shine stand outside the Paramount Theater and for five cents he used to sing the various selections on the jukebox at Stanley Cowell's hamburger joint. He'd sing the whole arrangement, everything, the brass, and the reeds. He'd take an arrangement like "Yard Dog Mazurka" by Jimmie Lunceford and imitate all the instruments. He claimed it was the genesis of what later became Lambert, Hendricks & Ross.

The other thing he used to do was crawl under the ten-cent coin-operated toilets in bus stations, unlock the door for the anxious patrons and receive five cents for his efforts. Later he made much more money singing on WSPD with a group called the Swing Buddies.[2] It was three o'clock in the afternoon and Jon Hendricks was still in his pajamas, a silk bathrobe, ascot, and slippers. He talked about why he wanted to come back to Toledo and live in the upscale village surrounded by Toledo called Ottawa Hills.

"Thomas Wolfe was wrong when he said 'You can't go home again.' I proved that and I had good reason. When I was 11, I and a friend of mine were walking along and the Ottawa Hills police stopped us for walking too slow and wanted us to leave. I decided right then that I was going to come back and live in Ottawa Hills.[3] My Dad was a friend of Reverend Thomas Waller, that's Fats Waller's father. They went to seminary school together. So Fats would be at our house often. One time he came when I was singing at the Waiters and Bellman's Club and he came in to hear me. He was knocked out. He told my folks that he wanted to take me back with him to New York. But my mother said, 'absolutely not.' I was too young. Later she told me that the real reason was that Fats Waller drank too much. And he died of cirrhosis of the liver not too long after that. He was in Toledo a lot. He loved to play the organ at the Rivoli Theater. When Fats went back to New York, he told everybody about me so when celebrities would come to Toledo, they would drop by.[4]

"Art Tatum was my biggest influence. He took me under his wing and got me to sing his chords on the piano. Every singer learns melody but only a few singers could sing chords. He taught me to do it with my voice like instruments do it. So it got so anything he played, I could sing. He really polished my ears. I sat with him at the Chateau La France. There were gangsters in fedora hats and sawed off shotguns in the audience. One time actor James Cagney walked in.

Well I sang around Toledo until I was drafted in 1942. It was the most miserable experience of my life. You're supposed to be fighting for democracy, teaching Germany a lesson and this we did under segregation, denying our whole purpose. Why it was reprehensible, and I am still angry about it. When I got out of the service, I married an Irish girl and took the GI Bill and decided that I wanted to be an attorney so I enrolled at the University of Toledo.

"In about 1950 the Charlie 'Bird' Parker Quintet came to Toledo fresh from the Royal Roost in New York. Kenny Dorham was on trumpet; Al Haig was on piano. Bird had heard a little bit about me so I got to sit in imitating with my voice all of the tunes that they did, 'Ornithology,' 'Groovin' High.' When I finished, Bird grabbed my coattail and said, 'Sit down,' and we had this conversation on the bandstand. He said, 'What are you doing?' I said, 'I'm going to be a lawyer.' He said, 'You're no lawyer, you're a jazz singer.' I said, 'What am I going to do about that?' He said, 'Come to New York.' I said, 'I don't know anyone in New York; it's a big city.' He said, 'Well you know me.' I said, 'But where would I find you?' He said, 'Ask anybody.'[5]

"I waited two and a half years before I went to New York. Parker was at the Apollo in Harlem. So I walked in while he was playing 'The Song is You' and right in the middle of the song he calls out, 'Hey Jon, how are you doing? Do you want to sing some?' And then he returned to the song. I almost fainted.[6] Parker was telling everybody about this kid from Toledo." Still Jon needed a full time job. He was having lunch one afternoon near Washington Square. Nearby a radio was playing. It was King Pleasure's "Moody's Mood for Love" where he sings James Moody's famous tenor saxophone solos. Hendricks was so taken by what he was hearing that when he got home, he wrote words to Woody Herman's "Four Brothers."[7]

Hendricks' recording debut was with King Pleasure in 1955. He asked Jon to put words to "Don't Get Scared," a Stan Getz/Lars Gullin tune.[8] At a party in Greenwich Village, Jon met Dave Lambert, a bop vocalist who had made some records with Gene Krupa. They made a record together on an off-label. Then Dave Lambert got the idea to add a British singer named Annie Ross who put words to Wardell Gray's recording of "Twisted." Thus began one of the most famous alliances in all of jazz, Lambert, Hendricks and Ross. Then Lambert talked Annie and Jon into doing an album of Count Basie tunes.[9]

Thinking about jazz in terms of language is natural. Some of Louis Armstrong's early trumpet solos were instrumental versions of Bessie Smith's voice. It wasn't until the mid-1940s that Eddie Jefferson and King Pleasure reversed the process when they converted some famous saxophone solos into words, a technique that came to be known as vocalization, not to be confused with scat singing which employs nonsense syllables and improvisation.[10] Vocalization is singing a story on a well-known jazz solo. The poet of this idiom is Toledo's second most famous jazz personality, Jon Hendricks, the John Dryden of jazz, equally at home in prose or rhyme. He once wrote an entire article in rhyme for *Down Beat* magazine.[11]

Putting words to a Count Basie arrangement with all the solos and ensemble parts was a Herculean task. It took Annie Ross, Dave Lambert, and Jon Hendricks six months, working long hours every day, to get the selections just right. The first track, "Blues Back Stage," can still send Hendricks into tears. Lambert, Hendricks & Ross made numerous albums including one of Duke Ellington's songs and another one of jazz classics, but none had the satisfaction of that first album. In September 1959, *Down Beat* called them the "hottest new group of jazz" and put their faces on the cover of the magazine. *Newsweek* called them "vocal lightning."[12]

Lambert, Hendricks & Ross is Jon Hendricks' crowning glory. Not far behind is his *Evolution of the Blues Song* which premiered at the 1960 Monterey Jazz Festival. "Jimmy Lyons was the director of the festival," said Hendricks, "and he wanted me to come up with something for the Sunday afternoon blues show, something different."[13] So Hendricks gathered a number of outstanding musicians, both jazz and blues, and went about telling this story. "So I decided to just talk and let the music just speak for itself. And following the advice of my mentor at the Univer-

Jon Hendricks with Claude Black on piano
Courtesy of El Myers

sity of Toledo English Department, 'write about what you know.' So I wrote about my ancestors' music that they sang throughout their lives, the spirituals. And I didn't stop there because the spirituals went outside the church to become the blues and through various horns to become jazz. In other words gospel and blues and jazz singing comes from the church and I ain't no liar. Dinah [Washington] and [Sarah] Vaughan come right out of the choir."[14]

Rave notices abound. Ralph J. Gleason of the *San Francisco Chronicle* called it a jazz version of Gilbert and Sullivan, and went on to say, "There have been few moments in this writer's lifetime in jazz, that have been as satisfactory as the Sunday afternoon session at Monterey. If in its three years, the Monterey Jazz Festival had done nothing but present *Evolution of the Blues Song*, it would have justified its existence."[15]

Evolution of the Blues Song which was recorded later by Columbia Records, was not a strict historical account of the development of jazz and blues in America, but as Leonard Feather said in his review "You don't go looking for facts in a story like this anymore than you'd look for exact photographic faces in a Picasso painting." This was the blues truth according to Jon Hendricks and a man with his gifts should be granted maximum poetic license.[16]

Hendricks in his early nineties is still going. His list of credits in Leonard Feather's *Biographical Encyclopedia of Jazz* is longer than any other Toledoan. He's been a jazz critic. He taught history of jazz at California State and also Stanford and the University of Toledo. He's written words to a number of jazz classics including "Little Niles," "Moanin'" and "Four" from his album, *The Swingers!* One of his best works is the relatively unknown album he did for Carmen McRae of tunes by Theolonius Monk.

Chapter 7
Jack Runyan – Thanks for the Memories

Before he was in the third grade, Jack Runyan knew he wanted to lead a band. Instead of collecting autographs of the Toledo Mud Hens, he was more interested in getting the autographs of local bandleaders: Jimmy Reemsnyder, Elliot Hoyt, Eddie Church, and Guy Shipman. Jack's first band was an offshoot of the Libbey High School orchestra, playing for proms and Bar Mitzvahs.[1] Jack Runyan never missed a night when a headliner came to the Trianon Ballroom, formerly Madison Gardens, and now a parking lot for the Toledo Club. It was a two-story brick building with a mock balcony on the side. The fire marshal's limit was 1500 people; but when Glenn Miller came to town, there were many more than that on the sixty by a hundred-and-eighty-foot maple dance floor.

Above was a giant crystal ball like the ones in *Saturday Night Fever*. The managers liked to brag that there were more marriage proposals there over a bag of peanuts and a Coke than any other place in Toledo. 25 cents got you in except on Wednesdays when it was only fifteen cents. Runyan said that he and other aspiring musicians would wait at the edge of the stage if some well-known band happened to be playing. The trumpet players had their own mouthpieces; guitar players with their picks in their pockets, drummers with their sticks in hand, "hoping against hope,"

Bob Hope and Jack Runyan at rehearsal
Courtesy of Julie Runyan

Jack said, "that a sideman would become ill or be called home, and the announcer would ask if there was any trombone players or saxophone players or whatever. But we would have fainted or soiled our pants if that were actually to happen."[2]

The dancers at the Trianon had their own pecking order and cliques. Imitators were given the cold shoulder. One of the best dancers was the cigar-chewing character named Boxie who had a unique shuffle he maneuvered forward, backwards, sideways, and in fast circles when the music got hot. Another memorable moment in the annals of Toledo jazz, according to Jack Runyan, was in April 1948 when Woody Herman brought his Second Thundering Herd to the Trianon for what was advertised as a dance but became a concert in powerhouse jazz. This was the Four Brothers Band because the whole saxophone section, Al Cohn, Stan Getz, Zoot Sims, and Serge Chaloff, were all the musical offspring of Lester Young. Shorty Rogers was on trumpet and the arrangements and compositions were by the brilliant Ralph Burns.[3] To get an idea of what that evening was like, listen to an album called *Woody Herman Road Band 48* released in 1978 but recorded about the same time the band was in Toledo.

In 1942 Jack Runyan was playing in the Paramount Theater pit band and that was how he got to play with America's greatest drummer, Gene Krupa and his Orchestra. "The wartime draft," said Jack, "was depleting the ranks of the big bands. The night before Krupa arrived, one of the sidemen was called to arms and I was graduated to the middle of the great Krupa sax section in my oversized uniform, so scared I could hardly blow a note."[4] It was Gene Krupa who brought the drums to center stage when he played his famous "Sing, Sing, Sing" drum solo in 1938. Krupa was Slingerland Drum Company's poster boy, a gyrating, gum-chewing, tousle-haired forerunner to Elvis Presley who had millions of fans, many of them women, who packed the Paramount Theater

Runyan Band
Courtesy of Marge Jay

the night they received three standing ovations from three standing-room only shows. Krupa was riding high from his role in the film *Ball of Fire* with Barbara Stanwyck and Gary Cooper. The musical sequences are worth the price of admission, especially the scene where Krupa exchanged his drumsticks for a set of matchsticks to light up the band.

"I felt I had really hit the big time when I was playing at the Paramount," said Runyan. "I firmly believe that when the city razed the Paramount, it took the heart right out of the town. People used to say it was like stepping into the Taj Mahal or an Arabian Nights adventure."[5] It was a massive monument to the days of silent film and vaudeville when Oriental opulence was the style. Marble statues, embroidered tapestry, and ivory columns graced the lobby. A squad of uniformed ushers in their golden shoulder braids and flashlights stood at attention. The 100-foot ceiling above the main floor was made to resemble a vast midnight sky complete with twinkling stars and moving clouds. The hydraulic stage allowed the audience to hear the performers before they actually saw them.[6]

Perhaps the biggest moment in Jack Runyan's illustrious career happened in Cleveland the first time the band backed up Bob Hope as a summer replacement for Les Brown. Hope may have worried about the quality of this unknown group from Toledo, Ohio, until he heard the first eight bars of his theme, "Thanks for the Memory." Wayne Ruihley was on baritone saxophone sitting just three feet away and never forgot the look on Bob Hope's face. "He started to quiver. I don't think he could believe that we could send a shiver up his spine, playing our own arrangement of his theme. We backed him up four or five times and Jack and Bob Hope became fast friends. The band kind of folded after Jack Runyan died, but it was a good band, a very good band. We had Bud Strawbridge who could play like Harry James. Bob Jay played very nice tenor but I always thought he preferred

Jack joining sax section on Stan Kenton's "Opus in Pastels"
Courtesy of Julie Runyan

Born to be a bandleader
Courtesy of Julie Runyan

to play clarinet. We had Paul O'Connor on trombone, a very, very gifted soloist, and of course vocals by Mary Ann Russo. So it was a fine band for many years."7

Every sideman who ever played with Jack Runyan loved to play for him. He may not have always gotten the tempo right but he gave the soloists plenty of freedom. His favorite band was Stan Kenton but Jack Runyan's band-leading style was more like the famous Charlie Barnett. Unlike his rival Johnny Knorr, Runyan was "loosely wired," as one of his trumpet players said. "You picture him in this easy-boy chair with a bottle of Buckeye [Beer] in his hand and Kenton album on his turntable. He was so easy going, if someone came in early or if somebody hit a clinker it was no big thing as long as the band kept swinging."8

Most of the arrangements for the band were done by the brilliant and very deeply missed Dave Melle. He would take a stock arrangement, re-harmonize it, and maybe put it in a different key, like he did on some of the Stan Kenton arrangements. The arrangement for "Thanks for the Memory" was by trumpeter Ron Wagner, Woodward High School, class of 1952, an extraordinary self-effacing man in a field littered with Mozart-sized egos.

To the surprise of everyone, Wagner disqualified himself from the trumpet section of the prestigious Toledo Jazz Orchestra one day because "I didn't feel I was holding up my end." He did the same thing in 1964 when Ray McKinley, who was running the Glenn Miller Orchestra, hired him. "Oh, Ray McKinley tried to talk me out of it. We had long, long talks, but I told him I just wasn't comfortable. I wasn't comfortable with some of the updated Glenn Miller evergreens, like 'Pennsylvania 6-5000' that Dean Kincaid, the new arranger completely re-harmonized.9

"The most comfortable group I ever played with in Toledo was with Eddie Abrams every Tuesday night at Rusty's. We had Frank Russo, fluglehorn. He played by ear, a very relaxed style somewhat like Miles Davis. Very cool. Bob White was on drums. One night after we finished a song, Eddie came over and said, 'I don't know what you've been doing, hiding yourself in those big bands with a talent like yourself.' Boy did I feel like a million dollars."[10]

Ron Wagner never got over seeing Les Brown at Centennial Terrace in August 1955. To the day he died, Wagner remembered every member of the band and most of the tunes they played that night. He went home and bought a copy of *Les Brown at the Palladium* and decided the next day to try arranging. He was happy to learn that *Metronome Magazine* named Les Brown and his Band of Renown as the best big band of 1955.[11]

Chapter 8
Centennial Terrace – "Some Enchanted Evening"

Jack Runyan's favorite venue, along with many other bandleaders, was Centennial Terrace. It was a different Centennial Terrace sixty years ago—a few white, cement block buildings, a concession stand, tiered sand piles, a man-made lake, an outdoor dance floor surrounded by a white fence. No glittering marquees to tell you Harry James was inside for one night only. You could drive right by it and some big band bus drivers did. In one of his last interviews, Les Brown, the leader of the longest lasting musical organization of the twentieth century, was talking about his favorite ballrooms and named the Hollywood Palladium, the Glen Island Casino, the Aragon Ballroom in Chicago, and "an outdoor ballroom outside of Toledo, Ohio."[1]

More than that, it was the largest outdoor ballroom in the United States or maybe the world, and until recently boasted of a checkerboard terrazzo dance floor—10,000 square feet of it—personally installed by authentic Italian craftsmen. Centennial was a rock quarry until 1931 when it was abandoned and filled with 25 feet of water. A guy by the name of Bob Burge leased it from the France Stone Company as a recreation area. He decided to build a dance floor in 1939 at the peak of the swing era.[2] If it were not for the Friends of Centennial Terrace, Inc., especially Johnny Knorr, Centennial would not have survived the 1970s: nobody cut the grass; and the dance floor was coming apart along with the canopied bandstand. The ring of lights that circled the dance floor was in various stages of collapsing. The whole place was in disrepair. It could have been torn down. Johnny Knorr gets sentimental when he talks about the importance of this idyllic setting. "There are people who met their wives and husbands here. They first danced here. They took their first dates here."[3]

Ray Anthony set the attendance record in 1956. He had his own television program called the *Chesterfield Hour*.[4] Owning copies of his albums, *Campus Rumpus* and *Houseparty Hop*, was the mark of a cool coed at the University of Toledo. His big band arrangements of TV themes from *Dragnet* and *Gunsmoke* made him even more popular and his recording of the "Bunny Hop" set off a dance craze similar to the conga twenty years earlier.[5] And many Toledoans remembered that exactly one year before, he married a Marilyn Monroe look-a-like,

Jack Runyan at Centennial
Courtesy of Wayne Rhuiley

in Toledo's Commodore Perry Hotel by the very Honorable Judge Frank Wiley.⁶ The previous attendance record holder was Johnny Long, a handsome left-handed violinist with a massive hit off which he lived for years called "Shanty Town." It is a Depression era song that says no matter if you are living in near poverty and your house is falling down, you could still have happiness and love. Saxophonist Jerry Sawicki said that "Long would arrive in Toledo with a lead trumpet player, a drummer, and a piano player and fill in the rest with locals. The book was so easy that any semi-competent musician in town could handle it."⁷

Ralph Flanagan

Centennial Terrace on the night of June 28, 1955, was a romantic's gourmet with all the trimmings: a warm summer breeze; the quarry below, glistening in the moonlight; the checkerboard dance floor above, overpopulated with college students in dinner jackets and evening dresses, bursting with hope and leaving a faint aroma of Shalimar and Old Spice in their wake. They were dancing to the most sought-after big band of the early 1950s—Ralph Flanagan and his fifteen cleanly shaven, freshly scrubbed, all-white sidemen. Flanagan estimated that when he retired in 1960, he had played 1001 one-nighters, mostly at universities as his early records would indicate, e.g., *Sophomore Splash*, *Junior-Senior Prom*, and an album of swing-styled college football fight songs called *The Old Ox Road*.

RCA Victor hired Ralph Flanagan to keep the dying big band business alive in light of the threat of rock and roll.⁸ Their plan was to bring back Glenn Miller, not the songs, but the sound,

Chapter 8 | 43

The bandstand where the best Big Bands played

The Way it Was

the clarinet lead and the muted trombone choirs, all of the qualities that made the Miller big band Number One. "Hot Toddy" of 1952, Flanagan's smash hit, was nothing more than a repeated figure over and over with little variation. It became the first big band tune to top the charts since 1942.[9]

Ralph Flanagan was a jazz fan. He arranged for Gene Krupa and Johnny Richards; and he had Benny Moten's "South" and Erskine Hawkin's "Tippin' In" in the band book. The Flanagan orchestra was the first one to do albums of musical hits from Broadway such as "Some Enchanted Evening" from *South Pacific*, "Stranger in Paradise" from *Kismet*; and every concert, including those at Centennial, had a twenty-minute medley from Roger's and Hammerstein's *Oklahoma*.

The band reached its height of glory when *The Glenn Miller Story* was released in 1954. The cute boy with the Colgate smile from Lorain, Ohio, was king of the hill. State troopers had to be called in to quell a riot at a public dance at Pennsylvania State College when the people from the first concert would not leave so that the people who had purchased tickets for the second concert could get in. Flanagan's face was everywhere, on billboards endorsing Chesterfield cigarettes, on the covers of teenage romance magazines, and on the label of a hair shampoo.[10] He had the celebrity status of a Bob Dylan for awhile.

Ralph was not a people person. Autograph hounds annoyed him. One overly aggressive bobby soxer who was tugging at Flanagan's pant leg for attention got a kick in the mouth for her trouble and Ralph had to be whisked away before her boyfriend could shatter that million-dollar smile. Nobody much cared for Ralph. The ballroom managers loved his music but loathed his personality. He incurred the wrath of his fellow band leaders by undercutting the standard fee for one-nighters. He tried to cheat his sidemen out of days off. He fought with the musicians union and got into a fist fight with a stagehand.[11] By the time he decided to quit, the Flanagan Band was relegated to making novelty records and Christmas albums.

Caruso with a Horn

Mercury Record's answer to Ralph Flanagan and RCA Victor was Ralph Marterie. Toledoans saw a lot of Ralph Marterie—sometimes twice in one summer. And in 1958, when he had saxophonist Joe Farrell and the fabulous Nick Ceroli on drums, he visited Toledo three times. Ralph grew up in Chicago listening to classical music, mostly to the greatest opera singer of his era, Enrico Caruso. By the time Marterie formed his first band in 1949, he had transferred the valiant bravura of Caruso to his Martin horn. *Down Beat* called him "Caruso with a Horn" and the name stuck.[12] A good example is Rachmaninoff's "Second Piano Concerto" from his *Love Themes from the Classics* album.

Ralph never liked jazz. In a *Down Beat* blindfold test with Leonard Feather, he offered these startling pronouncements:

"Roy Eldridge tries hard but nothing happens," "Miles Davis plays phony rhythm and blues licks," "Conte Condoli's vibrato is too wide," and "Louis Armstrong is vastly overrated."[13]

Three Toledoans played with Marterie: Jack Reidley, John Mast, and the very capable drummer Bob White. They all came pretty much to the same conclusion, that you could not feed chickens on what Marterie paid, and that there was more turnover on that band than at Burger King. "I was paid a 150 dollars a week," said White, "and I had to pay all of my expenses out of that. I got as far as Denver and headed back. He never talked to me or anyone else in the band. Not one word to me about my drumming. He was afraid you were going to ask for a raise."[14]

Ralph Marterie was a beefy, no-nonsense boss built like a barroom bouncer and not shy about getting physical. "He threatened to beat me up one night," said Nick Ceroli, "because he thought my solo on 'Caravan' was too long."[15] Marterie had two sponsors. Marlboro cigarettes in their battle with Chesterfield endorsed him, and he became known as Ralph Marterie and his Marlboro Men. *Down Beat* magazine adopted him after conducting a survey among college students. Ralph Marterie came out on top over Ralph Flanagan, Buddy Morrow, and Billy May. The magazine selected Marterie's band to spearhead the attack against the invasion of rock and roll.[16]

The executives at Mercury Records decided that if you can't beat them, join them. So the Ralph Marterie band was the first orchestra to fully incorporate the elements of both rhythm and blues and rock and roll: the twangy guitars, the heavily accented after beats, and the honking baritone saxophones. Now, Marterie was not only popular at the University of Toledo, but also with high school students. They bought millions of copies of "Caravan," "After Midnight" and "Crazy Man Crazy." Marterie's biggest hit was his instrumental version of Nat King Cole's classic, "Pretend." The effective use of call and response between the clarinet and the guitar stirred the passions of teenagers and octogenarians alike.

Woody Herman at Centennial

Woody Herman and his Thundering Herd is not the first orchestra that comes to mind in connection with the mambo, the dance craze that swept America from 1953 through 1956. When they first performed in Toledo, they were billed as "The Band that Plays the Blues." At Centennial in July 1955 they were the band that played the mambo. To his long list of golden hits such as "Bijou," "Apple Honey," and "Early Autumn," Woody added four mambo charts courtesy of the trumpet section which had just made an album with members of Machito's band.

Machito was the Duke Ellington of the mambo. He brought it from his native Cuba in 1949. In 1953 there were 200 mambo songs.[17] Pete Rugolo did "Jingle Bells Mambo." There was "Stardust Mambo" and Les Brown recorded "St. Louis Blues Mambo." There was even a "Marilyn Monroe Mambo." The best-selling

Sam Kallile with members of Woody Herman Orchestra, Mike Brignola and Frank Tiberi
Courtesy of *Woody Herman Newsletter*

single of 1955 was Prez Prado's "Cherry Pink and Apple Blossom White."[18] Like the bossa nova in the 1960s, and boogie woogie in the 1930s, every dance band had one or two mambo arrangements in their repertoire. There was a call for conga players, and timbales, claves and bongo drums became part of the instrumentation of jazz. By the end of 1954, it had become so ubiquitous that *Life* magazine did a huge spread with pictures under the title, "Uncle Sambo goes Mambo" and said it was the biggest dance fad since the Lindy in 1935.[19]

The mambo was the soundtrack for *Underwater*, a film starring Gilbert Roland and Jane Russell. There was even a documentary on network TV that discussed mambo addiction particularly among the Latin populations in cities like New York and Los Angeles.[20] Dance studios like Eddie Hanf's on Summit Street in Toledo and all over America, were flooded with requests to learn the mambo. Toward the end of the evening at Centennial, Manny Album's wild and frantic "Mambo the Utmost" set in motion two seasoned pros who put on a dazzling exhibition of the many moves of the mambo, twisting, writhing, and wiggling "like lizards on a hot slab."[21]

Toledo was a favorite stop for Woody Herman for at least three reasons: Dyers Chop House, the Commodore Perry Hotel, and a reunion with his best friend, Sam Kallile, who later became the oldest member of the Woody Herman Fan Club. "I was a fan of Woody Herman," said Kallile, "because I always thought the band was on fire most of the time. When they want to blow, it's like fire engines coming out of the station house. The band continues to meet the high standards of what Woody set. They better," said Kallile, "if they don't, I will have to leave town 'cause I have been spreading the word all over Toledo."[22]

Johnny Knorr

There is a paragraph from Frederick Lewis Allen's classic, *Since Yesterday*, that ought to have been above the mantel in Johnny Knorr's home. It goes, "If Benny Goodman could turn readily from the playing of 'Don't Be That Way' [his theme song]; to the playing of Mozart, so could many of his hearers turn to the hearing of Mozart. It may not have been quite accidental that the craze for swing accompanied the sharpest gain in musical knowledge and musical taste that the American people had ever achieved." Keeping that standard alive has been Johnny Knorr's mission.[23]

Knorr went to Jones Junior High School with the famous singer Helen O'Connell. Then he went to Libbey High School and at the time played with the big band of Jimmy Reemsnyder and sat next to the great Arv Garrison. Knorr may have thought of himself as the Glenn Miller of the Midwest; and, like his idol, Knorr was a tough businessman running a tight ship with strict rules. Be on time for the engagement. Be well groomed. No grandstanding. No smoking on the bandstand, and absolutely no booze. Ron Wagner, who played trumpet on occasion with Knorr's orchestra, said that you could not take a cup of water to your chair for fear Knorr would think it was vodka or gin. "I'm nasty" said Knorr, spoken with a sardonic grin, "and I don't mind telling you that it accounts for some of my success." In an interview in 2004 near his home in Oregon, Ohio, Knorr reminisced about some of the sidemen over the forty years he had had in his band.

"John Bud Strawbridge was with me for 25 years. He walked with a limp from a boyhood bout with polio. He could really play and in any style too that was called for, Harry James, Henry Busse, Clyde McCoy, a wonderful player. I tried to get Jimmy Cook but he said he doesn't like

Courtesy of J. Long (Johnny Knorr)

reading. But I did manage to get Ric Wolkins, an excellent player, and once in a while I'd get Gene Parker to sit in, especially if we had a show to do. He's a terrific musician. I had pretty good luck with drummers. I like a drummer who can take charge, like Bob Johnson who plays with us now. Clyde Yammick, who played with me for a while, did a stint with the Glenn Miller ghost band. Another very good drummer was Jerry Hartwig from University of Michigan who travelled down here to play with me. I guess the most interesting drummer I had was a black drummer named Aaron Purdy. He loved to solo, to show off, to throw the sticks in the air and behind his back; he'd put them in his mouth and then beat the tom-toms with his hands. Well, I don't usually go for this kind of thing, so I never encouraged him but the audience just went crazy. I remember one time he called me up hours before we were getting ready to do a date in Monroe, Michigan. He told me that he and his wife had a fight and that she took the car and left and he doesn't know if she was ever coming back. So we played without a drummer that night and we depended on the bass player for the beat. It was a guy from Wauseon who had played with the famous Russ Morgan Orchestra, a really good player, but he could never stop talking. He'd be talking and talking and telling the drummer how he should be playing. We used to call him Pappy, but Gabby would have been a better name. I finally had to let him go. He was driving everybody crazy."[24]

Knorr's son did the arrangements in 2004, but before that, the late Dave Melle did all those 1960s arrangements of "Sunny" and "Downtown." "John Mast was with me seven years playing piano and wrote some nice things," said Knorr. He was the ultimate perfectionist. He'd rewrite arrangements fourteen times, always changing a note here and a note there. Ya know, he thought he was pulling one over on me when he used to smoke on the stage. But I knew he was doing it and I caught him a number of times. The other piano player that I had who was very good was Howard Hill. He was with me for years. I probably had the best jazz soloist in Jimmy Riggs who ended up with Doc Severinsen. And I had pretty good luck with trombone players, Paul O'Connor for one and recently Mike Miller. You can hear him on Tommy Dorsey's 'Song of India' from my *Oh Johnny* CD.

"Tribute or theme nights when the band plays the music of Frank Sinatra or Glenn Miller draw the biggest crowds. Sometimes we do music of the big bands and play songs associated with Benny Goodman or Bunny Berigan and we even have part of the evening devoted to a medley of the songs of the sweet bands that we call Mickey Mouse time. That is when we let Bud Strawbridge loose in his imitations of Henry Busse and Clyde McCoy. Everybody really likes that."[25] When a newspaper writer once asked Knorr why there were hardly any people of color at Centennial Terrace, he replied, "I could never figure that out in all my years associated with Centennial."

Helen O'Connell "Those Cool and Limpid Green Eyes"

Johnny Knorr's classmate, the famous Helen O'Connell, had fond memories of Centennial Terrace, as she revealed to Seymour Rothman in an interview in January 1968. She was in town performing at the Hillcrest Hotel where Rothman's inquiry took place. With disarming frankness, Rothman admitted in the first paragraph, "You get so fascinated with the face, you lose track of what she is saying." So as she is telling him about her latest role on Broadway and about her life in Toledo, Rothman, in a series of asides, is telling the reader all about her eyes, her nose, her mouth, and her well publicized dimples. By the end of the fifth paragraph, Rothman had recovered from her spell and we learn that she was born in Lima, Ohio, came to Toledo at six, that she still had a cousin living in Toledo, and she went to Libbey High School for one year, and then when her dad died, she moved to Cleveland where she began her singing career to support her family.[26]

Band leader Jimmy Dorsey discovered her at the Village Barn in New York and matched her with Bob Eberly to form one of the most successful duets in all of popular music, on the level of Nelson Eddy and Jeanette McDonald or Dinah Washington and Brook Benton. A big year for both of them was 1941, starting off with "Amatola," and then "Yours," and in March she made her signature song, "Green Eyes." In October she appeared in a cameo role in a number of films, including one with comedian Red Skelton. In the summer of 1941 she recorded "Tangerine," with lyrics by Johnny Mercer. Then in 1943, with the help of Babe Russin on tenor saxophone and Johnny Guanari on piano, they recorded "Brazil."[27]

The result was that the readers of *Down Beat* voted her the best big band singer in America ahead of Ella Fitzgerald. Although she had limited range and tended to rush the beat when she got nervous, she sure could sell a song. Adding to her appeal was a childlike effervescence and the way notes seemed to explode as if, as one writer said, "someone was pinching her."[28] She came to Toledo again in 1973, this time at the Masonic Temple where she led the audience in a rousing chorus of "We're Strong for Toledo" and the Mayor decreed a Helen O'Connell Day.[29] She revived her career for a while in the 1970s and '80s when she went on tour with some of the ghost bands. Helen O'Connell died three years later at age 73. O'Connell never claimed to be a jazz singer. She comes close, however, with the Jimmy Zito Orchestra on some impossibly hard-to-find recordings done on the Coast Label in 1945.

Mary Ann Russo

Vocalist Mary Ann Russo was a raven-haired, lightly built woman with olive skin, almond-shaped eyes and a strong Italian bloodline. Class was almost always the first word to come out of the mouths of people who knew her. The kind you associate with Althea Gibson, Myrna Loy, or Peggy Lee. She could ride with any tempo, even flag-wavers, or turn up the volume on "I Love Being Here with You." However, it was those bittersweet love songs like "What's New," "My Old Flame," "The Nearness of You" that people remember best. Her singing style comes from a school of vocalists associated with the Stan Kenton, Les Brown, and Woody Herman big bands of the 1950s. June Christy, Lucy Ann Polk, and

Mary Ann Russo with Tony Celeste's band
Courtesy of Jack Walter

Mary Ann McCall are good examples. They were attractive, wholesomely seductive, and sang even better than they looked. They did not shout, and with the exception of Anita O'Day, they didn't scat. They didn't flaunt their sex appeal or call themselves jazz singers.

Russo's career started early. At age six she was singing on the *Kiddies Karnival* show on radio WSPD. At fourteen, as a student at Central Catholic High School, she was already singing professionally with the Jimmy Reemsnyder Band and later with Tony Celeste, Jack Runyan, and Johnny Knorr who said, "I was very fortunate to have had Russo for seven years. She is first-class and very particular about what she sings and how she sings it."[30] Knorr recorded an album called *Live at Franklin Park* in 1973 that featured Russo on "Watch What Happens."

Fred Kopp, a piano player in town, called her "Toledo's First Lady of Song." Tenor saxophonist Buddy Sullivan said that some of his most memorable moments were backing up Russo with the El Myers Quintet.[31] Pianist Preston Keys (his real name) was Russo's accompanist at the Hospitality Inn and remembered that she used her voice very expressively. "I am referring to glissandos and changes in timbre and tempo." Her biggest compliment may have come from saxophonist Jack Walter when he said, "I couldn't help admiring her and I don't as a rule like jazz singing. I figure if you want to play jazz, learn an instrument."[32]

In a telephone interview in 2004, she said that her favorite singer was Sarah Vaughn and her favorite arranger was Ralph Burns of Woody Herman fame. Duke Ellington's *Sacred Concert* was her favorite album. That recording, she later learned, was banned by three Baptist ministers for being anti-Christian and its leader Duke Ellington declared immoral for playing in night clubs.[33] When she got sick, Ramona Collins, Jean Holden, and others organized a farewell party called "Songs for Our Sister." Hundreds of people came: her family, members of the Toledo Jazz Orchestra, some from the Musicians Union where she was the first woman president, and some from the Toledo Jazz Society which she helped found. Carty Finkbeiner, mayor of Toledo, capped the evening when he acknowledged her many contributions to making Toledo a better place to live.

Russo always said that she preferred singing in small groups without the restraints of a big band, yet she seemed more at home at Centennial Terrace in front of Jack Runyan's big band in that baby blue evening dress waiting for the saxophones to come rolling in, the brass to come crashing through, and that six-note opening to "My Funny Valentine."

Chapter 9
Arv Garrison – Parker's Guitar

The bright splendor of Centennial Terrace was darkened on July 30, 1960, when Arv Garrison drowned. The headline of his obituary must have seemed like the final humiliation to those who knew him: "Ace Swimmer Dies In Quarry."[1] Arv was a very good swimmer, but he was a much better guitar player. Yet, there is hardly a word about his musical skills, nothing about the historic recordings he made with Charlie Parker, or about getting his picture on the cover of *Down Beat* magazine in 1946.

That was Arv's big year. *Esquire* said that he was one of the best young guitar players. Jazz writer Barry Ulanov went further when he called Garrison, "one of the great guitarists of our time." Django Reinhardt, whose name is as familiar to the world of guitar as Elvis Presley is to the world of rock, picked Arv as "the best of the new crop." That figures, because Arv came about as close to Django's style as anyone, including Les Paul, Oscar Moore, and all the rest. His specialty was the "tremelo gliss," a Django trick that guitar players to this day are trying to perfect. That is not bad for a guy who was not supposed to have any talent. That's what Arv's guitar teacher told him after a lesson one day: "Son, maybe it's time you thought about some other interests."[2] Aside from an occasional swim, Arv had no other interests, unless you wanted to count eating. There have been some big appetites in jazz, but

Arv's Toledo days
Courtesy of Vivian Garry

Arv practicing at home on Upton Avenue
Courtesy of Vivian Garry

not many to match Arv's. One night at Red Wells Restaurant, he downed ten roast beef and gravy sandwiches at a single sitting.[3] Nobody could understand why he never gained any weight. His dad thought it might be related to the mild seizures Arv had had when he was younger. Otherwise, he was a perfect specimen, a lady killer with blonde wavy hair, soft features, and a Sunny Jim smile that could make you say "yes." Add a Catalina wardrobe and a suntan like the one he had in the summer of 1945, and you are talking *Gentlemen's Quarterly*. Yet he was about as quiet and self-effacing as they came. Garrison wasn't exactly a worldly man. Guitar-simple might be more like it. Geography, politics, ball scores, even balancing a checkbook were beyond his scope. He was a mama's boy who never got around to leaving mom. She taught him how to read music and placed him in the center of the universe around which all things revolved. She took care of his daily affairs while Arv played along with his Django records from morning until night.[4] His mother was not even upset when Arv dropped out of DeVilbiss High School in the middle of his senior year. He was out of school more than he was in anyway, and when he was in, he was looking for some place to practice. Garrison was the "Basketball Jones" of the guitar.

Much of that time, he was working with Bill Cummerow who discovered Arv in 1938 at the high school variety show. "He must have been a freshman then. I guess I spotted a genius. We played quite a lot together after that. He was all music, but in my opinion he would never have gone anywhere without his wife, Vivian. She pushed him into the spotlight. She could be aggressive when she had to. I remember one night at a club somewhere, the owner walked over to Arv's chair and pulled as if to take it out from under him, saying, 'Stand up when you play here.' Vivian let him have it, 'Can't you see that his back is tired? Now let go of that chair or you are going to be wearing it.' I think we lost that engagement."[5]

In 1982, Vivian was selling time-shares in Lake Tahoe. Her platinum-blond hair, spiked heels, and long red fingernails brought to mind an ex-showgirl. "Everybody loved Arv," she recalled. "You know he taught me to play the bass and I became the first female jazz bass player. I was so crazy about Arv when I first met him that I used to follow him around to all of his rehearsals. I noticed that his bass player was having trouble getting the chords right, and I said to myself, 'Hell, I can do better than that,' so I went out and bought a bass from a guy who informed me that ladies did not play the bass fiddle. I took it home and put it in the middle of the front room. When Arv came home that night, I said, 'Teach me to play this, and we'll become famous.' I learned fast,

Early trio with Bill Cummerow, Vivian, and Arv
Courtesy of Bill Cummerow

so in a few weeks I was already better than Arv's regular bass player. "We picked up Bill Cummerow and called ourselves the Vivian Garry Trio, combining my name with Arv's. I contacted an agent, and we were off and running. Our repertoire included a lot of Nat Cole material. Wherever we played, the people loved us, so it wasn't that hard to get booked in Chicago at the Brass Rail. A lot of name jazz musicians were dropping by to hear this crazy trio with the chick bass player. One of them came up to me one night and told me that I played pretty well for a girl."[6]

By 1945 the Vivian Garry Trio, with new pianist, Teddy Kaye, was good enough to get work on New York's 52nd Street, known in those days as "Swing Street" and later as the "Street That Never Slept." It was a 24-hour non-stop jam session that began with the repeal of Prohibition and ended twenty years later. You could stand at one end of the street, look down, and see a sort of neon hall-of-fame rising above those canopied marquees announcing Jack Teagarden at the Club Downbeat, Coleman Hawkins at the Three Deuces, or Billie Holiday at Jimmy Ryan's.[7] Inside one of those brownstone buildings that lined 52nd Street was a jazz club the size

of a dollhouse called Kelly's Stables, where Viv and Arv had a nine-month contract. During that time, they entertained the best of the best, Duke Ellington and Ella Fitzgerald. Art Tatum came in one night. He stayed a set, but left without saying a word, unusual in that he and Arv had played together at the Waiters and Bellman's Club in Toledo. Arv was crushed until a few minutes later when Tatum's manager explained Art had had to go back to his job at the Onyx Club, but he wanted them to know how impressed he was.[8]

After that, they were on a roll; everybody wanted them. Their names began appearing in all the trade journals. Art Ford of WNEW invited them to play on his *Saturday Night Swing Session*, one of the most popular jazz radio programs in America. Then came their biggest break, a recording date with Guild Records.[9] The trio cut only two titles and they never did much, but having a record made it much easier to get booked out of town. "Relax Jack" on one side is a hep cat number, reminiscent of Page Cavanaugh, full of riffs and jive talk that would sound a little dated now. The flip side, "Altitude," with its intricate ensemble passages and thoughtful interplay, held up much better. Sometime before coming to New York, Vivian and Arv married. Vivian remembered that the ceremony was in St. Louis and was done more out of respect for Arv's mother than anything else. She was a strong and very possessive woman who had a complete hold on her only child. All I did was temporarily take her place. I fixed his soup and sandwiches twice a day the way she used to, arranged for all the hotel and travel accommodations, picked out all his clothes, and paid the bills. We were having a ball on the road together rehearsing, going to movies, swimming, but I don't know that we ever knew what love was. I could never crack the veneer between him and his mother. We were living for the moment without any long-term goals. We never talked about buying a home or insurance or current events or anything else substantial, and as I'm sitting here, I realize that I never knew him at all. Imagine being married to someone for ten years, someone you think you are in love with, and then you realize that you never knew him at all. It's kind of sad. Still, I'd have to say that those days were the highlight of my life, especially the Hollywood scene.[10]

The Vivian Garry Trio did well in New York, so when they decided to try Los Angeles, as many other jazz musicians were doing in 1945, their good reputation preceded them. Otherwise they would have been lost in Lotus Land, dwarfed by the number of jazz giants living there. There is a picture in a *Metronome Magazine* from that time showing Arv and Viv at a UCLA jazz concert surrounded by 22 of the biggest names in jazz, including Lester Young, Miles Davis and Benny Carter. The caption reads, ". . . an amazing cross section of the musical world." What's more, they were all living in L.A.[11] L.A. even had its own version of New York's 52nd Street called Central Avenue, a two-block cluster of jazz joints with signs out front saying "Bebop spoken here." For a short time you could hear the music on a dozen different radio stations programmed by some of the most outrageous disk jockeys ever to man a turntable, Steve Allen among them.[12]

Jazz fever was so high in L.A. when Arv and Vivian first arrived that club owners were hiring three name acts a night. Vivian remembered opening at the Royal Roost opposite Erroll Garner and Ray Bauduc. "We were all ready to make our debut when Teddy Kaye informed me that he wanted to go back to New York to be with his friend. I was furious. There we were, all ready to open, and no piano player. Then someone told me about Wini Beatty, who had been playing with Frankie Laine and Slim Gaillard. I wasn't sure how two girls would work out, but the audience loved us, and we

Top of the world—1945, Courtesy of Vivian Garry

Darlings of Sunset Strip. Wini Beatty, Arv, Viv, Courtesy of Vivian Garry

MONTE KAY
Presents
SYMPHONY SID'S WEEKEND

'BOP' Concerts

NO ADMISSION CHARGE · ONLY $1.50 MINIMUM

Fri., Sat., Sun., April 16, 17, 18.
Shows: 10-12-2 RESERVATIONS CI. 6-9559
STARRING

Allan EAGER   Kai WINDING
Lucky Thompson   Red RODNEY
&Introducing EARL COLEMAN vocalist on 'Birds' 'Dark Shadows'

Plus former star of the Dizzy Gillespie Band

Ray BROWN   Tadd Dameron
   Bass   Piano

Milt JACKSON   Joe HARRIS
   VIBES   DRUMS

:- ADDED ATTRACTION -:

SYLVIA SIMS   3 FLAMES
VIVIAN GARRY TRIO
with ARV GARRISON

ROYAL ROOST
1580 B'way cor. 47th St. opp. Strand Theatre
THE NEW JAZZ

---

were held over for a whole month. We worked at the Radio Room after that where we made those records for Lou Finston's Sarco Label. He wanted the arranger George Handy on piano rather than Wini because Handy had written some tunes for the date that Finston wanted to record.[13]

A few years ago, Onyx Records reissued the session under the name *Central Avenue Breakdown, Volume I*. Two of the selections, "Tonsillectomy" and "These Foolish Things," are among the best examples of Arv Garrison's style. The first is a complex "up and at 'em" chart that would make good background for a Tom and Jerry cartoon. Arv's guitar sound is crisp, his phrasing especially smooth as he breezes through his solo with such sure-fingered flair that it's hard to believe he had never played the tune before. "Foolish Things" is all Arv, everything from those high voltage twangs to the dive bomber runs into the

El Myers with Vivian at the Royal Roost
Courtesy of Vivian Garry

low register. Handy was so impressed with Arv's work that he asked him to play with Charlie Parker on the first of a series of bebop sessions for Dial Records.[14] Handy, the appointed leader of the date, wasn't the only one who wanted Arv. Parker wanted him too. He had played with Arv and Vivian on 52nd Street, and more recently at Billy Berg's in the heart of Hollywood. Moreover, Garrison had been a regular at the Finale Club, an afterhours bebop citadel where Parker was booking the acts.[15] Garrison was one of the few guitarists at that time who had the technique and imagination to play bebop. Most of the L.A. jazz community did not like the new music because of the stop-and-go rhythms, the slightly dissonant chords, and frantic tempos. One critic compared bop to being in a hardware store during an earthquake.[16]

Arv made four records with the Charlie Parker Septet, "Diggin' for Diz," "Ornithology," "Yardbird Suite," and "A Night in Tunisia." The last three became part of the basic library of jazz, but there is not much of Garrison. In those days, one side of a record was three minutes long maximum, meaning that in a seven piece group, no one was going to get much solo space. Arv's sixteen bars on the second take of "Yardbird Suite" is his longest statement. That amounted to half a paragraph, hardly enough time to develop an idea. Arv's role is to blend in with the ensemble, to keep things flowing and to lay down a good beat. He had a similar role on some little-known Dial recordings with Howard McGhee, one of the leading exponents of bop trumpet. More obscure are the sides Arv and Viv did with Vic Dickenson and Leo Watson, the madman of scat. Jazz critic Leonard Feather was the producer and Arv's most influential advocate. Chuck Wayne and Arv were his two favorite guitarists of 1945.[17]

The record Arv was most proud of was "Five Guitars in Flight," an arrangement he wrote for the brass-happy Earle Spencer orchestra. It was the first time a guitar ensemble had ever performed within a big band. Tony Rizzi, one of the five guitarists on that historic session, said that his current group, Five Guitars Plus Four, was an extension of Arv's original idea.[18] Meanwhile the Vivian Garry Trio had become the darling of Sunset Strip and a personal favorite of Lana Turner, Howard Hughes, and other Hollywood celebrities. *Metronome*'s Barry Ulanov heard the group at the Morocco and wrote, "The trio has a brilliant originator on guitar and two charming women to flank him with hipness in their voices and drive in their playing."[19] They were commercially and artistically successful, something that eludes most instrumental combos. In July, 1946, they made the cover of *Down Beat* magazine, a distinction that might compare to winning a Grammy these days. That was the summer they played on Catalina Island. It was the best three months of Arv's life. He was healthy, happily married, and one of the best jazz guitar players in America, on top of the world at age 25.

In October, pianist Wini Beatty noticed a change. "We were working at Slapsy Maxie's, a swank club on Wilshire Boulevard. Those were the days of live broadcasts, and we would go on the air for ten minutes. We were on the air one night, and right in the middle of an instrumental chorus, I happened to look at Arv's face. It went completely blank, and suddenly his hands fell down over the guitar, making a strumming effect. Viv and I looked at each other, and we must have turned white right through our suntans. We immediately jumped into the vocal part to try to cover it up. Nobody noticed anything, and all of a sudden, Arv recovered and everything was fine. That was the first time I realized that there was some kind of trouble there. I left the group not long after that, and Teddy Kaye flew out to rejoin them. They played in California for a little while, then all three returned to New York.

"I didn't hear from Arv again until 1956. I was working at the Howard Manor in Palm Springs when I got a call from Arv saying he was coming out west to see me and play a little guitar. I tried to discourage him because I knew there wasn't enough work out here for him, but he came anyway. When I went down to pick him up, I realized that this was a different person from the one I remembered. He was angry and foul-mouthed. He talked spasmodically while glancing off into space for fifteen minutes at a time. Worse, he was broke. I found him a place to stay and got him some food at a coffee shop. Then, very late one night, I let him sit in with me at the Manor. It was so pathetic; he couldn't play a lick. His hands were moving, but his coordination was gone. Finally, the manager came over and whispered in my ear something like, 'Get that creep who is trying to play guitar off the bandstand.' I made up a story about the strict union rules regarding guests so Arv's feelings wouldn't be hurt. After a week, I called his mother in Toledo and told her what was happening. She hung up on me. Nothing was wrong with Arv as far as she was concerned."[20]

Most of what was wrong had to do with the central nervous system. The epilepsy of his childhood had returned, but it was no longer mild. It was like a brief electrical storm going off in the back of his brain, causing him to black out and to lose control of his bladder.

The Vivian Garry Trio remained a top act in New York until 1949. The 1948 edition with Toledoan El Myers on piano was especially good. Myers, one of the best piano players in Toledo, reminisced about his days with Viv and Arv. "I was 22 when I joined them, and it seemed the most natural thing in the world for me to do. I had heard them in person and listened to all their records. I had Teddy Kaye's part down when I joined, which really impressed Vivian. We did a couple of weeks in Toledo, then we went to the Royal Roost in New York."[21]

The Royal Roost which is also known as the Metropolitan Bopera House was the epicenter of the bop universe when the Vivian Garry Trio was there. The Miles Davis *Birth of the Cool* band was born there. The Vivian Garry Trio shared the stage with the Charlie Parker Quintet with Max Roach on drums and Miles Davis on trumpet. "I was too young to realize the significance of what I was experiencing," said Myers. I was at the bar one night and Parker was there with three others and he said, 'Hey Man, buy me a beer. I'm a little short.' So we had a beer together, exchanged a little small talk until he had to go back to work. And as I'm walking away, I'm thinking to myself, here's little El Myers from Toledo, Ohio, having a drink with the great Charlie Parker—that is really something, isn't it!!?? A couple of nights later something happened to change my mind about being a full-time jazz musician. The Roost was in an old building and during intermissions I used to walk the long hallways for exercise. One night I noticed that one of the doors of a large storage closet was open and there was a glimmer of light coming through. I looked in and there was Bird

Program, Arv Garrison Memorial

Music is many things to many people

For Arv Garrison music was the greatest profession on this earth. His opinion never varied when it came around to the discussion of the importance of music. Nothing can replace the effect it creates in each of our lives. For some it gives an inner peace of mind, for others an excitement of spirit, and for a large majority of mankind, great happiness.

This is perhaps why we are now present at this concert. But when this concert is over, and you prepare to leave, we, the musicians of Toledo and the friends of Arv Garrison, hope that you take with you some of love and admiration we carry for this memorable musician and friend.

He was the greatest

Order of Performance

JACK RUNYAN'S ORCHESTRA
SAM SZOR, Master of Ceremonies
THE 5 BROTHERS
JACK REIDLING, TRIO
ART HILL, VOCALIST
JOE PRICE, QUINTET
MARY ANN RUSSO
CECIL HARRIS AND HIS JAZZ JESTERS
(Featuring Don Barnard, on Drums)

— INTERMISSION . . . 10 MINUTES —

STAN COWL TRIO
WINDY PEPPERS WITH ORCHESTRA
EL MYERS, QUARTET
(Featuring Buddy Sullivan)
MR. CLAUDE BLACK, PIANIST
VERN CHRISS WITH ORCHESTRA
(Featuring Miss Key To The Sea, Gloria Rehkopf)

FEATURED GUEST PERFORMERS
THE JOHN MAST, TRIO
THE FREDDY KOPP, SEXTET

Closing with
ARV GARRISON AND HIS GUITAR (Record)
Several Selections

---

getting a fix. I shut the door and got out of there but quick and decided right there that being a jazz musician would be better as an avocation. I love jazz, but not as a business. I don't think Arv's condition had anything to do with it, although he was having those twenty-second blackout spells where he would black out and become incontinent. I noticed they would come when somebody important, like Miles Davis or Dizzy Gillespie, was in the audience. So I always thought they were stress induced. When I left in the fall of 1948, I could have predicted what would happen."[22]

Soon after that, Vivian flew to California to see her ailing father and never flew back. She was ashamed of herself for doing that to Arv, but she had watched him have seizures for so long that she was having them herself. Week after week went by without any communication. Vivian would not return his phone calls or write him a letter. Then one day she received some divorce papers in the mail from his mother. Devastated and bitter, Arv returned to 3346 Upton Avenue in Toledo where he remained for the rest of his life under the watchful eye of his doting mother. It took years for him to get over Vivian, but he never recovered from the debilitative effects of epilepsy, a word his mother never used. She preferred attributing his mood shifts and migraine headaches to the medication Arv took for "a blow to his temple" that he had suffered in high school.

The worse he got the more he practiced. He played until he could not play anymore, sometimes falling asleep with the guitar still in his hands. By 1957, he was pretty much washed up. There were some flashes of the old Arv, but not many. The young guitar players who once came from all over the area to hear him sit in with Harold Lindsey at the M and L, or with Jimmy Jones at the Hollywood Cocktail Lounge, stopped coming. Many of the older musicians who would have been flattered to play with him when he was on top wanted no part of him now. Even his dad, who had always been so proud of Arvin's accomplishments, told a friend one day that he was sorry his son ever got into the music business for all the pain it caused him. Arv was having five or six blackouts a day. To make matters worse, he was mixing his medicine with uppers and downers and whatever else he could get his hands on. Swimming or driving a car could be fatal.

Garrison tried selling vacuum cleaners for a while and then went to work for the railroad. He lasted half a day. After that he gave guitar lessons. Arv could show you a chord or call you up in the middle of the night to play some newly discovered voicing, but he was not a teacher. Around 2 p.m. on July 30, 1960, Arv Garrison dove off the high board at Centennial Quarry. A lifeguard found the body three hours later in 25 feet of water. He had suffered his last convulsion. Pat Purcell was one of the last people to see him alive. She lived next door to Arv and dated him when he first came back from New York.

He'd be out on the porch playing his guitar, then suddenly the music would stop, and I'd look over and he'd be staring out into space like he was in a trance or something. After a few minutes, he'd start playing again. Toward the end he looked like a whipped dog, all bloated and out of shape. I remember the day he died as if it were yesterday. His folks really died with him. They went on breathing and all, but they never came out of their house after that.[23]

Vivian stayed on the west coast playing bass and singing with a new school of music called West Coast Jazz, the roots of which go back to the recordings of Lester Young, Miles Davis and Gil Evans. Most of its members, including Shorty Rogers, Bud Shank, and Frank Rosolino, had played with Stan Kenton. Their home was the Lighthouse at Hermosa Beach owned by a former Kenton bass player named Howard Rumsey. He named the group the Lighthouse All-Stars. They made a number of records and became one of the most talked about jazz groups in the country. To the delight of Jimmy Giuffre and Shelly Manne, Vivian became a regular substitute for Howard Rumsey, who according to Vivian, was not much of a bass player but a great manager and promoter. "So I sat in with the All-Stars often. I kept a good beat, no fancy stuff, and I made a record with them on the Skylark label."[24] Jimmy Giuffre, who she later married, was the leader and wrote the music. Vivian married several times after Arv, all of them except one musicians; and so many, that when she appeared at Shelly Manne's night club, he introduced her as "Vivian Garry and her all husband quartet."[25]

Arv's Guitar
Courtesy of The Truckees

Arv Garrison Memorial

Vivian received an invitation to the Arv Garrison Memorial but declined because, as she said, "I didn't have the nerve to face the past." The memorial turned out to be Toledo's first jazz festival. Eighty-nine musicians played, and many more came to the Civic Auditorium in September 1960. Arv's biographer, Jim Sheppard, El Myers, bandleader Jimmy Reemsnyder, and Jim Siwa of the musician's union planned and put the show together. Chase Clemmons of WTOD radio promoted it every day on his show. Toledo's music man, Sam Szor, was named Master of Ceremonies. Highlights were the Jack Runyan Big Band featuring Bud Strawbridge on trumpet, and Claude Black's thoughtful variations on "It Might As Well Be Spring" with Vern Martin on bass. Tenor saxophonist Candy Johnson, not yet a resident of Toledo, dropped by with drummer Swing Lee to shake the Civic's walls with Duke Ellington's "Cottontail." Fresh from the cafe lounge at the Lorraine Hotel, the El Myers Quartet featured the soft swing of Buddy Sullivan's tenor saxophone.[26]

Chapter 10
Buddy and El

Buddy Sullivan, a name that sounds as if it belongs on the sports page, is a bespectacled, mild-mannered accountant and super saxophonist. Before he moved to Cleveland in 1968, Sullivan and Harold Lindsey set the pace on the tenor saxophone in Toledo, Ohio. Sullivan is from a farm in Minnesota. He inherited a saxophone from his brother and learned to play by following a fingering chart given to him by a high school teacher.

"My first inspiration occurred when my dad took me to see the great Paul Whiteman band when I was twelve. That's when I saw Murray McEachren playing sax and trombone. I was enthralled and determined that playing saxophone was something I wanted to do." Sullivan's second inspiration was Glenn Miller's orchestra with Tex Beneke on tenor and vocals. Miller was on the air three times a week for Chesterfield cigarettes. "I used to play along with his solos from the radio. That's how I learned to play jazz. Tex was having problems breathing and could only sing when the Cleveland Orchestra brought him to town, so I got to play some of his solos from the Miller days right in front of him."[1]

"Later on I listened to the Black players like Chu Berry, Coleman Hawkins, and Herschel Evans. I played in some territory bands in the Dakotas and Nebraska. Then I went into the service. When I got out, I took advantage of my GI Bill and got a degree in accounting at the University of Toledo. That was one of the best moves I ever made. I had some offers to go on the road from name bands but you can't feed eight kids on a sideman's salary. In the late forties and early fifties I was playing with the Steve Snyir big band and the El Myers group. The turning point came when I heard Stan Getz' recording of 'Early Autumn.' That was over sixty years ago and it still takes you by surprise. I tried to get that light airy sound that Getz had. Also I liked Hank Mobley and John Coltrane, especially the *Kind of Blue* album. But Coltrane lost me on *A Love Supreme*."[2] The best of Buddy Sullivan on record is his solo on "A Night in Tunisia" from the Arv Garrison Memorial in 1960 and his sweet and lovely version of "Shadow of Your Smile," live, at the Lorraine Hotel in 1963. But it is doubtful that he ever played better than he did on "My Funny Valentine" with the El Myers Quintet one Friday night at Rusty's Jazz Café in the spring of 1985.[3]

Lorraine Hotel
Courtesy of the author

In the 1980s Sullivan was coming to Toledo five or six times a year either as a guest of the Toledo Jazz Orchestra, to play with Cliff Murphy and Claude Black at Murphy's Place, or most often, to play with El Myers and Jimmy Cook at Rusty's. "I quit for a while when I thought music was going in the wrong direction," said Buddy. "But it was El Myers, my very good friend of many years, who talked me into making a comeback."[4]

Over a spaghetti dinner one night, Elvin Myers, Toledo's Gentleman of Jazz, startled his dinner date by proposing a toast, "To poison ivy, my savior and the reason I am sitting here tonight. I got drafted in 1943 and took a test for the Army's Specialized Training Plan. No combat. However, it was disbanded suddenly and I was shipped for training to the 86th infantry division in Louisiana and given the title of lead scout. My job was to walk ahead of the platoon. The sergeant said to me, 'The enemy will shoot at you and then we will know where the enemy is.' 'But,' I said, 'I will surely be killed.' He said, 'Well you got to be good.' No way can I be that good, I thought. I was going to be the decoy, the fall guy in those cops and robbers movies of the 1940s. And do you know what saved me? Poison ivy. I was deathly allergic to it and we were stationed in Louisiana where it grew everywhere, and I got it so bad that when they saw how bad it was, they decided to keep me in the hospital instead of sending me overseas. I was shipped to Paris, Texas, eventually and ended up in an army band. I was so lucky. Two of my fellow pianists at DeVilbiss High School didn't make it back. One got killed in Okinawa and another in Italy. I spent D-Day in Rossford, Ohio, listening to Jim Ubelhardt, the Walter Cronkite of Toledo news. I'm thinking to myself, had it not been for poison ivy, I surely would have been dead and missed a hell of a life."[5]

From the very beginning Elvin Myers was the coolest kid in the classroom. He was every teacher's pet, and with that broad, beaming smile, every little girl's heartthrob. He was smart, good looking and very talented, the star of the 1942 Deviltries talent show, tap dancing, playing drums and piano. "My four years at DeVilbiss were some of the happiest years of my life. My parents supported me in everything I wanted to do. I had a car, almost before anyone in my class. I was popular with teachers and classmates. I can remember all the way back to Whittier Grade School the names of all my teachers and that was some 70 years ago.

"I was taking piano lessons from Mrs. Feldbach, and whenever I would improvise on my lesson a little bit, she would give me strange looks. I went to her 100th birthday party. I walked in and there she was in a wheelchair, so I walked up and introduced myself as Junior Myers, which I was called in those days. 'I am one of your oldest students.' She threw her arms up in the air and yelled out so that everybody could here. 'My God, this kid could dance!' She remembered after all these years that my dad had me taking tap lessons. She never said a word about my piano playing. As I got older I became self-conscious about tap dancing. The other day I heard a tape of Jo Jones, the drummer, talking about how tap dancers influenced drummers. I never had a problem with rhythm or time, probably because of those dancing lessons.

"I could not wait until Sundays when the name bands on their way to Cleveland, Chicago or Detroit would come through. I saw Gene Krupa with Roy Eldridge at the Paramount and afterwards as I was driving around, I saw Roy Eldridge standing on a corner with his trumpet case. I gave him a ride to the Waiters and Bellman's Club where everyone would go after a gig. It was not much on the outside, no marquee to tell you what it was. When you walked in, the place would be packed, the bandstand full of top-notch musicians. It was on Indiana Avenue, nothing there now but a vacant lot. It's funny, I can look out the top window of the Toledo Club, where I belong, and see a parking lot where the Trianon Ballroom used to be, where all the big bands used to play, right there on Madison Avenue.

"They had a big crystal ball over the spacious dance floor. Age was never a problem at the Trianon. I started going when I was sixteen. I saw the Stan Kenton Balboa orchestra there and Woody Herman's Four Brothers band, and that unforgettable Billy Eckstine bop band with Dexter Gordon, Gene Ammons, and Fats Navarro."[6]

Luna Pier today
Courtesy of the author

El Myers' biggest thrill was hearing Bunny Berigan at Luna Pier in the summer of 1941. "My dad took me. He sang a little and had all of Bunny's records as did many of his friends. So did trumpeter Jimmy Cook's dad. Jimmy told me one night that he was listening to Bunny Berigan when he was six years old. We didn't go into the dance pavilion because it was too crowded so we stayed on shore and listened from inside our car."[7]

Bunny Berigan recorded hundreds of records over his short life. Four of them were required listening for all serious trumpeters, "King Porter Stomp," "Marie," "Song of India," and his theme song, "I Can't Get Started." That became the national anthem of the swing era along with Glenn Miller's "In the Mood." "I Can't Get Started" was the record of the year in 1937. You can still find it occasionally on jukeboxes in retro restaurants. It was two sides of a 78 RPM recording. Louis Armstrong bought five copies of the record for himself and refused to record it because, he figured, you can't improve on perfection. "I Can't Get Started," was the theme song for John Huston's film, *Chinatown*, and part of the soundtrack for the 1974 film *Save The Tiger* with Jack Lemmon.

Berigan was the most wanted trumpet player in popular music, a white Louis Armstrong with rock star status. The businessmen, bankers and bartenders of Toledo and elsewhere knew about Bunny Berigan more so than Ziggy Elman, Harry James, or Roy Eldridge. Berigan personified the jazz playing trumpeter of the swing era, a nomadic, unstable, alcoholic genius in *The Bix*

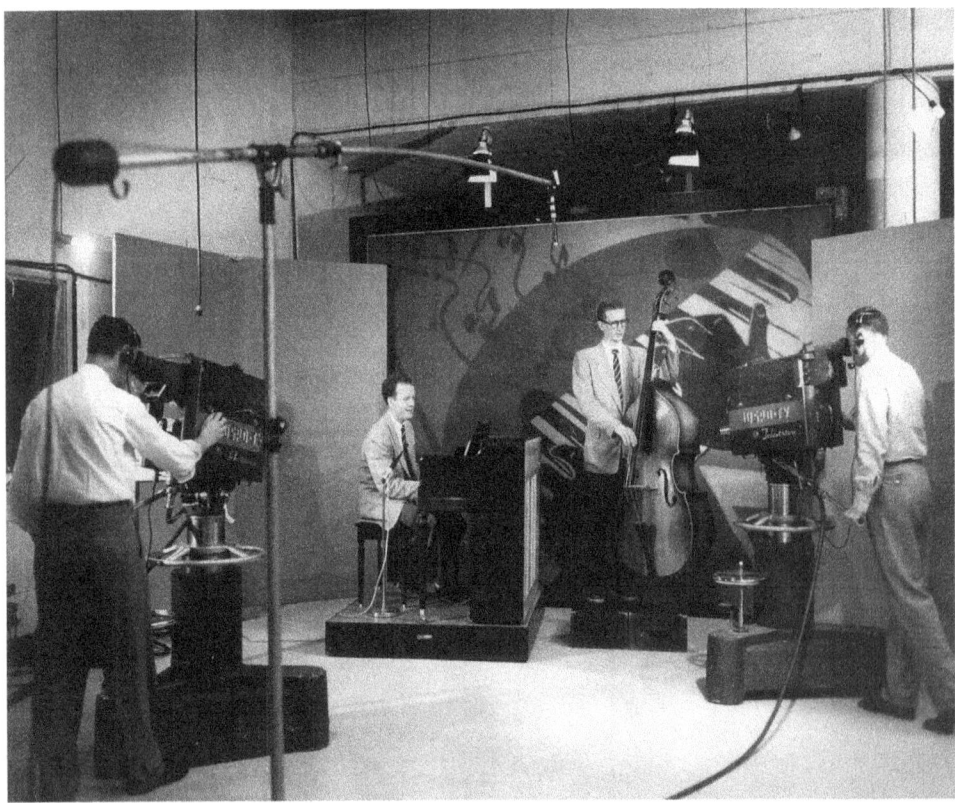

Bill Takas and El Myers on WSPD TV
Courtesy of El Myers

Beiderbecke Story, Part 2. Bunny Plays Bix is more than just an album title. Berigan was determined, as one writer said, "To follow his mentor's footsteps to the grave." When someone asked Berigan how he can play so brilliantly when drunk, he replied that he practiced that way.[8]

Berigan looked good up there leading the band, but that is about as far as it went. "Letting him lead a band is like giving car keys to a six year old," said writer George Frazier. "School was

Bill Takas with Billy May at Toledo University, 1956
Courtesy of the author

out when Berigan arrived."⁹ He played at the Trianon Ballroom when he came to Toledo. The last time was in early 1942, three months before he died of liver failure. Myers remembered that it had been sixty years but he could still hear the sound of Berigan's trumpet traveling over the waves "screaming with jazz."

"I have been fortunate to have played with some of the best bass players in the city," said Myers, "Bill Coyle, Jeff Halsey, Cliff Murphy. The strangest was Bill Takas. He worked with me at the Green Lite on Detroit [Avenue] and was my bass player on WSPD-TV's first jazz program. He left for New York not long after and became a first call bassist in New York."¹⁰ Takas, a Woodward High School graduate, was a gawky, pole-thin mechanical genius and automobile fanatic at home

Jack Walter, Buddy Sullivan, El Myers
Courtesy of El Myers

onstage or behind the wheel of a racing rig. He wrote the preface to a Datsun 510 manual, his favorite automobile of which he was a worldwide authority. Friends said he could hear a Datsun motor a quarter mile away. "He was always taking things apart and putting them back together, gerryrigging this and that," said his brother John, who also played bass. In New York he put his bulky upright bass in storage and helped design a graphite electric bass that could fold up like an umbrella and fit under his car seat.[11]

Bill Takas played on more recordings than any other Toledoan, including Art Tatum, Teresa Brewer, and Jon Hendricks. He had steady time, a great memory for tunes, and was adaptable enough to play Dixieland, bebop, as well as with rock groups like the Doors. He was in the house band at the Half Note in New York City, backing up the Al Cohn and Zoot Sims Quartet. He played with the Marian McPartland Trio for a while and was the bassist on Gerry Mulligan's five star recording of "I'm Gonna Go Fishin'." His most challenging assignment was with the Tal Farlow Trio in 1958. Takas is heard to his best advantage on a 1968 LP called the *Newport Jazz Festival All-Stars* where he supported the brilliant clarinetist, Peewee Russell, and cornetist, Ruby Braff who told everyone after that date that Bill Takas was the best bass player in New York.[12] The big band he most enjoyed playing with was Billy May, a dance band with plenty of talented jazz players such as Sam Donahue and Murray McEachren. May had a two-beat relaxed style reminiscent of Jimmie Lunceford. He was very popular with the ballroom dancers. His trademark was the slurring saxophones on such hits as "Lean Baby" and "All of Me." Noel Coward, the playwright, described the sound as a "wicked moan." The Billy May band with Bill Takas on bass played at the University of Toledo in 1956 during their tour of the Midwest. Takas lived on black coffee, fast food, and Camel cigarettes by the carton. He got his exercise by walking the streets of New York in the middle of the night, all the way from Harlem to the Bowery. He spent a lot of time in Paris where it was rumored he had a secret love. A close friend, actor Gordon Goodrow, looked after his apartment in Greenwich Village when he was gone. Goodrow described it as a disaster area, up four flights of stairs with no elevator to an unkempt, cluttered one room apartment with a leaky skylight and falling plaster. There was a collection of offbeat comedy records and a stack of hotrod magazines on a makeshift shelf and in the middle of the room all the parts to a Porsche engine.[13]

Takas had no ambition of ever being a leader. He was a confirmed sideman. For most of his career, he was the bass player for the songwriter pianist Bob Dorough, "the bebop hillbilly from Texas." They made many albums together. One of the best is called *Beginning to See the Light* that contained the classic "Better Than Anything." "We got along fine," said Dorough, "except for the time we drove his Datsun from San Francisco to Seattle for a club date. He would not allow me to drive or play the radio, or close the windows because he wanted to listen to the motor running and inhale the vapors. His hands were perfect for the bass violin," said Dorough, "mammoth hands with long spindly fingers, and gnarled claw-like nails." When he died of a heart attack in 1999, there was a memorial for him in New York. Dorough did the eulogy and Goodrow had the perfect closing when he sang Dave Frishberg's "I Want to be a Sideman."[14]

El Myers had the best of both worlds. He ran a spectacularly successful business and was one of the premier piano players in Northwest Ohio. In 1985, he was the guest soloist with the Toledo Jazz Orchestra. In 1999, he played opposite Kevin Eubanks of *The Jay Leno Show* at the

The Green Lite, just left of the jalopy
Courtesy of Rusty Monroe

El Myers, Bill Takas, Buddy Sullivan, Max Huffman on drums
Courtesy of El Myers

Centennial Jazz Festival. The high point of his musical career may have been the quintet he had at Rusty's Jazz Café in the mid-1980s starring Jimmy Cook and Buddy Sullivan. It was one of the best small combos to ever come out of Toledo. Rusty said in an interview in 2006 that she "could expect a full house every time they were booked."

There were two things about El Myers that never changed; he never ate at home and you never saw him without a tie and jacket, even in the middle of summer. He was old school. "As reliable as your phone bill," said a close friend, "with a strong contempt for what some musicians call 'aggressive sitter-inners.'" El remembered that "there used to be a guy in town who used to make me so mad because without ever asking permission, he would walk right up on the stage with his horn in his hands and tell me what tune we were going to play, and in what key. We usually complied but reluctantly."[15]

In the early 1950s, Myers was playing four nights a week at the Green Lite on Detroit Avenue with Sullivan, Takas, and Max Huffman on drums. Some of the biggest names in jazz would drop in after a dance date at Centennial or a concert at the Civic Auditorium: Wardell Gray. Lee Konitz, Art Pepper, and Shorty Rogers. "One night two sidemen came in from the Buddy Morrow Band. They never talked to anyone nor asked to sit in. They put their saxophone cases on the table in front of the stage and started to unlock them, getting ready to blow us away. I said to Buddy, 'Let's let 'em have it.' So we went into 'Have You Met Miss Jones' at a fast clip, not an easy tune at any tempo, and after Buddy's first chorus, they started putting their horns away. They knew they couldn't keep up with Buddy Sullivan."

El Meyers liked the big sound of open sevenths and inverted block chords. His style is more vertical than the horizontal horn-like lines of his colleague John Mast. The piano player he most resembled was Arnold Ross, a swing-to-bop member of the Jazz at the Philharmonic who made his reputation accompanying Billie Holiday and Anita O'Day. El would fantasize about backing up singer Diana Krall at some swank piano playhouse in New York, doing all those great tunes by Jerome Kern, Cole Porter, Richard Rogers, and George Gershwin, the ones El played on a solo CD he made shortly before he died.[17]

Chapter 11
Jazz Goes to High School (DeVilbiss)

DeVilbiss High School has had many outstanding jazz musicians. In addition to Arv Garrison and El Meyers, drummers Bob White and Charlie Mewhort went there. So did the highly regarded saxophonist Jim Riggs and the completely forgotten Brad Kinney, who always wanted to play trombone with Stan Kenton. Jack Tongring, the high school band director, thought Kinney was good enough.[1] He had everything, the tone, the technique, and the imagination. It was unclear why he did not do more with his gift. Dee Talmage, one of his girlfriends at DeVilbiss, thinks it may it may have been his loose living habits. "He lived like there was no tomorrow, staying up all night. I remember we used to listen for hours to his favorite album, *Four Freshman and Five Trombones*."[2] The caption under his name in his high school yearbook read, "Young man with a Horn" which was also the name of a bestselling book and movie about a character (played by Kirk Douglas) obsessed with the trumpet the way Kinney was with the trombone. It was difficult for anyone to picture him without it.

Howard Bellman, a bespectacled red-haired drummer in Jack Tongring's marching band, remembered him vividly. A retired arbitrator these days, Bellman recalled the effect Brad Kinney had on him. "We had this little band made up mostly of players from the marching band. We played stock arrangements like 'Perdido,' 'Moonlight Serenade,' and '720 In the Books,' songs like that. It's been a long time ago, but I think Jim Pugh was on piano, Jim French and Danny Lichtenwald on saxophones. I don't think we had a bass; I played drums. Bob Bruns might have been on trumpet and Brad on trombone. He was so much better than the rest of us it was ridiculous. It was like having an all-state forward playing on your neighborhood church team. I felt in awe just being around him. I felt so inferior that I actually had dreams about someday being able to play on his level, head and shoulders above everybody else. He was awesome."[3]

The jazz fan is often the most under-acknowledged member of the jazz community. They buy the tickets to the concerts; they buy the recordings and the trade magazines. Without them jazz could not survive. Ruth Ryan, a DeVilbiss graduate, was an office worker in downtown Toledo in 1952. She organized the Lee Wiley Fan Club.[4] Eventually she had everyone in her department

DeVilbiss High School
Courtesy of Toledo Lucas County Public Library

signed up. Wiley, the siren of the sweet-and-low-down school of jazz singing was so highly regarded that both Bunny Berigan and Louis Armstrong violated their recording contracts just to accompany her.

    The DeVilbiss High School class of 1955 had four of the most passionate and devoted jazz fans in the city. They had quite a bit in common: they were bright, they came from the same socio-economic background, they were fascinated by jazz musicians, and, with the exception of Clyde Kiker's modern problems class, they disliked school. They hung out at the Colony Record Store or at the Seligman Brothers and spent a large amount of money on jazz albums. They practically worshipped Dave Brubeck and never missed a Jazz at the Philharmonic (JATP) performance. Jazz at the Philharmonic, named after its place of origin in L.A., was the brainchild of Norman Granz, sometimes called the "P.T. Barnum of jazz." He took some of the most celebrated jazz musicians on worldwide tours playing in theaters, auditoriums and in the case of Toledo, the Sports Arena, so that anyone, no matter what age, could attend. In the 1940s, '50s, and '60s millions of people heard live jazz for the first time at a JATP concert.[5]

Seligman Bros. circa 1956
Courtesy of Rusty Monroe

Jazz Genius

    The most unforgettable character was Steve Calvert a sleepy-eyed loner with large lips and long, bushy hair that even at seventeen was on its way out. As far as anyone knew, he never learned how to play an instrument or had any formal musical training. He saw himself more as an errand-boy for jazz, a proselytizer, a self-styled critic blessed with an innate sense of what was hip and nothing was hipper in 1955 than modern jazz. He hated physical exercise, the American dream, and everything about the high school curriculum, especially math. A rumor floated around the pale green walls of DeVilbiss High School that he had publicly burned his algebra book in protest. Calvert had an Iago-like manner where everything was very confidential, like a bookie with a hot tip. His classmates avoided him like a bad habit. It was doubtful he ever spent more than fifteen minutes on homework in the four years he was enrolled at DHS. Some teachers gave him a D- just to get rid of him. But Steve Calvert found more impulse in eight bars of Charlie Parker than anything Rudyard Kipling ever wrote; more of life's meaning in Duke Ellington's "Black, Brown and Beige Suite" than in even the best of Brahms or Beethoven. He was not interested in the Magna Carta or how to diagram a sentence in Rose Bloom's English class; but on the subject of jazz, he was more than just well-informed, he was a walking encyclopedia. He listened to jazz on the radio, studied *Down Beat* and *Metronome* magazines like a scientist, plus all the trade magazines published in Great Britain and on the European continent. He could tell you who was playing where in all the major jazz cities in the world including Toledo. He read biographies and histories of jazz by such authorities as Leonard Feather and Marshall Sterns. He knew where Art Tatum lived and why he was called "the greatest piano player of them all." He knew the exact time and day when Charlie Parker died, a day he spent in the DeVilbiss High School library going from table to table whispering to anyone who would listen that "Bird was gone."

His evenings were spent either going to jazz concerts or hanging out on Indiana Avenue listening to drummers Swing Lee or Babe Borders at the Indiana Tavern. He was a regular at Tate's on the corner of Tecumseh and Ewing Streets where one night he saw Kenny Burrell and Tommy Flanagan bring the house down. Steve Calvert must have been the only one out of 1500 all-white students at DeVilbiss who had long-term meaningful contacts with the Black community. He felt at home there; he liked the food, the colorful expressions, the less inhibited nature of most of the people, and, of course, the music. Norman Mailer, the author, had someone like Calvert in mind when he wrote his famous essay, "The White Negro," describing an outsider who questions authority, champions the underdog, lives for jazz, and would rather be Black. Talk at the 50th DeVilbiss High School reunion was that he had eventually gone into law enforcement.

One of Steve Calvert's few friends was Howard Bellman. Bellman was taking drum lessons

The Heath Band - Waiting for Ted
Courtesy of Ted Hallock

from Hyman Hygait, a drummer in the Rivoli Pit Band, who taught many of the drummers in Toledo. "I was reading *Down Beat* religiously," said Bellman. "I had no mind of my own. Anything that got five stars I bought. I began listening to the Fire House Five, a Dixie group, and then I got into swing bands. And finally, with the help of Calvert, I graduated to bebop, especially bop drummers like Max Roach and Kenny Clarke. Steve made quite an impression on me. We used to go over to his house after school and listen to his record collection. He redirected my ears, told me what to listen for, and introduced me to the Charlie Parker Savoys. I found out what Dave Brubeck records to buy. You know, after 55 years I can still sing all the solos on 'Take the A Train' from the *Jazz Goes to College* album. About the only jazz on TV was Soupy Sales out of Detroit. He had some heavyweights on his show who happened to be playing in Detroit at the time."[6]

Sales, whose real name was Milton Supman, was a slack-jawed, dopey-acting host of a popular kids' TV show in the daytime and a jazz host at night. He had Chet Baker, Wardell Gray, the Marian McPartland Trio—anybody who was in Detroit appeared on his late night show. Not long ago a DVD of some of Soupy's shows of the 1950s was released; missing is the night that Charlie Parker visited. Another important event in the jazz education of Howard Bellman occurred during the annual senior trip to New York. "I escaped down the fire stairs of the hotel where our class was staying and walked all by myself to Birdland, the most famous jazz club in the world. The Modern Jazz Quartet was playing. It was my introduction to the big time. And I came back to Toledo wanting more than ever to be a jazz drummer and buying more records than ever, most of them from Seligman's Record Bar. I had a crush on the woman who worked there. I tried to impress her with my seventeen year-old sophisticated taste by buying those early Prestige and Blue Note albums."[7]

There will never be anything quite like Seligman Brothers. It was located on the north side of Sylvania Avenue about 75 yards west of North Lockwood Avenue. Actually it was two stores split right down the middle. On one side they sold appliances and sporting goods, everything from washing machines to fishing tackle. People in the neighborhood saw television for the first time when they witnessed Babe Ruth's funeral through the plate-glass front window of the store. The other side was called the Record Bar because the counter was in the shape of a tavern bar. But instead of napkins and ashtrays there were four 3-speed record players and instead of bottles of booze on the back wall, there were tiny shelves filled with thousands of 45s, the largest collection east of the Mississippi River. Around the edge of the ceiling hung

"That Feller McKellar"
Courtesy of *Metronome Magazine*

large colored publicity photos of Dinah Shore, Spike Jones, Gene Krupa, and other recording artists of the time. Sitting in the front window of the record bar was a life-sized replica of a Dalmatian, head cocked, listening to the voice of Enrico Caruso on a wind-up gramophone. It has been some thirty years since the store closed, yet jazz people still talk about the rows of record albums including such hard-to-get labels as Nocturne, Transition, and Storyville.

The store was owned by Hyman and Phil Seligman. They were two years apart in age but because they were exactly the same height and because they looked and dressed alike, people thought they were twins. Standing side by side, greeting customers at the door wearing that same bland half-baked smile, they looked more like Siamese twins. The Seligman brothers never showed much interest in jazz or any other music for that matter. How was it possible, then, that two seemingly indifferent businessmen could feature an enlightened selection so attractive that people came from all over to shop there?

The secret was in the source. And the source was the Black media. So Phil and Hyman read the *Bronze Raven*, the *Toledo Script*, and the *Toledo Sepia City Press* from cover to cover. They read the record reviews by the *Associated Negro Press* and ordered everything the columnist recommended. They paid close attention to the coming attractions in the entertainment sections, acts that did not appear in the *Toledo Times* or the *Toledo Blade*. For instance, if Bullmoose Jackson and his Buffalo Bearcats were coming to the Belmont Ballroom or Gatortail Jackson was coming to the Paradise Inn on Vance Street, the brothers would be sure to have two or three copies of all their recordings. To learn what to stock in the way of urban blues, they listened to Frances Belcher, "Lady B," from 4:30 to 5:00 p.m. every day on radio WTOD. That is where they first heard a young, and then unknown, Ray Charles.[8] When the first edition of Seligman Brothers died in the mid-1970s, hundreds of collectors came to pick over the remains of one of America's greatest stores, right up there with the Magic Flute in San Francisco, Filippi's in Seattle and Sam Goody's in New York.

Howard Bellman eventually ended up at the University of Cincinnati because he had read in *Down Beat* that it had more jazz than any other city of similar size. Also it had a fine Law School and an outstanding School of Music. Top-notch musicians were everywhere. "After a while I had one of those defining moments in life when I realized I was short on talent. I was five-foot-five playing in a six-foot-nine league. I kept picturing myself at fifty playing at the local Holiday Inn." Bellman chose Law School and ended up as a nationally acclaimed mediator. "I still listen to jazz every day," he said. "I still play those ten-inch albums I bought so long ago at Seligman's."⁹

Lee "One-Putt" Raymond was a six-foot-one, immaculately groomed golf prodigy. He had a coal-black carefully contoured crew cut, a hot temper and a garage full of shattered putters to prove it. Apart from being one of the best prep golfers in the state, not far behind Jack Nicklaus, Lee Raymond was crazy about jazz. It all started one Christmas when he received a portable 45 RPM record changer along with a copy of *Ted Heath's 100th London Palladium Sunday Concert*. Heath was and is the most popular big band ever to come out of Europe, a mix of Les Brown, Duke Ellington, and Stan Kenton. He had so many fans in the U. S., especially in Toledo, that the State Department put together a tour of major American cities in 1956. That first note on the *Palladium* album hit Lee Raymond like a ten-foot wave; and from that moment on he was hooked.

Within weeks he discovered all the jazz on the radio, Jam with Sam, Jack the Bellboy from Detroit, and his favorite, Phil McKellar, "That Feller McKellar," on CKLW in Windsor, Ontario. McKellar was *Metronome Magazine*'s Disc Jockey of the year in 1955, beating out Al Jazzbo Collins, Jimmy Lyons in San Francisco and Symphony Sid in New York. An ex-drummer with infallible taste, McKellar was on the radio from 11:30 at night until 6:00 in the morning five nights a week. Dentists, plumbers, symphony conductors, anyone with even a slight interest in jazz tuned in. He inspired more future jazz players, sold more records, and introduced more people to jazz than could ever be calculated. He called his first hour of the show "The Choice Ones," the ones whose sound is so unmistakable that they could be identified in a couple of bars, for example, Ben Webster, Paul Desmond, and Theolonius Monk. On the night he featured Erroll Garner's Concert by the Sea, the station had to bring in extra people to man the phones. Phil McKellar knew more than anyone how to make radio the "theater of the mind." He could make it seem like you were there in person, front and center, in some smoky afterhour cafe listening to Erroll Garner play "Misty."¹⁰

On the weekends, Lee Raymond listened to NBC's *Monitor* and that is where he discovered Alex Kallao. What a year Alex Kallao was having! RCA Victor hailed him as their new star and

spent a lot of money promoting his album, *Evening at the Embers*. He made numerous appearances on television shows including Soupy Sales in Detroit and the *Steve Allen Show*. *Time* magazine had a short article telling all about this blind, classically trained pianist currently living in Detroit who was gaining such a large following.[11] Alex Kallao was all over the airwaves, not just in Toledo and Detroit. Seligman's, Grinnell's, and Larry Meng's fine record store could not keep the albums in stock. In his white dinner jacket, black bow tie, and dark shades, Kallao looked more like a well-fed Middle Eastern oil baron than a jazz pianist, "as if he had just stepped out of an Esther Williams musical," exclaimed one writer.[12] His piano style was a blend of Bach, bebop, and show tunes, not unlike George Shearing. He made one more record live at Ottawa University for an offbeat label and then vanished, turning up years later in California, still thrilling audiences with his version of "The Man I Love."

One of Lee Raymond's friends going all the way back to McKinley Elementary School was Fred Lutz. Long before Lutz was writing spirited reviews on books and films for the *Toledo Blade* and even longer before he became infatuated with the major American writers, Lutz was a serious jazz fan. His love affair began when Fred Sr. brought home a copy of Billy May's "Lean Baby." Fred liked the easy two-beat swing of the rhythm section and the sexy sound of the slurred saxophones. He was sixteen when he saw Stan Kenton and Dizzy Gillespie at the Sports Arena, "a place better suited for hockey, wrestling, and circuses than jazz," Lutz complained. The highlight of the concert was June Christy. She had just recorded her best-known album, *Something Cool*. Fred wore out his copy within a couple of weeks. He played it every day after school and before he went to bed. "Cute as a bunny's ear with a voice that aroused my libido," he remembered.[13]

The following summer he heard Les Brown and his Band of Renown at Centennial Terrace. That was the night that saxophonist Dave Pell took a seven-minute solo on "Montoona Clipper." Fred spent most of the evening riveted to the edge of the stage. In a 1985 conversation at the Toledo Press Club, Lutz, bearing a strong resemblance to actor Don DeFord, said he almost did not graduate from DeVilbiss High School. "Between girlfriends, jazz concerts, and movies at the Colony Theater, I finished third from the bottom of my senior class."[14]

Lutz spent a lot of time inside the Colony Theater that was at the east end of the Colony Shopping Center. Every Wednesday afternoon you would find him in the back row of the theater

Fred Lutz, 2nd from left on top row, with members of the 1956 TU Phi Kappa Psi pledge class;
Jazz pianist Bruce Kinney is front row, far right
Courtesy of Toledo Lucas County Public Library

making mental notes of the current attraction. His favorite film was *The Wild One* starring Marlon Brando as a rebellious leader of a motorcycle gang about to take over a small town. But it was not Brando's acting or the story that fascinated Lutz. It was the jazz score by Leif Stevens and performed by fuglehornist Shorty Rogers and His Giants. Fred, who was always reading, called it "the consummate marriage of jazz and film." He became the unofficial president of the Toledo chapter of the Shorty Rogers Fan Club.

Rogers was one of the pioneers of a school centered in Los Angeles called West Coast Jazz (1951-1957). He wrote clever melodies with hilarious titles like "The Chinook that Melted My Heart," "Tale of an African Lobster," and "Sweetheart of Sigmund Freud." What endeared him most to Lutz became one of the best put-ons in all of popular music. One afternoon in 1952 Shorty, Shelly Manne, Jimmy Giuffre, and the rest of the Giants went into the RCA studio and recorded "Shortnin' Bread" and "Blockbuster" under the pseudonym Boots Brown and His Blockbusters. It was a joke, a musical parody of some of the worst features of rock and roll. Shorty and RCA conspired to market it as the real thing and aimed it at millions of teenagers with big allowances. Disc jockeys fell for it. So did just about everyone else. High school students went batty over the screaming saxes, the monotonous riffs, and sledgehammer drumming. Every jukebox in every tavern, malt shop and hamburger joint in West Toledo had a copy of "Blockbuster." Somebody even put a dance step to it. When a planning committee at Ohio University tried to hire the Blockbusters for their Senior Prom, they discovered to their surprise that they never were.[15]

Lutz' interest in jazz peaked in 1956 when he was a freshman at the University of Toledo. His English composition instructor told him he had a "flair for writing" and for a couple of weeks he thought about becoming a jazz critic. He could "write his butt off," as he used to say, and had a natural contempt for received opinion, especially the opinion of most jazz critics. But becoming a complete critic seemed out of reach. He thought that jazz critics should know about jazz history, have a couple of years of basic piano, some familiarity with the instruments of jazz, and more than just a passing acquaintance with classical music. Writing about movies, however, was something he was certain he could do.

Chapter 12
Jazz Goes to College

In the winter of 1956 the University of Toledo and the Toledo Museum of Art brought to town four of the biggest names in jazz, Stan Kenton, Don Shirley, Duke Ellington, and the number-one small combo in America, the Dave Brubeck Quartet. Even in 1956 Brubeck had accomplished enough to be in the Hall of Fame. He won all the major polls, sold millions of records, had his picture on the cover of *Time* magazine,[1] and introduced thousands of people to jazz. He courted the college crowd by going on tour for fifty weeks a year, playing concerts at colleges and universities, some of which were recorded and became bestsellers. The *Jazz at Oberlin* album was the first time jazz was played on their campus. Brubeck recorded *Jazz Goes to College* at Ann Arbor just forty miles away from Toledo.

In February of 1956, the Brubeck Quartet was at the Peristyle, an auditorium audiophiles called one of the most perfectly designed music halls in the world, on the same stage where the Budapest String Quartet had played, and where heretofore jazz producers had feared to tread. It was an electronically free evening to remember, just one mike, no elaborate sound system, a three-piece set of drums, a grand piano, a saxophone, and a bass violin. They played from their recent album, *Jazz: Red Hot and Cool* that featured a tune that Brubeck wrote for Duke Ellington called "The Duke." Brubeck was the leader, but altoist Paul Desmond was the star. He had a dry, delicate, vibrato-less tone that sometimes teetered on the brink of a clarinet. In an interview in 1978, Brubeck said that he had to push Desmond into the odd time signatures like "Time Out" and "Take Five" and "Time Further Out." "His favorite period was 1955-1957. He liked the older tunes, the four bar exchanges, the things we used to do harmonically and the counterpoint."[2] When Desmond was not playing, he stood stone still in his rumpled suit, fingers clasped around the bell of his horn, head bowed like a monk in meditation.

On Saturday, February 11, the Don Shirley duet took the stage. Shirley specialized in rhapsodic interpretations of romantic ballads such as "Tenderly" and "Stardust." He had a Boston Pops appeal for those people who were not sure what jazz was. Jazz people were divided on whether this conservatory-trained musician was playing jazz. One French jazz pianist thought

Brubeck Quartet at Peristyle 1956
Courtesy of University of Toledo

Shirley would be better off picking carrots.[3] Duke Ellington, however, thought it was some of the most beautiful piano music he had ever heard, made even better by the accompaniment of his bassist Richard Davis. *Esquire* magazine wrote that "Shirley plays fat notes that fall soft as velvet and small ones that tinkle like ice in a martini glass."[4] Shirley's appearance on *Arthur Godfrey Time* brought him to the attention of a national audience. Godfrey, a 1950s Oprah Winfrey, had been plugging Shirley's first album, *Tonal Expressions*, for weeks.

In the middle of his concert in Toledo, Shirley suddenly began to sway back and forth violently, his hands flapping up and down like wild birds. He almost fell off the piano bench. Was he having a nervous breakdown in public? Were the people at the Peristyle witnessing the disintegration of a brilliant artist? Hardly. It was part of the program to lead the audience one way and at the last second, just when it appeared Shirley had gone over the edge, he paused, and went into "How Much Is That Doggie in the Window?" The whole place erupted with laughter and applause. Of all the big bands that ever came to Toledo, none had the impact of Stan Kenton. He came to Toledo several dozens of times, usually at Centennial Terrace or the Trianon Ballroom. The camps and clinics Kenton directed in the 1960s and '70s inspired the Toledo Jazz Society to educate elementary and secondary students on the nature of jazz. The Toledo Jazz Orchestra, a gathering of some of the best and brightest musicians in the area has kept the Kenton spirit alive with annual tributes. One of the first local bands to come under the Kenton charisma was the Jack Runyan Orchestra with brilliant arrangements of "Opus in Pastels," "Dinah-flow," and "Love for Sale."

Stan Kenton was forever uncovering new or unrecognized talent. He discovered the Four Freshmen and the Al Belleto Sextet whose vocal arrangements were Xerox copies of the Fresh-

Bill Coyle with El Myers on piano
Courtesy of Jerry Sawicki

men. For some reason, they had a following among coeds at Michigan State University who arrived in droves the night Belleto played at Leroy's on Dorr Street near Secor Road. The reverence for Stan Kenton sometimes seemed extreme. One barkeep in California had his tavern decorated to look like the inside of the Stan Kenton band bus. Another loyal fan in Portland, Oregon had Kenton's Contemporary Concepts album played at his funeral.[5] Bill Coyle, a fine bassist, and Toledo's foremost authority on Stan Kenton, flew all over the United States to attend concerts. Some years ago he flew to Los Angeles for a four-day Kenton reunion of his fans and alumni. They came from all over the world to celebrate the music and life of one of the most innovative and courageous figures in jazz.

Another Toledoan crazy about Stan Kenton was big Charlie Mewhort who had a dream that someday he would play with Stan Kenton. It could make him nervous just thinking about it. "The drummer is the quarterback. The other sidemen in the band depend on the drummer to punctuate and underline various parts of the arrangement and above all to keep a steady beat. You have to know when to play loud, when to play soft, when to use sticks, when to use brushes. In the Kenton band you had to have strength and endurance." Gary Hobbs, a drummer who played with Stan Kenton for much of the 1970s, said it was "murder on your body, like chopping wood for two hours."[6]

At Centennial Terrace in 1964, Charlie's dream came true. According to pianist Mark Kieswetter, "Kenton's regular drummer was going to be late for some reason and Stan Kenton was frantic. Word traveled around the audience that there was a good drummer by the name of Charlie Mewhort in attendance. Of course Stan was skeptical, but you can't play without a drummer

Charlie Mewhort
Courtesy of Jerry Sawicki

in Stan Kenton's band. Well, Kenton started out with his theme "Artistry in Rhythm" and went into Bill Holman's "The Opener" and after a few bars Kenton knew there was nothing to worry about. From listening to so many Stan Kenton records for so long, Charlie Mewhort filled all the breaks and ushered in all the solos. Stan was really impressed. Charlie, of course, felt like a million dollars."[7] Charlie Mewhort died early, but he died a rich man with loads of friends, lots of love, and those fifteen minutes with Stan Kenton. Many Kentonites think the 1956 band, the one that came to Toledo, was Stan Kenton's best band. He had Mel Lewis on drums. Bill Perkins, Carl Fontana, and Lennie Niehouse were his main soloists. And in Bill Holman and Johnny Richards, he had two of the most adventurous composers/arrangers in jazz. Richards had just written *Cuban Fire!*, a blend of Afro-Cuban rhythms and American jazz. After all these years, it is still one of his best albums.

The Kenton concert was sold out before his loyal fans discovered that Kenton was not going to play at the Peristyle, the Paramount Theater or even the Civic Auditorium, but instead, inside the University of Toledo's ROTC armory, a steel, glass and concrete building, with a linoleum floor where, hours earlier, cadets in full uniform had marched in formation to commands of Cap-tain Cushing. Kenton fans were outraged; one compared this humiliation to putting Arturo Toscanini and the NBC Symphony in a junior high gymnasium. If Kenton was annoyed, he certainly did not show it during the concert and the band played on gallantly. The centerpiece of the festival series was Duke Ellington, one of the indispensable figures in jazz history. For more than fifty years he maintained an orchestra with almost no turnover. Francis Williams, the only Toledoan to play with Ellington, stayed for seven years off and on. Ellington has written hundreds of songs, many that have become jazz classics or part of the American popular songbook. He is one of the main links in the evolution of jazz piano, beginning way back in the 1920s when he was playing in the stride style of Willie "The Lion" Smith, to the 1940s and '50s as a modernist influencing Theolonius Monk and Cecil Taylor. Ellington's face was on a postage stamp but it was

doubtful many people could tell you why.[8] A walk down the halls of Scott High School in the 1950s might yield a portrait of Marian Anderson or Booker T. Washington, but you would never find one of Duke Ellington despite a sizable following in the Black community that went back to 1930 when he played at Luna Pier in Lakeside, Michigan. That was the Cotton Club Band also known as the Jungle Band with those growling trumpets, snarling trombones, moaning saxes and Oriental gongs. One of the stars of that band was Freddy Jenkins who took a strong liking to Toledo. He played at Chicken Charlie's and even co-wrote a tune called "Toledo Shuffle."[9]

One of the great moments in Toledo jazz happened at 8:00 p. m., June 6, 1945, when Duke and his men riding high on an elevated stage emerged from the basement of the magnificent Paramount Theater playing "Things Ain't What They Used To Be." A recording of that evening is available on the Fairmont label.[10] The band that the University of Toledo brought to Toledo was the band that broke up the Newport Jazz Festival six months later with its version of "Diminuendo and Crescendo." Duke had his picture on the cover of *Time* magazine in 1956. So imagine the dumb-faced shock when the people who had been at the Peristyle that night read what the reviewer of the *Toledo Blade* had to say: "a carnival of uncouth vulgar sounds, Jazz hounds should not be allowed to profane the sanctity of the Peristyle."[11] The *Toledo Blade* was flooded with letters calling the reviewer "snide, condescending and nasty." One wondered "how a reviewer for the *Blade* could review a concert if he leaves at half-time."[12] One could only guess what Duke had to say. He probably responded the same way he did in 1952 when a *Down Beat* critic slammed a particular Ellington performance. "I'll just have to try harder next time."[13]

Chapter 13
The Case Against Jazz

Resistance to jazz was everywhere in the 1920s, in the schools, the universities, magazines, newspapers, and music teachers. Except for Langston Hughes and a few others, the Black intellectuals of the Harlem Renaissance decried it.[1] They preferred strings to saxophones, Paul Whiteman to Louis Armstrong, Marian Anderson to Bessie Smith. They asked, "How could something nurtured in brothels and barrelhouses have any musical value?"[2]

Most music critics thought it was crude and obscene, musical graffiti played by "intoxicated clowns" imitating the uncouth sounds of farm animals. One article in *Toledo Blade* called it a "foolish fad."[3] A letter in the January 1921 issue of *Variety* magazine from a musician's union in Pittsburg predicted the Death of Jazz. Also in January 1921, the whole town of Zion, Illinois, banned jazz.[4] There was even a campaign to outlaw playing by ear. Some psychiatrists thought it produced neuroses. *Ladies' Home Journal* wanted to take the "sin out of syncopation." The writer, Ann Faulkner, said that jazz is nothing less than a violent reaction against law and order. She claimed it was part of the Bolshevik element of society, "striving for expression even in music."[5] Even the Salvation Army was down on jazz. They tried to block the construction of a movie house next to a home for unwed mothers, fearing that jazz coming from the theater's piano would "implant 'jazz emotions'" into the unborn baby.[6] Most of the Black middle class and the community leaders did not want to be associated with

Lafayette Street - Chicken Charlie's is last building on the block with white oval sign
Courtesy of The Blade

the primitive sounds and the promiscuous dancing of southern migrant Blacks. Art Tatum's close friend, Harold Payne, a banjoist turned businessman, said, "My folks cared nothing for jazz. I had to sneak a copy of Mamie Smith's 'Crazy Blues' into our house. They thought it was the Devil's doing."[7] Bassist Cliff Murphy, a name synonymous with jazz in Toledo, said that his dad, a minister, preached to him on these dens of iniquities called nightclubs where the temptation for wine, women and drugs was everywhere.[8]

You might imagine how unpopular jazz was in the neighborhood taverns and beer halls of the many ethnic groups that made up a large part of Toledo's population. Jazz was the music of the Black, non-union people brought north by Willys-Overland and allied industries to replace the Hungarians, the Italians, the Polish, and the Germans, when the U. S. Immigration laws of WWI and later resulted in being locked out of their jobs. Not to mention the invasion of heretofore all-white neighborhoods by Black people playing "jungle music."[9] But the most aggressive opposition to jazz came from the urban reformers, from the Daughters of the American Revolution who wanted to sanitize radio with the help of the federal government to prevent jazz from being played on the radio,[10] and the Women's Christian Temperance Union, who lobbied authorities to crack down on the gangsters, to uphold the laws of Prohibition and to shut down all the jazz clubs.[11] The Juvenile Protection Agencies worried that jazz was an aphrodisiac and would filter into the schools.[12] Foremost among the anti-jazz element were the fundamentalist ministers and their congregations, some of whom were people, as columnist H. L. Mencken said, who "were haunted by the fear that somewhere, somehow, someone is having a good time." Elwood A. Rouser, pastor of Toledo's First Westminster Presbyterian Church, came very close to losing his job when he invited a "jass" orchestra to play for his congregation. "Saxophones in the choir" said the *Toledo News-Bee* headline.[13]

The enemies of jazz targeted the tenderloin districts. One district was Canton Avenue from Cherry Street to Spielbusch Avenue called "Wildcat Shoot" where poor Blacks and poor Jews

Front view of Chicken Charlie's
Courtesy of the author

lived side by side. It was one of the toughest neighborhoods in the city. On one side of the street was the Armory Field, the site of brutal football games. The other side was lined with bottom-of-the-bin saloons, called "blind pigs," selling bottom-of-the-barrel booze, such as Ben Goldstein's place at 2011 Canton Street, a smoky fire trap that reeked of stale beer and disinfectant. There was a cigarette-scarred piano with some keys missing, and the only light in the place came from a sin-

Front of the Dixon Hotel, 1998

Back of the Dixon Hotel, 1998

gle bulb hanging from the ceiling. On Friday night after payday, the place would be jammed with traveling salesmen, off-duty cops, painted women and itinerant musicians.[14] The pesky reformers, however, were more interested in what was going on down the street at Chalky Red Yaranowsky's Black and Tan nightclub, where on the second floor, to the utter repulsion of "decent people," Blacks and whites were dancing together cheek-to-cheek and navel-to-navel,[15] primitive and obscene dances, many of them named after animals, like the kangaroo dip, the chicken scratch, the monkey glide, and the grizzly bear.[16]

The other target was the Lafayette area, now called the Warehouse District in southwest Toledo. Many Blacks settled there after they arrived at Willys-Overland to replace the dwindling number of European immigrants. Reformers set their sights on a four-block area of night clubs, pool halls, hotels and hospitals embracing Lafayette, Erie, Washington and St. Clair Streets. The Temperance Union called it "the Badlands." Twice they tried to close it down, begging City Hall to stop the gambling, jazz music, alcohol and arrest those "powder haired harpies" and "dusky damsels of the night" who were seducing young men and ruining their lives with drugs and alcohol. The city's watchdogs worried that the returning soldiers from WWI would be vulnerable to the venereal. "They succeeded in getting it closed down only to open two days later," said McGowan. "City Hall could not afford to lose the large amount of graft coming from these unlicensed businesses." McGowan said, "I started to go there when I was 17 years old. I saw all the bands and groups that came into Chicken Charlie's, owned by Noble Boyd. Every week I watched the bag guy, named Big Clarence, come to collect the paybacks, and every week all the prostitutes would be hauled in for inspection at the hospital on Lafayette. Lafayette Avenue was alive those days. Most of the action was from about St. Clair to Erie. Except for a large oval sign over Noble Boyd's, there really wasn't much to tell you what was going on, just two-story brick buildings, no advertising. The respectable church people kept it out of the papers."[18]

Only a couple of buildings remain from the time when Lafayette Street was the main entertainment strip in Toledo. One is the Dixon Building, a three-story brick building on the corner of Lafayette and St. Clair Streets. It was built by Charles Dixon in 1885 as a brothel when Italian architecture was in style. Pressure from the anti-saloon league closed it in 1920. So Dixon turned it into a novelty museum of nature's mistakes, two-headed calves, petrified bearded women, and flying chickens.[19] It became a furniture store in 1937 and in 2000, a hardware store with expensive condominiums upstairs. Its best years were during the Black expansion in Toledo from about 1915 until it closed in 1920. Russ McGowan said, "They had the best prostitutes in town, anything you wanted, Black, white, and for more money, an Octoroon."[20]

The Dixon Hotel was about the size of a basketball court with 39-foot ceilings, and an eighty-foot-long bar. Originally, there was a small stage for strippers and musicians and enough room for a large dance floor. To the rear of the first floor was a belt-driven hand-pulled elevator made in Toledo. In the middle of the downstairs was a sweeping staircase with a hand-carved banister that led to a second floor of tiny, independently heated rooms, with peeling wallpaper that went back generations and just enough room for a cot and a chair. It was the same on the third floor except in the back near the elevator was an escape hatch through an open window to a ladder down the back of the building.[21]

Chapter 14
The Willard-Dempsey Fight

The Guardians of Godliness were not happy to learn that on July 4, 1919, Toledo would be the site of the heavyweight boxing championship of the world. Boxers were barbarians, a notch below jazz musicians. The Guardians were concerned about all the riffraff that would pour into the city. They noted that the police chief had already issued a warning about pickpockets in large crowds.[1] Mayor Cornell Schreiber may have feigned agreement, but could not help thinking how much money the hotels, theaters, and restaurants would make. It would put Toledo on the map as a major city if it hosted the world's greatest sporting event of the twentieth century.

Addison Thacher, a junk dealer who became Toledo's mayor in 1931, may not have known the difference between a trombone and a trumpet, but he did more for the advancement of early jazz in Toledo than he ever knew. More than anyone, he convinced the city officials and promoters of the fight that Toledo was the ideal place for such a world class event. It had easy access; it was the gateway to the Great Lakes, and a crossroad between Chicago and New York.[2] It was an inland seaport where tourists from all over the world would bring money into the city beyond what they would gain from the fight proceeds. Addison Thacher knew the perfect place, Bayview Park out on Summit Street. Tickets would run from $6.00 to $10.00. At the end of Memorial Day, the city operated as though it were hosting the Olympics or the World's Fair. They built a wooden arena the size of a Roman Coliseum to accommodate the

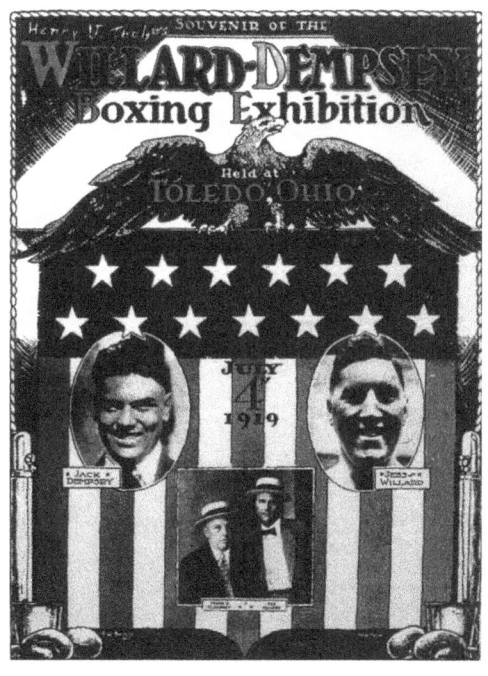

Courtesy of *The Blade*

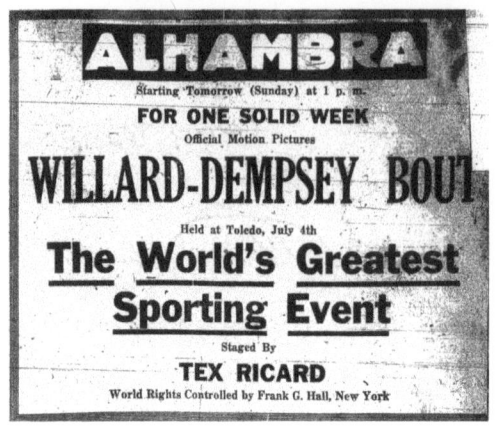

Courtesy of *The Blade*

100,000 people they expected. There was a need for more beds, for more hotel rooms. Gymnasiums and theaters were changed into sleeping quarters. There was a great need for maids, cooks, and waiters. WWI veterans in uniform were called in as ushers.[3]

When the fighters arrived for training, there was not a corner or a vacant lot in downtown Toledo without a concession. Celebrities came from everywhere, actress Ethel Barrymore, writers Damon Runyon and Hart Crane, and ex-boxing champions like John L. Sullivan and James Jay Corbett.[4] And what would all these invading people be looking for beside the Canadian whiskey? Entertainment. So an All-Points-Bulletin went out for singers, strippers, dancers, territory bands, ragtime pianists, jazz and semi-classical musicians; some, like pianist Elise Young and drummer Velmar "Fats" Mason, stayed in Toledo.[5] It was a Cecil B. DeMille spectacular. David and Goliath. Jess Willard was the Great White Hope who had beaten the Black heavyweight champion, Jack Johnson. Willard was a six-foot-seven, two hundred and fifty-three pound man-mountain who towered over his opponent, Jack Dempsey, who was 66 pounds lighter, seven inches shorter with a reach disadvantage of five inches. However, Jack Dempsey was a raw-boned killer with an iron jaw and fists of cement.[6]

The fight itself was a disaster. It lasted three rounds; it should have been stopped after one. Willard was no match for Dempsey's youth and speed. It was one of the worst beatings ever in the history of boxing. Willard's face looked like a piece of raw beefsteak. Another reason for the disaster was the weather. The temperature reached 104 degrees on July 4. There were 100,000 people expected. 20,000 showed up. It was so hot that the glue in the coliseum seats started to melt.[7] Despite that, the city made a lot of money because although many people did not go to the fight itself, a lot of money was spent, some of it on jazz and cocktails.[8]

Chapter 15
Jimmy Harrison – "The Toledo Terror"

The boss of the jazz trombone for most of the 1920s and one of the excellent musicians who came to Toledo around the time of the Willard-Dempsey fight was Jimmy Harrison. Not much has been written about him, no books and just a few articles that were done many years ago. Even in a field crowded with forgotten giants, Harrison stands out as one of the most neglected figures in all of jazz, perhaps the most important jazz musician not in the Hall of Fame. Not long ago his face was absent from a deck of baseball-like cards celebrating the pioneers of jazz. Two of his disciples were included, but no Jimmy Harrison.[1] He is so infrequently mentioned, so seldom thought of these days; it's as if he never existed. One reason is that he died before he ever made a record under his own name. Martin Williams, jazz historian emeritus, said that until J. J. Johnson came along in the 1940s, there was not all that much that happened in the evolution of the trombone since Harrison.[2] Rex Stewart, ace cornetist with Duke Ellington, called Harrison the "Father of Swing Trombone."[3] Count Basie, who played with Harrison in New York, said that he was the most complete player of his time.[4]

James Henry Harrison, whose presidential name befits his place in jazz history, rescued the trombone from its tailgating, oom-pahing function as a kind of brass bass and brought it into the modern period. And he did this by adapting the trumpet style of Louis Armstrong to his trombone. Harrison was born in Louisville, Kentucky, and moved to Detroit when he was six. He picked up the trombone at age seven and began teaching himself. At fifteen, he started impersonating the singing monologues of Bert Williams, a Black Tom Lehrer who exposed the corruption and hypocrisy in America.[5] Harrison was in Toledo for about two and a half years, living at 337 Vance Street, a couple of blocks from Lafayette Street.[6] The Anthony Wayne Trail was built where the house once stood. Like most of the other homes in that area it was starting to fall apart, with bad plumbing, poor insulation, and leaking roofs. The Great Migration of Blacks from the South during WWI and restrictions called red-lining by real estate companies put housing at a premium in the Pinewood District. Landlords charged rents three times higher than before WWI. To make ends meet, people would sublet.[7] A house made for two families now accommodated four, making crowded conditions that Black historian, LeRoy Williams, compared to "rabbits in a warren."

Rex Stewart, who nicknamed Harrison the "Toledo Terror," said when Harrison was in Toledo he played first base for a local baseball team while working in his father's restaurant. Harrison had an enormous appetite. Night after night he would put away huge helpings of candied sweet potatoes, baked spareribs and quarts of ice cream. His father had to fire Jimmy for eating up all of the pastries.[8] Harrison booked a lot of out-of-town jobs. He liked to play with Hank Duncan in Detroit, and in Louisville, Kentucky, his birth place, at the Ebbs Hotel. Sitting in the audience one night was another trombone player and future star of the Count Basie Band, Dicky Wells. "He was just playing with the piano and he got angry if anyone wanted to sit in," said Wells. "He'd cross his legs and that boy would blow more blues on a hot day than the law allows. I never heard that from a trombone before. He influenced Jack Teagarden, because I used to see Jack in the audience when Jimmy was playing in New York and there would be a big smile on his face."[9]

Early Jimmy Harrison
Courtesy of the author

Jimmy also liked to play at the Elephant's Café in Atlantic City. To enter this funhouse you walked under a simulated rear end of an elephant. In Atlantic City he polished up his comedy skits and Bert Williams impressions. After a couple of trombone choruses, Harrison would put on a seedy old frock, a dilapidated hat, a pair of lensless glasses, slip on some white gloves, and standing on his band chair, become a stuttering stumble-bum, spewing out hellfire and whiskey. It bought the house down.[10]

In late 1919 there was an unprecedented gathering of jazz immortals in Toledo. They liked to play at Louis Herman's in the general vicinity of where the Spaghetti Warehouse is today.[11] A sign in the window read "soda pop and confectionaries" meaning bathtub gin in

Dicky Wells
Courtesy of Unwin Paperbacks

the back room. You drank at your own risk; Prohibition made people want it more than ever. There was a bar, a dance floor, and a set of drums and piano downstairs. Rooms for rent were upstairs.[12]

Joining Harrison was Juice Wilson, the second-best jazz violinist in America. Drummer Sonny Greer came to Toledo for a short stay just months before joining Duke Ellington. Greer was no Gene Krupa or Sid Catlett. He wasn't a soloist; he was an ensemble drummer, a colorist, who provided the exotic effects that made Duke Ellington's Jungle Band so successful. Pianist James P. Johnson, cornetist June Clark, and trombonist Lee Baxter came to Toledo after they were stranded while playing a tent show in Tennessee.[13]

Piano Starts Here by Art Tatum is one of the most mistitled albums in all of jazz. Tatum would not have allowed Columbia Records to use that title had he been alive. Tatum knew that Willie "The Lion" Smith and, above all, James P. Johnson were the real beginnings of jazz piano. Johnson is the father of the Harlem Stride piano style and one of the brightest and most versatile figures in all jazz history. He wrote symphonies, operas, and his QRS piano rolls were primers for young piano players, including Tatum.

James P. Johnson is the author of the "Charleston," the song that became a dance craze and the national anthem of the 1920s. Johnson put the swing in jazz piano and is as important to its development as Art Tatum who was eleven years old in the winter of 1920 and was then living not far from Lafayette Street.

June Clark, a follower of King Oliver, became Jimmy Harrison's best friend. They left Toledo separately but reunited in Flint, Michigan. Then they went on tour with a couple of territory bands before arriving in New York in 1923. They planned to put together a band based on the records of King Oliver's Creole Jazz Band with Louis Armstrong, an essential selection in any basic library of jazz. Fidelity aside, these recordings represent the epitome of New Orleans jazz, tight ensemble work by a group who believed that the whole sound was greater than any soloist.

Harrison found a copy of "Mable's Dream" in a record store on Broadway, brought it home, and he and June mem-

June Clark
Courtesy of June Clark

orized the breaks and interplay between King Oliver and Armstrong, the way Johnny Dodds' clarinet weaves in and out of the melody, and the solid 4-4 beat of Baby Dodds. Harrison would play Louis Armstrong's part and Clark, King Oliver's. They added Jazz Carson on drums, Prince Robinson on tenor sax, Benny Carter, one of the fathers of the alto saxophone, and either Willy "The Lion" Smith or Count Basie on piano. They called themselves the Gulf Coast Seven. They found work at Small's Paradise, home of the tap-dancing MC, strutting waiters and wacky dust, so vividly portrayed in Carl van Vechten's controversial *Nigger Heaven*. It was the first Harlem night club to attract a white clientele. Soon the Gulf Coast Seven became the talk of Harlem and within months, it seemed every trombone player on the East Coast was coming under the domination of Jimmy Harrison.[14] Jimmy Harrison played with a lot of very good bands from 1926 until his death in 1931. He was with Duke Ellington for a while; he made a couple of records with Charlie Johnson and some with Bessie Smith. Fletcher Henderson bought Jimmy's contract with Charlie Johnson at the end of 1926.

Harrison made a number of recordings with Henderson and the offshoot of the band, the Chocolate Dandies. Most of these are available on compact discs. Four performances stand out. "Hop Off," is a driving muted solo based on the chords to "I'm a Ding Dong Daddy" and "Somebody Loves Me," an arrangement by Benny Carter. The growls, the snarls, the stop time and swing make "Oh, Baby" another one of his best solos. "Dee Blues," after seventy years, is still a model of how to play the blues on the slide trombone. Just before his death, he made one more recording, this time with Chick Webb, on a Louis Armstrong tune called "Heebie Jeebies." With the Henderson band, Jimmy could sing, play heartwarming solos, and do comedy routines. He was the trombone triple threat, a rare breed like the late Frank Rosolino with Stan Kenton in the early 1950s. He loved a put-on, such as coming to work complaining he was too sick to play; and then, slumped over in his chair, he would pretend to be asleep until his solo came around. Suddenly he would leap up, point the slide of his trombone to the ceiling and blow the daylights out of "King Porter Stomp."[15]

It was no laughing matter in 1930. He wasn't feigning illness anymore. An untreated stomach ulcer resulting from his terrible diet for so many years became malignant. In July 1931, the man who brought the trombone front and center, who expanded its range, and gave it a voice was dead. Epitaphs and condolences poured in from all parts of the jazz community. Benny Carter wrote, "He played as naturally as he breathed and his singing had the emotions of a Louis Armstrong."[16]

The Great White Hope on the trombone in the 1920s in New York was Irving Milfred "Miff" Mole. One jazz critic said Mole reminded him of a quizzical owl. Until Jack Teagarden came to New

Coda
Miff Mole

York in 1927, Mole was Jimmy Harrison's main competition. He was conservatory-trained, a better technician and more versatile than Jimmy Harrison. Mole could perform in a gin house one night and with Arturo Toscanini in the NBC Symphony the next. Tommy Dorsey, famous bandleader and trombone player, called Mole the "Babe Ruth of the trombone." Glenn Miller spent a good part of his life trying to catch up with Miff Mole. As a white trombonist, Mole got more exposure and more opportunities than Jimmy Harrison. Mole was first heard on some recordings made with the Memphis Five.[17] His two best solos are with his own group, Miff Mole and the Molers. One is "Crazy Rhythm," and what might be his best solo, "Dixieland One Step." A comparison with "Hop Off" done the same year by Jimmy Harrison shows the subtle difference between these two trombone titans.

Chapter 16
Action at the Green Mill

The most dynamic aggregation to play on LaFayette Street was the Synco Septette, later known as the McKinney's Cotton Pickers, one of the three best big bands of the 1920s, according to some jazz historians.[1] Most of the members came from Springfield, Ohio, a veritable fertile crescent of jazz talent in part because it was the home of Wilberforce, a post Civil War Black college with an outstanding music department. The Cotton Pickers began as a trio led by drummer William McKinney, with Milt Senior, a saxophone clarinetist, and Todd Rhodes on piano. Milt Senior who spent most of his life in Toledo, was truly one of the essential pioneers of Toledo jazz.[2]

The dancers and managers of ballrooms and dancing academies like Cassidys on Adams Street wanted a bigger sound. So the McKinney's Cotton Pickers added a trumpet, a trombone, a banjo player-vocalist named Dave Wilborn, and some saxophonists to make a septet.[3] Russ McGowan was there the night Chicken Charlie's, called Nobles then, was raided and the band was hauled away. "Of course, they were let out right away," said McGowan, "and Nobles was open the next night, like what always happened. It was just to satisfy the solid citizens of Toledo. You know, I knew the trombone player, Claude Jones, because he was here a lot when his dad was a preacher in town."[4] Claude Jones learned to play the trombone while he was at the student army training base during WWI. After that he went to Wilberforce University for three months, originally to study

Cuba Austin
Courtesy of Unwin Paperbacks

Woodshedding at Devil's Lake

law before he decided on music and joined the McKinney's Cotton Pickers. Jones graced the trombone sections of Duke Ellington's, Chick Webb's, and Fletcher Henderson's bands. His solo with Cab Calloway on "Nagasaki" became a classic. Jones once said of the Cotton Pickers, "I reckon it was the best band I ever played with."[5]

Jones' idol was Jimmy Harrison, the "Toledo Terror," who, like Jones, was the band comedian. Wiggy was his nickname because he wore a hairpiece to cover his congenital baldness. He had some clever tricks to lighten things up. One was playing trombone with just his feet, something he got from Jimmy Harrison. He billed himself as "Hot Lips Jones – The Laughing Trombone Player – Plays With His Foot."[6]

Around 1923, William McKinney realized he was better suited for a marching band than for a jazz band. He went on the hunt for a replacement so that he could be the manager, a position with which he felt much more comfortable. He found exactly who he wanted in Cuba Austin, a rubber-wristed sparkplug from Charleston, West Virginia.[7] Austin's innovations took the Cotton Pickers to another level. He would sit down at his drum set, adjust the height of his various cymbals, twirl his drumsticks like miniature batons, and kick off a flag waver that had the dancers running for cover. Gene Krupa, the world's most famous drummer was flabbergasted the first time he heard Austin.[8] He could not believe the press rolls ala Art Blakey 27 years later, the clever ways Austin advanced the use of the sock cymbal, and above all, his showmanship, like tap dancing on his tom-tom while juggling his drumsticks. It was crazy.

Before coming to Toledo, the McKinney's Cotton Pickers had a long engagement at Manitou Beach on Devil's Lake. Austin said, "That is when we really started to improve, because of John Nesbitt, who joined our band in 1925. It was here that 'woodshedding' got its name. It meant going off by yourself into the woods and practicing until you got your part right. He taught us all how to read."[9]

Nesbitt was a five-foot-eight, pitch-black composer, arranger, and trumpet player from New Orleans. He replaced Milt Senior as the brains behind the band, and he was a close friend of Bix Beiderbecke whose playing he resembled. Gunther Schuller, the jazz historian, devotes many pages to John Nesbitt in his book *The Swing Era*.[10] Nesbitt left in 1930 when he felt the band was becoming more commercial. Like his close friend Bix Beiderbecke, Nesbitt was a two-fisted drinker, consuming more than a quart of gin a day. When he was on the bandstand, he had a pint of white lightning and a straw in the vest pocket of his band jacket so he could sip between solos. Nesbitt was the author of "Stop Kidding," "Nobody's Sweetheart," and other Cotton Pickers favorites.[11] The Green Mill was, as the management liked to say, "Broadway on Superior where every night

was Saturday night and every Saturday night was New Year's Eve." It was located at 418 Superior Street next to where Georgio's Restaurant opened in the mid-1980s. A parking lot is there now, but in the mid-1920s, it was Action Central.[12] It was owned by two gangsters. John Chilton described the Green Mill in his book about the McKinney's Cotton Pickers as "a tough gangland place . . . . Often there were fights and sometimes shootings on the dance floor."[13] People sat in tables alongside the dance floor giving easy access to comics and shake dancers. The Syncos, soon to be the McKinney's Cotton Pickers, prospered financially under the glaring lights and pandemonium of the Green Mill. This raucous, sometimes violent atmosphere required a bigger sound so McKinney added a saxophone and tuba.[14]

Drinking was the top priority at the Green Mill, music came in second as was evident one night when the portly proprietor stopped the Syncos in the middle of a song to make this announcement: "Ladies and Gentlemen, there has been a silver flask lost here tonight by a patron half full of gin." Besides extending a cordial welcome to all the arrivals, the maitre d' at the Green Mill was also the screener whose job it was to let the managers know who happened to be in the club that night, movie stars, war heroes, gang leaders, and famous entrepreneurs like Jean Goldkette.[15] Goldkette was a French classical pianist with an appreciation for big band jazz. So he became a talent scout, a band leader, and an impresario. He sponsored, created, and managed more bands than he knew what to do with. Goldkette controlled the big band business in Detroit, and much of the Midwest. He took pride in his ability to spot talent and the Green Mill Syncos lived up to everything he had heard about them. He hired them right off the stage, took them to Detroit and booked them for the famous Greystone Ballroom. He got them on the radio where they broadcast nightly. Then he changed their name to the McKinney's Cotton Pickers. He got them a record contract and then brought in one of the most important figures of the swing era, the ace arranger and saxophonist Don Redman, who eventually took them to New York. By the time they opened at the Trianon Ballroom

Milt Senior
Courtesy of John Chilton

in Toledo in 1932, it was a different band. Many of the original members had left, most notably, John Nesbitt, Claude Jones, and the founder Milt Senior.[16]

Chilton discussed Senior's departure in his biodiscography of the Cotton Pickers. "In 1929 another early member, Milton Senior, also left the band. He had married a school teacher from Toledo, Ohio, who was anxious that Senior should quit the touring life and settle down. Eventually he acquiesced and left the band. He joined Wesley Helvey's Band [from Cincinnati] for a residency, before leading his own unit at the Luna Pier in Toledo. Later his marriage broke up, but by then there was no vacancy in McKinney's Band. Little went right for the saxophone player thereafter, and the unhappy man committed suicide in the late 1930s. His playing had been much respected by his ex-colleagues. Claude Jones gave him supreme praise when he said 'Now Don Redman was a good musician, but he wasn't Milt Senior.'"[17] Milt Senior recorded his only solo on "Forgetting You" with the Jean Goldkette Orchestra. The Jean Goldkette Orchestra from Detroit, under the direction of Frankie Trumbauer, was the first and best all-white big band. Some high ranking authorities such as Artie Shaw and Benny Goodman thought it was the best band of its time, better than Duke Ellington or Fletcher Henderson or the McKinney's Cotton Pickers.[18] Red Norvo, vibraphone pioneer, never saw anything like it. "So clean," he said. "So swinging." It was a dream team of outstanding soloists, Bix Beiderbecke, the Dorsey Brothers, and Eddie Lang on guitar. One of the great injustices in all of recorded jazz was their omission from *The Smithsonian Collection: Big Band Jazz From the Beginnings to the Fifties*. The Goldkette Orchestra lasted about four years. Then the payroll just got to be too much for Jean Goldkette and the egos got a little too large, so they disbanded.[19]

Pearl Barber

One of the McKinney's Cotton Pickers' biggest supporters was Pearl Barber, a handsome coffee-colored playboy, pimp, and high-stakes gambler. Defiant would be the best way to describe him. He was a Black man with a Jack Johnson complex who could and did pass for white. He lived in Eagle Point Colony near Rossford, Ohio, in a palatial residence with the best of everything, furnishings, paintings, and a library stocked with first editions by some of America's greatest authors.[20] He liked lots of jewelry, loud clothes, and luxury automobiles that he used to drive down Superior in the middle of the day so everyone could see his white wife.[21] Barbour was the original big spender. He would rent a nightclub like the Tabernilla on Bay Shore Drive and invite all of his friends to a champagne dinner and dancing to either the McKinney's Cotton Pickers or the Milt Senior Small Combo with Teddy Wilson on piano. His rich and infamous life came to a screeching end in November 1930 when a drunk driver hit Barbour head on. He was sixty years old.[22]

The *Toledo Blade* summed up his life this way, "In death Barbour wore that same look of disdain he'd always given society. He believed himself to be superior to the herd, whether colored or white. Years ago he turned his back on the most powerful politicians in the city. They couldn't drive him out of business. He outsmarted them by being the first to obtain a club charter for his gambling place on the 400 block of Monroe. Can it be maintained that a man for thirty years could weather the political and social storms of a big city admittedly at the head of an unlawful profession and not somewhere in him have the perverted strain of genius?"[23]

Opening
Monday · April 9

{ MUSIC
DANCING
& DINING }

Changed to the Original Name of

La Tabernilla
EATING HOUSE
East Bay Shore Road . TAylor 2998

Chapter 17
Cakewalkin' at Tony Packo's

Where would one go to hear traditional jazz in the 1970s and '80s? Tony Packo's was the place, home of the high-voltage frankfurter, a Hungarian restaurant made to look like an upscale saloon out of the Roaring Twenties, somewhere between New Orleans, Kansas City and Chicago. Real Tiffany lampshades, a spittoon, pool tables, and an old fashioned bar provided the authenticity. In the middle of the bandstand was an ancient drum kit complete with side snares, wood blocks, some cymbals, and a bass drum that said "Cakewalkin' Jass Band," a name taken from a famous recording done in December 1924 by one of the fathers of the saxophone, Sidney Bechet and the first great jazz soloist, Louis Armstrong.

The Cakewalkin' Jass Band was the most popular band ever to come out of Toledo and the most enduring. Every weekend for 33 years, from 1968 to 2001, the Cakewalkin' Babies had a standing-room-only crowd, listening to eight all-white musicians in bow ties, suspenders, and high-collared shirts playing music of the Black bands of the nineteen-teens and '20s. The Cakewalkin' Babies played in hundreds of jazz festivals all over America, including the Bix Beiderbecke Memorial. Apart from their weekends at Packo's, they did weddings, private parties and funerals, New Orleans style, playing a deep-down dirge like "Rock of Ages" on the way to the graveside and then breaking out into an all out joyful version of "Didn't He Ramble" on the way back.[1] Ray Heitger is the leader and clarinetist of this band and has produced dozens of records. One of the best albums was recorded live at Packo's on a weekend in March 1972. Included are "Honeysuckle Rose," "Clarinet Marmalade," "Muskrat Ramble," all performed with the rhythmic precision of a well-oiled combustible engine. Two events gave rise to the reawakening of early jazz. One was a revival in San Francisco in 1941 with names like Turk Murphy and Bob Scobey. They felt jazz had lost its way and needed to go back to the roots.[2] The second event was the release of a 1955 cult film called *Pete Kelly's Blues* starring Jack Webb of *Dragnet* fame as Pete Kelly, the leader

Courtesy of Tony Packo's

of an eight-piece combo playing in a setting remarkably similar to Tony Packo's. In the film, Pete Kelly is trying to survive the gangster controlled clubs of Kansas City. Ella Fitzgerald made a cameo performance singing the title song and Peggy Lee was nominated for best supporting actress at the Academy Awards. This is still worth seeing.

Chapter 18
The Joy of Sax

Todd Rhodes, one of the founders of the McKinney's Cotton Pickers, had another career later as leader of Todd Rhodes and His Toddlers. They were stationed in Detroit and a big favorite in Toledo thanks to Jack the Bellboy, a daytime disc jockey on WGR in Detroit. He plugged the band after seeing them at a club in Paradise Valley. In return, Todd wrote "Bellboy Boogie" which became the Bellboy's theme song. Ed Mackenzie, Bellboy's real name, was the first broadcaster to push off-label companies called Indies. They were sprouting up everywhere—fly-by-night shoebox operations on a shoestring budget.[1]

The reason was the recording ban of 1942-43 and again in 1948. The ban, along with the shortages of WWII, were the beginning of the end for the big band era and the rise of rhythm and blues, bebop, and gospel music, categories that had been neglected by major companies. The recording ban was the doing of one man, James Caesar Petrillo, heavy on the Caesar, a rotund, cigar-smoking dictator of the American Federation of Musicians. He was the John L. Lewis of music who could sit back in his leather La-Z-Boy chair and declare war on anyone who would cheat his 85,000 members out of their earned income. "No more free music," was his drum cry. His enemies' list included the major record companies, radio stations who used more canned music than "live music" and jukebox manufacturers. Petrillo demanded that "live music" be played in back of all commercials; but small stations, like Toledo's WSPD, could not afford live music. He decreed that recordings be labeled "for home use only." Also, there would be no more canned music for traveling stage shows. Worse, he banned all jam sessions and sent agents to various nightclubs as enforcers.[2]

When Decca, RCA, Capital and Columbia would not agree to his demands for a higher percentage of records sold, he prohibited all instrumentalists in the American Federation of Musicians from making records. The ban lasted eleven months. It killed some of the big bands that depended on records. Will Bradley and Billy Eckstine's bop band were among the casualties. Decca Records was the first to surrender and the other major companies followed.[3]

Enter hundreds of Indies to fill the void in the wake of the record ban. The Toddlers' first recordings, as well as those of Toledoans Claude Black, Candy Johnson, and Cliff Murphy, were on the Sensation label in Detroit. Todd said, "We didn't have any arrangement, there was no music, man, just heads. Guys would start a riff and we'd all join in, that's about what they were." In 1947, Todd and his Toddlers were voted Number One in the rhythm and blues category of a Detroit poll.[4]

Paul Williams

The second place in the Detroit poll went to the band of King Porter. He had a baritone saxophonist named Paul Williams who would drive the audience up the wall each night by honking on one note for a chorus and then holding that same note for a half a chorus before changing its pitch and density. Musicians call it tattooing. Honking among saxophonists spread like the Asian flu. The principle shouters and wailers in Toledo were Candy Johnson, Choker Campbell who played at the old Thomas Hotel on Front Street, and a saxophonist with Cecil Harris and his Jazz Jesters who went by the name of "Cranberry."[5] Many well known mainstream musicians also indulged: Johnny "the Little Giant" Griffin, Sam "the Man" Taylor, Willis "Gatortail" Jackson, Hal Singer, and even John Coltrane had a spell. They discovered they could get more money and get more attention by becoming exhibitionists.[6]

Teddy Reig of Savoy Records heard about the King Porter band and dropped in one night. He did not care for the band, but he was fascinated by this handsome baritone saxophonist named Paul Williams. He took Williams to a coffee shop next door and told him, "Look, I don't want

Hawley Café
Courtesy of Rusty Monroe

Courtesy of Rusty Monroe

Indiana Tavern
Courtesy of Rusty Monroe

the whole band, I want you and I can make you a lot of money but I don't want you to play no sax. All I want is one note, one note."[7] Reig put together a backup combo and took Williams on the road. They came through Toledo on the way to Baltimore. In Baltimore, the microphones were placed below the level of the stage. When Williams dipped way down and hit a low E Flat, it rattled the whole auditorium. Williams said, "Word got out I had blowed the microphones right through the floor and soon we had a line waiting to see us that went right around the corner as far as you could see."[8]

Paul Williams was not just the honking king of Detroit but also the "author" of "The Hucklebuck," a melody he lifted from a Charlie Parker B Flat blues called "Now's the Time." Williams stole the tune and then wrote some lyrics which explained how to do the Hucklebuck dance. Frances Belcher, "Lady B," played it every day on WTOD in Toledo. Suddenly everybody was doing the Hucklebuck. Benny Goodman had a bop version of it. Columbia Records released an album of nothing but "The Hucklebuck," twenty minutes and sixty-three choruses of it.[9]

The center for jazz, jump, and rhythm and blues in Toledo was the Pinewood District, where there were some streets that never went to bed for ten years, where the tenor saxophone was king; and what someone said about the trumpet in New Orleans could be said about the saxophone on Indiana Avenue. "It practically blew its self." Jon Hendricks was not exaggerating when he said that much of the time it was better than New York. It was sort of a jazz and blues village with its own radio station and disc jockeys, its two newspapers and music columnists. It had its own night clubs, taverns, ballrooms, and auditoriums and its own record stores: the Plumbers Appliance on Ewing Street, Sherry's on Dorr Street, the home of the Earl Bostic Fan Club, and a satellite in West Toledo called the Automatic Sales Company where they also handled used records, a fragile commodity in the age of the 78 RPM. There were certain performers who were linked to particular clubs. Guitarist Neil DeBoe and pianist Jack Jackson were the house band for months at the Hawley Café. The Indiana Tavern was home of the ten-minute blood and thunder drum solos featuring Swing Lee and Babe Borders. The Green Lite Night Club on Detroit Avenue was a favorite place for Arv Garrison and Harold Lindsey. Tate's Midway Café on Tecumseh Street was where Tommy Flanagan, George Benson, and Calvin Frazier had a popular run in the early 1950s. Frazier made his reputation in Detroit playing with the T. J. Fowler Band. Alto saxophonist George Benson talked about his days in Toledo at Tates, "We would play jazz for the first set or two until more people came and then we would break out and play rhythm and blues. Frazier had a long cord so he could walk and play all over the club. We had the place packed every night."[10]

The most talked about club, and the number one destination for out of town musicians, was the Waiters and Bellman's Club where the best after-hours jam sessions took place. Pinewood District even had its own promoter, the indefatigable Lucius Huntley who did his best to bring the headliners to the Belmont Ballroom and the Civic Auditorium.

Dinah Washington came to the Civic Auditorium at the height of her popularity. Washington was a 1950s Bessie Smith with a penchant for pink Cadillac convertibles and suggestive lyrics. "Evil-gal Blues" and her version of "Love for Sale" were intimations of immorality to the conservative radio stations, which refused to play her records. She countered by making a recording of "Record Ban Blues" with Cootie Williams on trumpet. Washington was a triple threat; she was tops in jazz, popular music, and, for five years,

in the top ten on rhythm and blues charts. Esteemed writer Leonard Feather said he'd "heard the folk roots of jazz in her fabulously flexible voice."[11] She was billed with Tab Smith who arrived in Toledo plugging his two big hits, "Because of You" and "You Belong to Me," Tab's melodramatic tribute to Tony Bennett and Jo Stafford. This was a different Tab Smith from the one who came to Toledo playing his alto-saxophone and arranging for Count Basie. When the big bands went under, Tab Smith, either unwilling or unable to play bop, went into the real estate business. Now he was back in the spotlight again, thanks in part to the early success of Earl Bostic, another alto-saxophonist who turned lusty balladeer.[12]

Earl Bostic

Earl Bostic played at the Civic Auditorium in November 1954. He had a raspy, raw sound full of sand and fury that appeased the bodily appetites of adolescents. Of all the hot selling records he had, nothing compared to his version of "Flamingo." John Coltrane played with Bostic for a while and said he learned more about music from Bostic than anyone. Bostic was the most musically literate of all the R&B leaders. He was a student of theory and harmony with a degree from Xavier University.[13] He arranged for Lionel Hampton and had his own swing band for a while. Then when bop replaced swing, like Tab Smith, he decided on a more commercial and infinitely more lucrative career.

Big Jay McNeely

Big Jay McNeely and his brother, or as their detractors called them, the McSqueely Brothers, came on with two phosphorescent saxophones that would light up when someone dimmed the lights. As an encore, Big Jay would march his whole band through the auditorium, through the doors and outside where on some nights there would be a patrol wagon conveniently waiting to take them to jail for "disturbing the peace."[14]

Lynn Hope

The most bizarre act to come to Toledo was Lynn Hope, "The Maharajah of the Saxophone" and his all-Muslim all-family band. While he was playing a long engagement in Cleveland, he recorded "Tenderly" for a small Indie company called Premium. It was an immediate hit and sold a million records, mostly to white middle class high school students. It was one of the early examples of crossover music, that is, music intended for a black audience but it ended up being even more popular among white middle class teenagers. Hope's song list would include jump numbers such as "Eleven 'Til Seven," ballads sometimes with a rock beat and lots of triplets, Latin numbers, and Middle Eastern music as in "Morocco," which Hope said was based on belly dance rhythms. Lynn Hope took his religion seriously. He was never without his jeweled turban and a copy of the Koran. He spoke Arabic fluently and gave ten per cent of his income to his mosque. One time he was arrested in Central Park for bowing to Mecca in his pajamas. Bebop musicians

and hip comedians put him down, calling him Lynn "No Hope."[15] You can be assured that when he came to Toledo on Christmas Day 1952 at the Belmont Ballroom, it would have been packed to the rafters. Hope was not a screamer and did not throw tenor tantrums like Big Jay McNeely nor engage in tenor battles. He was an erotic saxophonist, one of the lusty ones like Earl Bostic.

The Clovers

Another favorite among white teenagers, especially members of the underground high school fraternities and sororities in Toledo, was the gospel-rooted Clovers, a deceptively simple doo wop group that along with Ruth Brown put Atlantic Records into the rhythm and blues business with such chart busters as "Good Lovin'," "One Mint Julep," "Blue Velvet," and "Devil or Angel." Each one was filled with sexual candor and creamy saxophone solos usually by Willis "Gatortail" Jackson who came to Toledo often with his even more famous wife, Ruth Brown.[16]

Tiny Bradshaw

Tiny Bradshaw, a drummer bandleader from Youngstown, Ohio, played the Belmont Ballroom frequently. He led the last of the instrumental jump bands which began in the late-1930s with small groups like the Savoy Sultans and ended when vocal groups took over and it became rhythm and blues. His recording of "Soft" for King Records was on the top ten best selling R&B record list for many weeks. Of all the bands that came to the ballroom at that time, Tiny Bradshaw had more to offer jazz fans. His groups were stocked with name brand jazz figures such as Sonny Stitt, Gil Fuller, Carl Perkins, and Toledo's Candy Johnson.[17]

Chapter 19
Candy Johnson – Two Sides of the Street

Of all the Detroit ex-patriots to include Johnny O'Neal and Claude Black, the most entertaining and the most controversial was Floyd "Candy" Johnson. As a fellow saxophonist said of Candy Johnson, "He walked on both sides of the street, the jazz side and the rhythm and blues side." On Friday nights in the late-1970s, he might be walking the bar at Tate's Midway on Tecumseh Street all decked out in his barber pole uniform. He'd be honking on his saxophone with one hand tied behind his back, while his sidemen, the Peppermint Sticks, threw candy canes to the howling, hysterical mob.[1]

On Saturday nights he liked to be at the Commodore Perry Lounge with just Eddie Abrams on piano. One night years ago, he played a 45-minute ballad medley ending with "Until the Real Thing Comes Along," his signature song. It was a tribute to the elusive lady in beige who would quietly slip into the lounge every Saturday night always dressed in beige, always alone, stay for one set and then just before intermission would escape into the night. "I never did catch up with her," Candy admitted.[2] On weekdays you would find Mr. Floyd Johnson, head of music at Spencer-Sharples High School, teaching students how to play the saxophone. You wonder if any of those students sitting around the music room had any idea of just who they were listening to. Candy Johnson was born in Madison, Illinois, but moved to St. Louis fairly early and became very close friends with Milt Buckner, the piano player and organist. Candy played in some territory bands and then traveled to Springfield, Ohio, to attend Wilberforce University, an incubator for the jazz talent of tomorrow. He moved to Detroit just in time for the birth of the rhythm and blues rage. Detroit was one of the centers. Candy did not have any trouble finding work, mostly in Paradise Valley where there was a cluster of nightclubs with signs outside saying "King Porter," "TJ Fowler" and other jump and rhythm and blues groups.[3]

Candy's group, the Peppermint Sticks, was a sax-dominated jump group, playing swing riffs, bop licks, and urban blues, all calculated to get dancers on the floor. But Candy, still holding on to his reputation as a jazz name in Detroit, made a couple of appearances, one with Charlie Parker and another with Wardell Gray that was reviewed by George Hoefer of *Down Beat* who

Candy Johnson
Courtesy of Candy Johnson

called Candy's playing clichéd and exhibitionistic.[4] Then he made one of his first trips to Toledo's Belmont Ballroom to take on Big Joe Burrell and Scott High School's Dave Seaman in a battle of the saxes. In 1960 he took time off to play at the Arv Garrison Memorial.

From 1958 to 1962, Candy played with the Bill Doggett Combo who had the hand-clapping knock-out hit, "Honky Tonk." The high point in Candy's career, and in his life for that matter, came in 1952. He received a draft notice from Count Basie, which was like getting called up by the New York Yankees. Count Basie spread the gospel of jazz all over the world by performing in every possible setting from Buckingham Palace to rodeo corrals. Dave Brubeck, George Shearing, and Woody Herman were popular; but no one had the pedestrian appeal of the "Li'l ol' Groovemaker" from Red Bank, New Jersey. He cut across individual tastes like a baby's smile, subduing Juilliard graduates and musical illiterates alike. It was said that if you didn't like Basie, you probably didn't like music. What was the secret to his success? In part, simplicity. Most of his arrangements like "Jumpin' at the Woodside" and "One O'Clock Jump" were no more than arrangements made up on the spot, called "heads." Basie must have had a couple of hundred of these in the book all approximately the same structure: repeated musical phrases called riffs, played over a twelve bar blues pattern.

So seemingly elementary is Basie's style that many bands over the years tried to copy him in an attempt to ingratiate themselves with the general public. They followed his time-tested formulas carefully, recreating his every nuance, but it was never quite the same. That was the secret behind the Basie mystique. In the first place, no one has ever been able to duplicate the Basie piano, a sort of Chico Marx-like style, complete with pistol finger doodles, succinct single line exclamations, glissando runs, and a sense of time that defies imitation.[5] Count Basie performed at the Sports Arena in Toledo, Ohio, in January, 1956, with a band many think was his best. At the end of July, they recorded the famous *April in Paris* album starring Frank Foster's saxophone and Thad Jones' cornet. Sitting in the trombone section that day was Bill Hughes. When Basie died in 1984, Hughes was one of the alumni who took over the band. In 2009, he brought the Basie Band to the Franciscan Center in Sylvania as part of the Toledo Jazz Society's concert series.

Candy was with Basie for only a few months and in that time he had only one solo on "Fawncy Meeting You," a Buster Harding arrangement. Candy Johnson was the only Toledoan ever to be hired by Basie and he didn't mind telling you about it.

In the 1960s Candy played at the Aku-Aku, an upscale attempt at Las Vegas, located on the corner of Bancroft and Monroe Streets. Cliff Murphy was on bass and Swing Lee on drums. Fred Kopp was the piano player. Kopp remembered Candy as a "big bald very amiable guy, didn't smoke, didn't drink but loved being the whole show. Your solo time was limited because it was Candy's show and he liked to go table to table honking and lying down with his feet in the air and then pedaling like he was on a bicycle while playing his saxophone. People would just go crazy. He preferred the standards but couldn't resist the attention he got doing crazy stuff. I could never get into his head, never could figure that guy out."[6]

Bob Pavkovich was Candy's drummer for a while. He remembers that "Candy didn't want any bombs or any kind of punctuation and no drum solos. He told me just to play straight time and he would do the rest."[7] Pavkovich learned by playing along with Paul Smith and Dave Brubeck records on a homemade drum kit in his basement. He was self-taught and had almost no technique. He could not read music and was deathly afraid of drum solos but put a metronome beside his drums and the beat would never waver. Some musicians in town felt that Candy Johnson was threatened by some of the young up-and-comers who were into John Coltrane and Wayne Shorter, a more modern approach to the saxophone. They thought that

was why he never let anyone forget that he was with Count Basie; and it probably accounted for his occasional overbearing behavior, such as what happened one night at Alfie's, a fashionable restaurant and nightclub in the 1970s. Pianist Mark Kieswetter tells it this way: "Candy would bolt into the lounge, unannounced, uninvited, saxophone in at his side, sometimes in the middle of a song and announce to the house band and to the stunned audience, always in the third person, 'Candy's here, Candy's here, Candy's here, let Candy play,' and he always wanted to play 'Sophisticated Lady,' and the bandleader would always yell out, 'In what key?' and Candy would say, 'Candy plays in any key.' This happened a number of times.

"To gain revenge on these annoying intrusions, the members of the band came up with a plan. See, the song is almost always played in A Flat, but Steve, the bandleader, decided to put it in E Major which would put Candy in F Sharp, which is the absolute worst key for horns and it's a tough song anyway. Well they waited and waited and sure enough one night Candy shows up, same old thing, 'Candy's here, Candy's here' and 'Let Candy play' and the whole thing, 'What key' and 'Candy plays in any key.' So Steve yells out again, 'Any key, Candy?' And Candy replies, 'Candy plays in any key.' 'This key?' And they went into E Major and Candy sounded like a junior high school kid. When he got to the bridge he had messed up so bad, he just walked away."[8] The best of Candy Johnson can be found on two albums, *Midnight Blues* and *Candy's Mood* on the Black and Blue label out of Paris.

Milt Buckner in Toledo

Milt Buckner was Candy Johnson's best friend and one of the most influential piano players in jazz history, although his name is usually missing from the list of the major stylists. He came to Toledo for the first time in 1932 when he was 17 years old with a band from his hometown in Detroit that included his brother Teddy. After their dance date, they headed for Angelina's brothel where Art Tatum was playing on the mezzanine. Buckner liked to say that he "was deflowered by the music of Art Tatum."[9] He was discouraged and disgusted that he could never play like Art because his hands were too small. So he went back to Detroit and began experimenting with his hands locked at the wrist, playing four-part chords with the top note repeated an octave below, known as the block chord style. Now he could jack up the volume and be heard in a big band. He would fly over the keyboard, sometimes in unison with the trumpets or saxophones. He was the Pancho Segura of jazz.

Block chords spread faster than honking saxophones. George Shearing was one of the first. Then the great Lennie Tristano and Dave Brubeck used them to their advantage. Herman Foster, the piano player with Lou Donaldson, used them almost exclusively as did Toledoan Mozart Perry. Buckner was also one of the head arrangers for the Lionel Hampton band. He contributed "Hamp's Boogie," a piano primer for the young at jazz, and "Flyin' Home" featuring Illinois Jacquet, a number that many critics think was a start to rhythm and blues. Milt Buckner was in Toledo frequently. He liked to play at Lee's Sensation on Miami Street, but he spent most of his life in Europe where he was treated as royalty. Seymour Rothman of *The Blade* discovered that when he went to Defiance, Ohio, for Milt's funeral. Jazz VIP's were everywhere: Paul Quinichette, Freddy Green, Joe Newman from the Basie Band, and Charlie Shavers. "There were eulogies and there was music," said Rothman. "A group of Detroit jazz musicians with backgrounds from here to McKinney's original Cotton Pickers were on the church steps playing for Milt . . . Jack Jackson, Toledo's fine organist played; David Wilburn, one of the original Cotton Pickers . . . sang 'My Buddy.' Toledo jazz saxman Floyd (Candy) Johnson spoke of his great friendship with Buckner and, dissatisfied with trying to put his message into words, picked up the sax and played 'Ebb Tide,' a number which the two had recorded for a European record company . . . . The greatest eulogies to this talented musician—pianist and organist—were delivered in the corners where his friends gathered . . . . Mr. Bakker, a seller of wines and groceries with an interest in radio and television, is collaborating with a Swiss writer, Otto Fluckiger, on a biography of Buckner.

Candy's solo with Count Basie

"'Why am I writing a book?' he said. 'Because people don't know what we have in Milt Buckner, and I want them to know. In Europe he is a great artist. No one there would have to ask why I am writing a book. Our countries take a different attitude toward jazz. Here you listen, you applaud, and you forget about it. In Europe we want to know more about the people who make this jazz. Who are they? What are they like? How to they come to create such beauty? We appreciate the person as well as the music'"[10]

Chapter 20
Claude, Cliff, the Detroit Connection

Claude Black

The story of Claude Black is the story of two cities, his formative years in Detroit and his remaining years in Toledo where he was part of the Detroit Connection, the name of one of his albums. Black said he grew up in a house with two pianos, his mother's in the living room and his uncle's in the basement. He saw Jimmie Lunceford and many of the big bands at the Paradise Theater in Detroit. But other than his uncle, his main influence was two records, "After Hours" by Avery Parrish and "Hamp's Boogie Woogie," with Lionel Hampton and Milt Buckner.[1]

Black started piano lessons when he was eight years old with Miss Shambly, who was all classical music with no understanding of, or willingness to listen to jazz. Black went to Cass Technical High School and then later at Northern Senior High School, two reasons why Detroit had more jazz talent per square mile in the 1940s and '50s than any other city. Talent nurtured in the soil of Detroit's public education system which put undue emphasis on a musical education that turned out hard boppers, like Claude and his classmates, Paul Chambers, Sonny Red, and Tommy Flanagan.[2] They took their inspiration from Charlie Parker, Dizzy Gillespie and Bud Powell, but mixed more muscle with the roots of gospel music. Black also benefitted from the many places in Detroit to hear jazz musicians; such as Phil Hill at the Blue Bird Inn, Will Davis and BuBu Turner at Parrots Lounge, and the patriarch of Detroit piano, "The Dean," Hank Jones at the famous Baker's Keyboard Lounge, a club that started in 1934.[3] One of Claude Black's earliest dates in Toledo was in 1956 at the Waiters and Bellman's Club on Indiana Avenue when he had Benny Cook on drums and Vern Martin on bass. In 1960, he gave a sparkling rendition of "It Might As Well Be Spring" at the Arv Garrison Memorial.[4] After that he joined Eddy Harris who had a big hit called "Exodus." From 1965 to 1967 he was Aretha Franklin's piano player.

Claude made his first record on the Sensation label, one of those short-lived Independents in Detroit with the wonderful Donald Byrd on trumpet and bassist Gene Taylor who was born in Toledo and made a name for himself with the Horace Silver Quintet. Claude lost the record many years ago and he never found another copy. He was in Switzerland on tour with ex-Basie sidemen

Claude Black with saxophonist Sonny Stitt
Courtesy of the author

Al Grey and Buddy Tate, an occasion Claude named as one of the high points of his career. Claude said, "We were just getting ready to play when this guy comes up and said, 'I have something for you' and he pulls out this cassette with the Sensation date on one side. How it got from Detroit to Switzerland, I will never know."[5]

When Claude returned to the United States, he made an album that some think is his best called *The Detroit Jazz Tradition*. The album was under the leadership of drummer JC Heard, but it is Claude who steals the show on "Never Let Me Go," "If I Should Lose You," and his own tune, "The Poor People Bossa Nova." Another high point in his career was playing at the Village Vanguard in New York City backing up some of New York's finest musicians. Then there was the time he accompanied Sonny Stitt and Milt Jackson at the Baker's Keyboard Lounge in Detroit. To that you would have to add February 25, 2000, at the Peristyle, "a night of dazzling jazz", said David Yonke of *The Blade*.[6]

Claude Black died in January 2013, a victim of cancer. Susanne Scott, his ex-wife took care of him. "A pair of benefit concerts last year to raise money for his health-care costs led to an outpouring of support,' Ms. Scott said, 'They came out of the woodwork when it came to those concerts last year,' she said. 'He was absolutely flabbergasted—and it never stopped.'... 'Some people could hear his technique, but there was something in Claude and his heart was in it and it was so deep. He couldn't help but pull people in.'"[7] Pianist El Myers said, "Everybody loved Claude Black, but what impressed me the most, even more than his music, was when I heard that when he had lost his piano, he would walk all the way to the music department at Toledo University so he could use one of the practice rooms. Snow or sleet he would be there."[8]

Another admirer, and fellow piano player, Mark Kieswetter, said, "I could be in a room and listening to twenty other piano players and still be able to pick out Claude, not his harmony or his ideas, not even the sound of his piano, it's where he puts the notes that gives it away. I saw him at Murphy's one night with Cliff Murphy on bass on one of those nights that happen so infrequently when you don't have to think about anything. It's like a story that just tells itself. You play for these moments when you are in the zone. They were in that zone that night, deep in a groove. The golden pocket, I call it, a high like no other."[9] About the only knock against Claude Black was that he intimidated his cohorts. Preston Keys remembered that he was overwhelmed the first

Claude Black, piano; Milt Jacson, vibes; Roy Brookes, drums; Ralph Armstrong, bass
Courtesy of the author

time he heard Claude Black.[10] Johnny O'Neal, whose career included a stint with Art Blakey and the Jazz Messengers, is another Detroiter who took Toledo as his second home. He played in Carnegie Hall in front of Oscar Peterson. He portrayed Art Tatum in the movie *Ray* but still said, "My knees were shaking that night when I was going to play a duet with Claude at Murphy's, just the two of us trading off fours and eights. He has this command over the nuances that always get your attention. What I've learned is that you can never figure you've arrived in jazz, because the horizons are so vast.[11]

"The other thing I have learned is you never know who you are talking to. Let me give you an example, there was this obnoxious looking and acting guy who used to come into one of the clubs in town.

Courtesy of Claude Black

The Claude Black Trio at Murphy's with Cliff Murphy, bass; Sean Dobbins, drums
Courtesy of El Myers

Johnny O'Neal Trio with Cliff Murphy, bass; Sean Dobbins, drums
Courtesy of the author

He was an albino with pink eyes and scabby skin that was flaking all over the place. It seemed like he never took a bath. You could smell him about a block away from the club. He was something out of a Stephen King movie. He looked inhuman, grotesque. Every time he walked into the club, he would yell out something like, 'Hey Baby, I've got some superimposed altered chords that will screw with your head, Baby.' Well I put him off as much as I could. He always wanted to sit in. The management didn't know what to do, so I decided one night that I would let him play. I thought that I would just let him make a fool of himself and he would never come back. So one night he comes in and said, 'Hey man, let me play, let me play.' He sat down at the keyboard; I turned my back. I was just about ready to put my hands over my ears when I couldn't believe what I heard: Bud Powell, Phineas Newborn, the guy was a whiz, an amazing guy. I never found out his name. He just disappeared after that night.

"Toledo has more of these fine piano players than I can even name, and not all are jazz players. Eddie Abrams took me downtown one night to the Commodore Perry Lounge to hear Jim Gottran. I call him 'Hank Jones by candlelight.' He plays high society, penthouse jazz like Eddie Duchin or Joe Reichman or Cy Coleman. There is no improvisation and he really doesn't swing. It's just beautiful piano. Gottran is the piano doctor in Toledo. There is no furniture in his apartment, just rooms full of Steinways, Yamahas, and Baldwins he's working on. I trust his assessment. He'll tell me if I had an A, B, or just C performance at Murphy's. What a critic he would have made.

"My own influence was my dad, who got me to listen to Miles Davis' piano player, Wynton Kelly. Of course I was influenced by Art Tatum and most of all by Terry Pollard. She adopted me since that day when I was fourteen when I walked down a few blocks to the club she was playing in and heard all that piano. Later I found out how to sneak into the club. That was the first time I had ever heard live jazz. She made a big impression on me."[12]

In 1955, Pollard was voted by *Down Beat* as the new star on both vibes and piano, mostly on the strength of her work with the Terry Gibbs Quartet. In 1957 she appeared with the Gibbs Quartet at Toledo's Paramount Theater in a festival called the Birdland Stars of Tomorrow. It was the greatest assembly of jazz giants in Toledo history: Count Basie, Bud Powell, Zoot Sims, Sarah Vaughn, and Chet Baker just for starters.

A Gathering of Eagles

From L to R - Don Hales, Claude Black, El Myers, Cliff Murphy, Bob White
Courtesy of the author

Cliff Murphy

Claude Black and Cliff Murphy have been linked together for so long and so often that some people think of them in the plural, like the Everly Brothers or Ferrante and Teischer. They met more than fifty years ago at the House of Israel on Stickney Avenue. Both of their fathers were ministers who had zero tolerance toward jazz. "An invitation to ruin," they called it.[13] Since about 1954, when he had a group at the Paradise Inn on Vance Street, Cliff Murphy was the number one bass player in Toledo. He is one of the last musicians to have played with Arv Garrison. "Arv was slipping badly," said Murphy. "We'd be sitting there at intermission and he would be sipping coffee and suddenly he would be spilling it all over himself and then in a few seconds he'd continue on as if nothing happened."[14]

Pianist and composer Harry Gregory arrived in Toledo in the mid-1920s and said there were tuba players like Bert Cobb and June Cole with the McKinney's Cotton Pickers but few bass players; the only two he could remember were Bass Johnson and Hank Durham.[15] All bass players and especially Cliff Murphy owed a great thanks to Jimmy Blanton of the Duke Ellington Orchestra for liberating the instrument. In 1940 Jimmy Blanton changed the role of the bass from simply a harmonic and rhythmic foundation to one that could improvise melodies like a trumpet or saxophone. A more immediate influence on Cliff Murphy were Detroit bass players like Doug Watkins, Will Austin, and the Glover Brothers, four brothers all of whom played the bass. "John Mast and I would go to this huge mansion in Detroit that only let cats in who could play. You

L to R - Jim Gottran, Buddy Sullivan, El Myers, Cliff Murphy, Jack Walter, Bob White, Claude Black

Courtesy of El Myers

could go to this hip 'hotel' at four a.m. and somebody would be playing jazz. It was all day, all night, big names too, just before some of them went to New York: Billy Mitchell, Kenny Burrell who was in Toledo quite a bit, the Jones Brothers. So you might say that the Detroit tradition of hard bop got to me early."[16]

Cliff said he was destined to be a musician from the first time he sat on Art Tatum's porch listening to him practice. He had a very rewarding career in music, but he has had one regret—that he did not learn to read music earlier. Had he passed a simple test when he was drafted into the army, he would have avoided a horrible experience in the infantry that caused him to go AWOL. He ended up in a bar in Columbus, Ohio. Standing next to the jukebox was a blind sixteen-year-old saxophonist in dark glasses playing along with the selections. It was Roland Kirk. They became fast friends and in ten years, Kirk was a familiar name in international jazz circles. Years later they had a reunion when Kirk played at the M and L Rendezvous on Indiana Avenue.[17]

Murphy was always eager to learn. It was John Mast who taught him how to read music. "We worked on classical stuff," said Murphy. "And once I started something, he wouldn't let me stop and do a passage over, mistakes be damned."[18] Preston Keys, the pianist, said once that Cliff Murphy was born to play the bass, with those huge hands and that big warm tone. "I thought we got along very well," said Preston. "I was a bit stronger harmonically, but he was rhythmically way ahead. And what I liked also was that he never overplayed. Now I had five bass players, two of them were really fine bass players, before Cliff came along, but there was too much interplay.

L to R - Jim Gottran, Claude Black, Johnny O'Neal, El Myers
Courtesy of El Myers

The Bill Evans Trio was not what the audience wanted or the management for that matter. Some bass players get carried away with their Scott LeFaro licks. We were playing for an audience who wouldn't know Wayne Shorter from Wayne King."[19]

In the early 1970s, Cliff Murphy went on the road with the very popular piano player Glen Covington, and then had the opportunity to join the Buddy Rich Big Band when they played a date in Toledo. "It was Sunday," said Murphy, "and the band was in the parking lot getting ready to head out when some guy calls me and said 'Buddy wants to see you.' I said, 'What does he want with me?' So I went to see him and when I got there and entered the bus, he was chewing out the band, challenging everyone, firing some, and challenging others to fist fights. When he saw me, he yells out, 'Can you play?' I paused and said, 'I'm not prepared tonight or ever,' and got off the bus as fast as I could."[20]

Cliff Murphy and his partner, Joan Russell, owned Digby's Jazz Club before opening Murphy's Place in 1991. Murphy's closed twenty years later. It was a split-level jazz theater in-the-round located in the basement of a downtown hotel. After Rusty's Jazz Café closed, it was the main jazz club in Toledo, bringing in nationally known acts of the caliber of Wynton Marsalis, Milt Jackson, and hometown prodigy Stanley Cowell. Joan took care of the business end of it, while Cliff Murphy and Claude Black, the house pianist, provided the entertainment. In the twenty years of business, there were some acts that brought down the house. One of them was in February 2005 when Fathead Newman, formerly of the Ray Charles Band, was their guest.

At the time he had the number one jazz hit on the Billboard charts. On the day of the concert, they rehearsed for four hours which was unheard of. Newman wrote a song for the occasion called "Cookin' at Murphy's" which is also the name of the CD that came out afterwards.

Johnny O'Neal called Murphy one of the fathers of Toledo jazz. "He's like a roadmap, a guide, a guy you can take risks with because if you get lost, you know that Cliff will lead you out of the jungle. You can listen to him on *My Reunion at Murphy's* CD. That's what I'm talking about."[21] Cliff Murphy never paid much attention to compliments. He said, "I know how well I've played or didn't play. I'm my own worst critic." He didn't mind, however, being compared to west coaster LeRoy "The Walker" Vinegar. At the end of an interview in 2004, a newspaper reporter asked Cliff Murphy, "Of all the people living, who would you most like to have coffee with?" "Hillary Clinton," replied Cliff, "Fascinating woman."[22]

Chapter 21
The Man Behind the Mast

John Mast exploded one night when a music writer asked him if he had been ready to play with such luminaries as Zoot Sims, Carmen McCrae, and the legendary Dick Haymes. "What kind of stupid question is that? Ready? Ready? Do you know who you're talking to, for Christ's sakes?"[1] Like the child prodigy, Ruth Slenczynska, John Mast was destined to play the piano. His father, Clare, was a classically trained, highly respected pianist in Toledo who worked six nights a week in various show clubs and theaters. "When I was a baby," said Mast, "My dad would hold me in his lap at the piano and take my fingers with his hand and guide them on to the keyboard to whatever pop song or light classics we happened to be listening to." By the time John was three, he was playing by ear. He started taking lessons in first grade from Elizabeth Gould. He continued with her until the end of his freshman year at Indiana University's fine musical department.

A drummer friend introduced Mast to Charlie Parker and Dizzy Gillespie's "Hot House" and "Groovin' High." Then he discovered the saxophone battles between Illinois Jacquet and Flip Phillips on the *Jazz at the Philharmonic* recordings. When he was fourteen he went to New York as a contestant in a talent show called the *Big Break*. He finished second. The winner was, coincidently, another Toledoan, a Waite High School student named Teresa Brewer.[2] She became Toledo's most successful entertainer since Joe E. Brown. In the early 1950s she had six, count them, six million-seller recordings, each one delivered with the piercing exuberance of a cheerleader on Jolt. In the fall of 1950, "Music, Music, Music" was blaring out of every car radio and jukebox in Toledo. She made a couple of records with Les Brown which evidently gave her the idea she wanted to sing jazz. She made fifteen records, one with

L to R Buzzy Jasinsky, unknown, John Mast
Courtesy of Buzzy Jasinsky

Duke Ellington and another with Count Basie. They received lukewarm reviews. Critics had trouble getting "Ricochet Romance" out of their ears. "What was so remarkable about the trip to New York," said Mast, "was that the night before the concert, I snuck out of the hotel and found a jazz club in Times Square where Lester Young was playing with Billie Holiday. I had my first taste of beer that night."[3]

In 1951 Mast performed Rachmaninoff's "Tonight We Love" at the Peristyle in Toledo. Much to his father's regret, it was his last classical concert. "It broke his heart," said Mast. "He had no understanding of jazz." That summer he joined the Fred Dale Band at Lake Hamilton, Indiana, where he had a reunion with some of his classmates at Indiana University. That is where he met flautist and alto saxophonist, Bob Wynn, an enormously talented musician who later led one of the best quintets on the West Coast. "One day after band rehearsal, Wynn stayed around for over an hour just listening to me play. There is no higher praise than that. It may be the highest compliment I ever got. I have had some nice things written about me in the paper. *The Blade* once in a while gets someone who at least can listen, but I've gone to some concerts that have been panned and came away with the feeling that most music writers are not qualified to judge something as complex as jazz."[4]

In 1955, John Mast found work in Chicago that eventually led to him backing Carmen McCrae at the Prelude Club. Mast recalled, "She was just getting started then, and during intermission we used to walk around the Loop telling stories and exchanging smokes." In 1957, Mast was back in Toledo working with a few roughhouse tenors by the name of Dave Poulin and Candy Johnson. In 1958 he went to New York and stayed for two years. He bought a loft there and invited the mysterious and very tasty drummer, Ronnie Free, and the highly valued bass player, Ben Tucker, to move in with him. "Word got around," said Mast, "that there was this loft on East 23rd with a great home-based rhythm section, jam sessions all night long with people like Freddy Hubbard, Zoot Sims, Warne Marsh, and those Detroit guys I used to play with at the Blue Bird, Thad Jones, Donald Byrd, and Curtis Fuller."[5]

Harry Gregory, John Mast, Preston Keys
Courtesy of Rusty Monroe

Harold Lindsy at Fifi's
Courtesy of El Myers

Fellow Toledoan, Bill Takas, enjoyed a similar experience in a loft near his apartment on Bleecker Street. "Because basses, pianos, and drums are so much harder to move, any place with a rhythm section would attract horn players from all over town. We'd put the word out and you never knew how many would show up —two, three, or twenty-five horn players. The masters might be there, or cats you'd never seen before."

"The standard American songbook," said Takas, "was a key ingredient of the sessions. You had to have a common repertoire. If you didn't know tunes like 'I Got Rhythm' and 'Indiana' you couldn't make it in those sessions. But in the 1960s, the 'everybody is creative' hippie movement really changed things. Nobody had the common repertoire anymore. Nobody knew the standards."[6] Playing with the best and brightest in New York City filled Mast with confidence and pride. The skinny, slightly hawk-faced kid from Toledo was doing all right. He then went on a six-month tour out of New York with the Billy May band under the direction of Sam Donahue. For a while he played with Si Zentner, later with Ralph Marterie, and an unforgettable three weeks in Miami Beach with the Zoot Sims Quartet.

High on the list of John Mast's achievements would be accompanying Dick Haymes, the pretty boy crooner and movie star of 1945 with a rich baritone voice that housewives wanted to cuddle and their husbands wanted to throttle. "He wasn't a happy man," said Mast. "Everything was closing in on him. Everybody wanted his money, including the IRS for back taxes. There were threats to deport him to Argentina where he was born. His many divorced wives wanted money. The Press always disliked him. They thought he was a spoiled snob."[7] In the 1960s, long after John Mast and a dozen other pianists had gone, Haymes was fighting to get applause in Las Vegas. He felt like a blacksmith in the age of V8 engines trying to sell bittersweet love songs of the 1930s to an audience that wanted Bobby Vinton instead of Jerome Kern. He was always going to make a comeback, but it never happened. He was Miniver Cheevy, who could not escape the past when teenagers mobbed him and music critics ranked him just below Frank Sinatra and Bing Crosby; back to 1945 when he sang "It Might as Well Be Spring" to Jeanne Crain in the film *State Fair*. So it was Bloody Marys in the morning, afternoon and evening. He began forgetting the lyrics to songs that he had sung hundreds of times. Mast said, "He was completely absorbed and very self-destructive. He was reckless, like the time we rode in his convertible from New York to Toledo in record time averaging ninety miles per hour, Haymes laughing in the wind, blurry-eyed, half drunk, his mistress wrapped around his shoulders. I was huddled in the back seat in a fetal position thinking every moment was going to be the last."

"Dick Haymes was a pro in every sense of the word," said Mast, "I had no trouble accompanying him. He was aloof, to be sure, offstage, but once you got on the bandstand, it was a different world. You became part of a very creative adventure. It was a beautiful feeling, a moment in time that won't happen again and I'll never forget it."[8] "After playing all over the country and parts of Canada and living for short periods in cities like Las Vegas, San Francisco, and Dodge City, Kansas," Mast said, "I came home to Toledo again and continued to work steadily until the early eighties and I saw that electronic instruments were taking over. I gave it a try. I played on a couple, but I knew I would never enjoy playing on a dummy keyboard that was unresponsive to the touch, the very thing that identifies Hank Jones and Tommy Flanagan who was in Toledo quite often by the way."

In the fall of 1982, Mast became the musicians' union president for six years. After that, he played for private parties and worked as a salesman in Western Michigan and Toledo. Dealing with nightclub owners was always a hassle for Mast. A good example happened in about 1952. He said, "I was just getting started and this guy who had read about me in *The Blade* offered me a job. I was up for it until I took a look at the piano in his club. It had never been tuned, and some of the keys were missing and the action was all fouled up. So I told him, 'It would sure be great to work for you, but the piano is unplayable,' thinking that he knew what I meant. He assured me that he would fix the piano to my satisfaction. So I came back in about two weeks. The gig was

Arv Garrison, Skip White, Harold Linsey, unknown pianist
Courtesy of Vivian Garry

already advertised in the paper. I walk in and the guy said, 'Look, I got a big surprise for you.' He was a Greek guy. So I walked into the room and there was the piano, resplendent in the only shaft of light in the whole place, a royal blue. So, I went over and the keys were still missing. It was so out of tune that anything you tried to play would be a laugh. I started to walk out and he said, 'Look what I done for you and you don't even appreciate it. I had it painted, didn't you notice?'"9

Some might remember a fall night in 2006 at Fifi's, a New York style supper club and piano lounge located in a strip mall on Airport Highway. There was a black state-of-the-art grand piano greeting customers as they entered. At the keyboard was John Mast and he was on a roll, just as he had been the night Johnny O'Neal first saw him and was blown away by his long, seemingly interminable lines. "Secret Love," "Long Ago and Far Away," "Snowfall" with the Debussy touch, "Every Time We Say Goodbye," and by the fifth number the place was hushed. The dinner crowd stopped chatting and only the cash register and the cocktail mixer competed for attention. Mast was just beginning another love song when suddenly, someone from the very back of the club yelled out, "Hey John, stop making us cry." Mast turned in the direction of the voice, smirked, and plunged into "Happy Days Are Here Again." Not much of John Mast's work was recorded, just a couple of tapes, one done at Fifi's, and another one from the Arv Garrison Memorial. He has a long solo on "Baby Doll" from an out-of-print recording by Johnny Knorr called *Let's Go Dancing*.

Mast's finest two hours happened in 1994 at the Franciscan Center in Sylvania, Ohio. It was his "A Tribute to Two Harolds," Harold Lindsey and Harold Jaffe, two of the most important people in all of Toledo jazz. With the backing of Dave Melle and the eighteen-piece Toledo Jazz Orchestra, Mast played the "Jaffe Variations," a suite in five movements.

    The state of jazz in Toledo, Ohio, would have been different without Harold Jaffe and his sons. Harold must have believed, as one famous essayist put it, "The true measure of a healthy society is the use of its leisure time" and Harold's idea of the best use of our free time was to cultivate an appreciation of the arts. This humble jeweler, who used to bid farewell to all of his friends by telling them "to think good thoughts and drink plenty of V-8 juice," gave generously to the arts: to the Toledo Museum of Art, the Toledo Opera, the Toledo Symphony Orchestra, all the visual arts, the Toledo Ballet Association, and most of all, jazz. In 2003, thirteen years after his death, Harold Jaffe Jewelers was honored by the Governor's Award for the Arts in Ohio for his support of the arts. As a spokesman for the Ohio Arts Council said, "It is difficult to find an arts-related event or program in the greater Toledo community that has not been supported by Harold Jaffe Jewelers through in-kind support, financial contribution, or staff volunteers." He helped support the Toledo Jazz Orchestra, and was one of the people who started the Toledo Jazz Society. He bankrolled dozens of festivals so that the biggest names in all of jazz could visit Toledo.[10]

    As a tribute to Harold Lindsey, John Mast wrote "Smooth Stuff and Funky Dunk" to illustrate Lindsey's two styles. "The melodic member of the cool style but who once in a while would throw in a little funk," said Mast. When Lindsey died in 2012, the title of his obituary read "Musician a fixture in city for decades,"[11] as if longevity and permanence would be his only legacy. He displayed a big bluesy sound in the manner of his idol, Gene Ammons, a sound that could warm up a concert

El Myers, Jim Gottran, Buddy Sullivan, Harold Lindsey
Courtesy of El Myers

hall faster than central heating. Lindsey did not honk or showboat. He never tried to sell himself or hog choruses in a jam session; it was doubtful that he ever made a single enemy. He was the only horn player welcome at Fifi's and probably the only one she ever hired.

Harold Lindsey discovered the saxophone at Libbey High School and it soon became his best friend, never out of his sight. One of his first jobs was at the Gaiety Club with the Brown Buddies, starring the DeBoe Brothers. Then he worked at the 3-D Club on Broadway and South Streets with his own quartet, and perhaps his favorite time was with Arv Garrison at the Green Lite Night Club on Detroit Avenue. Tenor Don Arnold a former member of the Scott High Five, thought that Lindsey could have played with the best of them. "He could have gone to L.A. or New York and made it, but he loved Toledo and the city was better for it."[12] Harold Lindsey was the most generous, most pleasant cat with the least ego in all of Toledo. "A better person never walked the earth," said Gene Parker, "and the notes he played were like huge brush strokes of a master painter."[13]

Chapter 22
Gene Parker – The Head Master

Gene Parker is a curly haired, cocksure saxophonist. Many think he is Toledo's outstanding musician and heir apparent to Jim Riggs who left town years ago to join the faculty at North Texas State. His ability to raise his playing to another level sets Gene Parker apart. At the Tri-State Festival some years ago, he stood shoulder to shoulder trading choruses with the co-inventor of bebop, Dizzy Gillespie. Gillespie was so impressed with this "little fat kid from Toledo" that he offered him a job and a trip to Europe as part of his quintet. Gene would have gone if it had not been for the return of the eminent James Moody. However, being the best musician in Toledo, Ohio, will not be Parker's legacy. His ability to communicate to aspiring instrumentalists will be.

Gene Parker
Courtesy of Rusty Monroe

Most cities with a jazz history usually have one or two master teachers, people who believe that music is heaven's highest calling and who impart that feeling to their students. In Seattle, Washington, the man to learn from was Jerry Grey. In Portland, Oregon, it was Gene Confer about whom one pupil said, "He inspired you. That is what a teacher is supposed to do, isn't it? Inspire you."[1] James Lee at Central High School in Cleveland, Ohio, knew how. He managed to get free passes for all his students to the big band matinees at the Palace Theater where they saw Benny Goodman, Tommy Dorsey, and Jimmie Lunceford. Lee made playing in the stage band as

Young Gene Parker on piano with Buzzy Jasinski on drums, and leader Lou Sands
Courtesy of the author

Unforgettable!!
Courtesy of Rusty Monroe

prestigious as playing on the football team. Louis Cabrera, at Miller High School in Detroit, put together a fourteen-piece dance band that included Milt Jackson and Kenny Burrell. The band travelled to different high schools every week for which they were paid seven dollars a night.[2]

Gene Parker is the supreme music educator in Toledo. His students talk about his ability to put the vocabulary of music into plain English. They compare him to a demanding coach. You have to keep up, and as soon as you get one concept, he gives you another so that you are always challenged. He has turned out dozens of fine musicians. Guitarist Dan Faehnle studied with him; Parker does not even know how to play guitar, but he has a certain success teaching guitar players. When the fabulously successful Jerry Sawicki wanted to get back to the saxophone, he looked up Gene Parker. "I have to laugh when I think of this pudgy red-haired kid who we had to shoo away at Tony Packo's because he would always be pestering us to sit in and he ended up being my teacher. The guy is a class act, the most multi-talented musician I've ever known and that goes for everyone. You get theory and technique, and he takes you right back to the basics. When I came back, I didn't even know what a diminished chord was. He looked at me and said, 'no problem, it's simple' and that was the way lessons went."[3] The song, "I Thought About You" from Sawicki's *Second Time Around* album is dedicated to Gene Parker.

Zoot's Last Stand

One of the most moving concerts Gene Parker ever witnessed was Zoot Sims playing with the Toledo Jazz Orchestra. Every tenor saxophonist within fifteen miles packed the Clarion Hotel on Secor Road to hear the man they called "The Natural" who one critic said "could singlehandedly swing a Shriner's band." Parker remembered the evening as if it were yesterday. "He was in a wheelchair. His vision was going. I hardly recognized him, he had lost so much weight. But he had to play because he was completely broke; and worse than that, he was locked out of his house. We didn't even rehearse, but he played great, and despite his condition you couldn't even get him off the stage until he signed every autograph."[4]

Coda

Don Arnold, Zoot Sim's number one fan in Toledo, was there that night. Arnold was one of the Scott High School Five that included Dean Austin, Jack Walter, Dave Seaman, and John Mast. In fact Walter was with Arnold the first time he ever heard Zoot Sims. Arnold remembered, "It was in a small record store on St. Clair, right between Rivoli Theater and the Palace. I think it might have been called United Music. There was a heavy-set red-haired lady that owned it that liked us and let us try out all the records

Don Arnold with idol Zoot Sims
Courtesy of Don Arnold

we wanted before we spent our hard earned cash. One was called *Zoot Sims Plays the Blues*. That's how it started. From that moment on I wished I could play like he does. I still have the record along with many others as I followed his career from Stan Kenton to Woody Herman. Oh, he looked awful that night at the Clarion, so weak from cancer that he could hardly carry his saxophone case. My wife started to cry when she saw him. He still played great, mostly on soprano which was easier to handle. I don't usually do this, but I just had to tell him how much he's meant to me all these years. So I managed to get enough courage after the concert to walk right up to him and asked if my wife and I could take him to breakfast the next morning. I never thought he would have time, but he said 'Yeah, yes.' So the next day we took him across the street from the Clarion where he was staying to Frisch's Big Boy, and you know, I was so excited about what was happening that I can't remember what we talked about, only the sight of him eating bacon and eggs."[5]

Chapter 23
Jack Walter – In the Land of the Giants

Most jazz musicians remember one or two nights that stand out above the rest. For El Myers it was trying to keep up with Wardell Gray at the Waiters and Bellman's Club. For the master educator and saxophonist Gene Parker, it might be trading fours with Dizzy Gillespie; and Jimmy Cook never forgot the night in Flint, Michigan, when Stan Kenton offered him a job. For Jack Walter, saxophonist at large, it was a Sunday night in early January 1954. His favorite musician, Lee Konitz, was playing at the famous Storyville club in Boston. Sitting across from Jack at a small candlelit table was the woman whose letters kept him from going crazy during the worst days of the Korean War. They met immediately upon his return from the army. She was more attractive and smarter than he had ever imagined, and she collected jazz records. "First thing she did," said Jack "was whisper in my ear that 'we could get to know each other later. But right now I have tickets for Lee Konitz.'

"It was the happiest day of my life. If I could have stopped the world then and gotten off, I would have. I have a CD of the Konitz Quartet about the time we were there. I memorized all the songs we heard that night: 'Hi, Beck,' 'Foolish Things,' 'If I Had You,' that was going to be our song. I should have stayed in Boston. I really wanted to, but I needed the money so bad. I got a job the next day with the Bernie Cummings Band out of New York for a series of one-nighters. Sometimes they were 300 miles apart and we were on the road all the time. It is not like now where there are cell phones everywhere. We were just on the go all the time and I should have written but I let it go for a few weeks. And finally I got a letter from her, a 'Dear John' letter

Jack Walter
With the Murphy's
APRIL 22
Murphy's Place
151 Water Street
Toledo OH
419.241.7732

Dean Austin, unknown bassist, Jack Walter
Courtesy of Jack Walter

saying that she had met someone else. I could hardly get out of bed the next morning, I was so devastated. We were meant to be. I've had a lot of relationships since and nothing has ever come close to that. I wish I would have acted. I still haven't gotten over it and it has been fifty years. She is probably not even alive."[1]

Several photos of the girl that got away surround Jack's tiny basement apartment in South Toledo. Memorabilia of his musical past fill the room: the picture of Jack playing lead alto with Tony Celeste at Aku-Aku, another of him with Phil Woods and Arv Garrison at the M and L Rendezvous, and one of him with the great baritone saxophonist Pepper Adams when they roomed together in New York. There was a huge poster of his return to jazz at Murphy's after a serious stroke. Walter said he knew he wanted to play the saxophone after he heard the instrument for the first time when his aunt bought him tickets for 75 cents to the Paramount Theater. When he got there he sat through two performances of Wayne King, the waltz king. Jazz musicians called him the Schmaltz king. "The show came on, here comes this guy with an alto sax," said Jack, "and when he started playing, I don't know, something happened to me." When he came home he told his aunt that he wanted a saxophone for Christmas, and that is how it all started.[2] He began by trying to imitate Wayne King's wide, sugary vibrato. That all changed when he went to high school. He met a talented group of students known as the Scott High Five: Dave Seaman, Don Arnold, John Mast, and Dean Austin, in Jack's opinion, the best small drummer Toledo ever had. "He was a mix of two drummers, Dave Tough, especially his work with the Clam Bake Seven, and Shelly Manne. And like Shelly Manne, he was a third horn, very melodic, subtle. He didn't overplay. He was the perfect drummer. Great taste, great time. For big bands, I always preferred the

rock solid beat of Bob White or Charlie Mewhort. Last time I saw Charlie it was at Rusty's. He walked in with a girl and I knew he hadn't been well. Rumors were floating around. Mewhort sat down and started talking a mile a minute like he always did and continued on for a while. Finally I stopped him, and I said, 'Charlie, give it a rest. Tell me how do you feel?' He put his hand on my shoulder, didn't say a word, for about a whole minute not one word. Two months later he is gone."[3]

When Walter was eighteen, he and pianist John Mast went to Detroit to see Charlie Parker. After the first set, they went up to talk to Parker who invited them to sit in. John Mast jumped at the chance, but Walter shied away. "Charlie Parker is the father of the saxophone, inventor of bebop," Walter said. "When he asked me what I played, I looked down at the floor and said alto sax. He then asked if I wanted to join him in the next set. He was serious. I wish I had, just so I could say I did it, but I just didn't have the confidence, in fact, I really never had the confidence. Because of that I've missed a lot of opportunities. I just wasn't willing to take the risk. Now I regret that."[4]

In 1956, Jack got a call from Arv Garrison asking him to join him in a group at the M and L Rendezvous. "That night the place was just packed. It was packed every night, mostly Blacks, but there were some whites," said Walter. We were just ready to start our second number when the door opened and in walked trumpeter Kenny Dorham, alto saxophonist Phil Woods, and Conte Candoli. They walked in and began taking out their horns, and I got offstage as fast as I could. The big boys had arrived. I was still shaking when I found a seat next to my friend. He couldn't understand why I was so nervous. He wondered why I didn't take the opportunity to sit in. I said, 'Phil Woods is the closest thing to Charlie Parker.'

Pat Carroll
Courtesy of Jerry Sawicki

Claude Black and Jack Walter
Courtesy of the author

"I was in the land of giants and I had to tell Kenny Dorham how much his playing had meant to me. I had his first record on Debut. So anyway, I approached him and told him how much I loved the album and I had memorized all the songs. He looks at me like he is questioning my judgment.

"He put his thumb on his lapel and said, 'How do you like my new suit?' The last thing he wanted to talk about was that album. When they started to play, Phil Woods, as a courtesy, went over to the piano and yells out into the audience, 'Hey Jack, get up here, c'mon.' Oh, I didn't have the courage. There was no way I would play. I was in the land of giants."[5]

Walter was with Tony Celeste at the Aku-Aku the night they played opposite Glenn Miller. The band was under the direction of Buddy DeFranco who was veering away from the Miller evergreens and introducing new material like "Theme from the Odd Couple." "I was sitting at the bar at intermission," said Jack, "and one of the trumpet players and one of the saxophonists came over and said to me, 'We don't believe you, the way you play lead alto. Man, you sound like Marshall Royal with Count Basie.' Well, my ego was running over, and then they offered me a job. 'Why don't you join us? We love the way you play lead alto.' 'I can't,' I said, "I haven't played the clarinet in years and the clarinet lead is the Miller sound. And they said, 'Well Buddy will give you plenty of time to adjust.' 'Play in front of Buddy DeFranco? The clarinet king of America?'" DeFranco, the successor to Benny Goodman, was arguably the only clarinet player able to keep up with Art Tatum as he demonstrated in the album they made together in 1955.

Jack spent 1957 and '58 in New York living with Pepper Adams who he met at one of the jam sessions in Detroit. Pepper Adams and Nick Brignola brought a renewed interest to the baritone saxophone since the days of Gerry Mulligan and Serge Chaloff. Adams was voted the new star of 1956 by the jazz critics of *Down Beat*. He played with the Stan Kenton Orchestra in the late 1950s. In the 1970s he was with Thad Jones and Mel Lewis Orchestra, where he earned the nickname "The Knife" for the way his harsh sound, like a Mac truck in first gear, cut through the ensemble. Walter admits that "I didn't even take my horn. That wasn't my purpose for going. When money got short, I ended up working in Gimbles Department Store. What was so thrilling was that Pepper introduced me to all of the biggest names like the Miles Davis Sextet, the same group that made the *Kind of Blue* album, with Cannonball Adderley, John Coltrane, Bill Evans."[6] Jack spent many nights at the Five Spot Café in Greenwich Village where Pepper had a quintet of mostly Detroiters. On April 15, 1958, they made a live record for Riverside Label that is still available. When Walter arrived back in Toledo, he took account of that experience.

"I realized what it did for my playing and I realized I could never play like Gene Parker or Jimmy Riggs, but it offered me a glimpse into the difference between honesty and dishonesty. There are some who are just playing a game and I began to tell who they were. The ones with conviction and the ones who are always boasting about themselves. I realized, especially about vocalists, that I really don't like vocalists generally and I am not the only one. Oh, I make an exception for Pat Carroll with Tony Celeste's band. She was great and so was Mary Ann Russo and they didn't try to scat like some vocalists. I can't stand that. That is why I was never a fan of Ella Fitzgerald. I remember Jon Hendricks asked me what I thought of his last album which had to do with a vocalization of Count Basie. I

Jack Walter, unknown drummer, Jimmy Cook on trumpet, Preston Keys, piano
Courtesy of the author

told him right off. I didn't like it. If you want to play jazz, learn to play an instrument. I know my limitations. I know myself as far as music is concerned, but still my ego has been well nourished. I remember one time at Bud and Luke's where a group of us liked to hang out, nothing fancy, just home-cooked food served by waitresses who didn't call you honey, and there wasn't any loud rock and roll in the background. We were just getting ready to eat and Jim Riggs who was at the table said, 'You know, I used to go to the M and L almost every night to hear Arv Garrison and you, Jack, and one night you went into the first eight bars of "My Funny Valentine" that went straight to my heart. I still think about it. I came close to breaking into tears, right there.' It's the nicest thing anybody's ever said, especially from Jim Riggs.[7]

"I remember another incident. Preston Keys had just come into town and right away the buzz among the musicians was that he was playing very much like Bill Evans. So one night we were playing a set together, and Preston said, just as we are getting off the stage for intermission, 'Jack, why don't you stay up here. Let's play a duet together, how about "For All We Know."' He knew that was the song I played when any of our friends died. And my God, the way he fed me chords; he really knows how to feed saxophone players, where to put the chords, knew exactly where I was going. It was one of my career highs. You could hear a pin drop when we were finished and then there was kind of an eruption of applause. Just as I was getting off the stage for a drink, Preston whispers, 'see Jack, you did it again.'"[8]

Chapter 24
Fred & Preston - Last of the Lounge Players

Like the department store elevator operator and the uniformed theater usher, the lounge pianist is practically extinct and the grand piano and popular song form with them. "Stardust" doesn't mean much to a generation suckled on KISS and Michael Jackson. Lounge pianists used to be everywhere: wedding receptions, supper clubs, nightclubs, cruise ships, hotels, and all the Holiday Inns. Amtrak hired a couple in the 1970s for their club cars. In the Nordstrom chain on the West Coast there was a piano player in every store. There were even movies about solo pianists, *The World of Henry Orient*, with Peter Sellers, *The Fabulous Baker Boys*, starring Jeff and Beau Bridges, and *The Only Game in Town* with Warren Beatty.

Lounge pianists have been replaced by the guitar, karaoke, and the electric piano, an instrument not popular among Toledo pianists. John Mast would not play one. Fred Kopp, the pianist at Fifi's for more than twenty years was even more emphatic. "I hate electric pianos," said Kopp. "There's no touch, there's no response. There's nothing personal about them. Nightclub owners love them because they don't have to pay money to have them tuned. But Fifi wants to hear popular standards on acoustic pianos."[1] Kopp, sporting a head full of snow white hair was looking prosperous, but worried. He had had two strokes and was legally blind. His wife had to drive him everywhere, including to Fifi's every weekend. "It's a day-by-day situation," said Kopp. "Fifi, God bless her, told me that as long as I can still play, I have a job. That's really something these days, isn't it? I cried after she told me that. But she has her rules. There's no sitting in with few exceptions, no horns, no drums, and absolutely no singers, and tableside crooners are given the stare. You see customers come through the door, they'll yell something at you. You are their entertainment for the evening. I know most of them, their jobs, what they drink, their birthdays, their favorite song, which I try to sneak in when they are not looking. It is kind of like a family, a second home. I am not there to play jazz but to provide romantic background music for dining and drinking. Now when no one is there or I think no one is paying attention, I can stretch out. That happened the other night on a tune called 'I'll Take Romance' when I thought no one was listening. I gave it quite a run. When I finished there was a muffled 'Yeah' from someone at the back of the bar. It made my weekend.

Buzzy Jasinski, Jerry Sawicki, Fred Kopp, Arv Garrison
Courtesy of Fred Kopp

"My first teacher was a farmer from Wauseon, Ohio, named Uncle Dud. No kidding that was his name. No, that was his nickname. His real name was Alexander Hamilton. He came to our house once a week during the school term, and I went to his farm during the summer. I was about thirteen or fourteen. It was all classics. No pop, and he hated jazz. He didn't even want me to listen to it. Once I brought in some sheet music by George Shearing and he refused to help me learn it. On the other hand, if it were not for Uncle Dud, I wouldn't be a professional piano player. I have to credit him for that.

"I started at Libbey High School and was in the stage band for a while. I switched to Macomber because I had every intention of becoming a tool and die maker like my dad. All that changed with the service. I was thrown in with some guys from L.A., really talented guys who became part of that West Coast movement in the early fifties. I came out at the top of my game. I was sitting in at the Waiters and Bellman's Club regularly. And whenever I could, was listening to guys like Jack Reidley from Fremont or John Mast who was at the Tivoli and El Myers at the Lorraine Hotel also Howard Hill at the 3-D Club. I really admired Howard's playing and that he was such a patient teacher. Howard would play these things that I couldn't do, and I would ask myself, 'How does he do that?' and I'd come home and work on it and then be back the next night to see if I could figure it out."[2]

Fred Kopp has been a solo piano player most of his career. He did have his own group in the 1960s with Dave Seaman and Jack Walter on saxophones and Frank Russo on flugelhorn. Kopp also played with the Dave Poulin Quintet at the Friendly bar on 17th and Adams Streets. The feature soloist was guitarist John Justice who Kopp said was second only to Arv Garrison. Kopp also had a stint with Candy Johnson, Cliff Murphy, and Swing Lee at the Aku-Aku. "Candy was a big friendly guy but confounding. I could never figure him out, a real enigma. Course he had to be the whole show every night, but he'd never let you get close enough to really let you get to know him."[3] Other than Fifi's, Fred Kopp's favorite places to play were Ka-See's on Lagrange Street and Kin Wa Low's downtown. There was not a lot of jazz, mostly floor shows, but they brought in big talent like The Inkspots, Bobby Darin, and The Crew Cuts. Helen O'Connell set an attendance record there. Kin Wa Low's, in the words of one of its customers, was "Chinatown in Toledo. For $2.75 you could get a six-course meal and a floor show, for lunch, a $.95 plate of steaming Chop Suey."[4] The Blade's best storyteller, Seymour Rothman, wrote about it in an article. "To get from the dressing room to the audience, entertainers made their way through a dimly lit corridor, through little doors, up a rickety flight of stairs directly onto the stage. The dressing rooms were known in the trade as the catacombs. Ella Fitzgerald, the most expensive talent ever brought in, used the staircase once and then almost walked out of the engagement because she could barely fit through the stairway and the narrow confines were a threat to her beautiful wardrobe. The stage was another Kin Wa special. It moved up and down by a hydraulic lift. For dancing, it was kept at ground level. When the floorshow started it was raised to table level."5

Preston Keys is an introverted, soft-spoken piano player with a name Sinclair Lewis or Walt Disney might have thought up. Preston doesn't talk much. Two hundred words a day would probably be the maximum and jive talk is not a part of his vocabulary. When he does have something to say, you know he has put a lot of thought into it, like the time someone asked him why he thought Rusty's Jazz Café

Howard Hill Trio: John Takas, Howard Hill, Jim Lair
Courtesy of John Takas

was so successful. "Not a labor-management situation," replied Preston. The best way to bring him out is to tell him he sounds like Bill Evans. Preston said, "A light went on when I heard Bill Evans for the first time. It was 'My Foolish Heart' from the *Waltz for Debby* album."6

What is it about Bill Evans' style that is so attractive, beguiling, and fresh? What is it about his playing that makes him and Bud Powell the two most influential jazz piano players of the last part of the twentieth century? "People go to his concerts," as British writer Brian Priestly said, "not so much to listen, as to worship."7 It is the way he infuses fragments of Debussy, Bach, Bartok, and Chopin into his improvisations, the clever passing tones, and rhythmic displacements. It's the long original lines Evans got from listening to Lennie Tristano and a floating sense of time that isn't on top of the beat nor behind it, but suspended to bring a unique kind of tension and release to his performances.

"There was a guy in town" said Preston, "who told me that Bill Evans does not swing like Oscar Peterson. I said, 'I suppose that is why Miles Davis hired him.'" So deeply is Preston Keys into the Evans mystique that for a hobby he transcribes Evans' solos right off the record, every little nuance, and then sells them to other Evans disciples. "I enjoy doing more and more of this as I get older. Of course it helps to have perfect pitch, which I explain by saying that it is like seeing everything in high color or infrared. That is how I hear notes, in infrared."8 Preston grew up in Santa Monica, started on accordion, and then when he was thirteen he began piano lessons. His inspiration was a Dave Brubeck album *Jazz: Red Hot and Cool*. *The Glenn Miller Story* with

Fred Kopp, John Justice, Howdy Lehman, Dave Poulin
Courtesy of Fred Kopp

June Allyson and James Stewart made an even bigger impression on young Keys. "It was the right movie at the right time. I saw it seven times. It was very powerful even though a big part of his life was left out and part of it was weepy Hollywood melodrama. Inaccurate, but it was the first time I had ever seen Louis Armstrong and Gene Krupa. I enjoyed the marching band sequence when they play 'St. Louis Blues March.' I bought the soundtrack right away."[9] Preston attended UCLA for one year majoring in music theory in a music department that wanted nothing to do with jazz, calling it street music. The one salvation was Glenn Miller's alumnus, Paul Tanner. Tanner's History of Jazz class, three hours a day, three times a week, was the most popular course on campus. It was a favorite class of Kareem Abdul Jabar, also known as Lou Alcindor. He took it his senior year when he was the best college basketball player in America.

The Lighthouse Café at Hermosa Beach was a favorite destination for students from UCLA. Preston spent many evenings sitting in the front row semicircle listening to Howard Rumsey's Lighthouse All-Stars with guests Hampton Hawes, Maynard Ferguson, Art Pepper, and Miles Davis, with the great Lorraine Geller on piano. There was even better jazz radio than New York. Sleepy Stein had a very popular program and on a clear night you could pick up Jimmy Lyons from San Francisco.

Around 1960, Preston became the third member of a sensational rock and roll group called The Diamonds who had two top of the chart hits, "Little Darlin'" and "The Stroll." In 1977 Preston joined the roaring Buddy Rich band. Mark Kieswetter tells how it happened. "Tom Warrington was a bass player from Oregon, Ohio, who was playing with Buddy Rich and going with

Bill Coyle with pianist Preston Keys
Courtesy of Jerry Sawicki

Preston Keys
Courtesy of Preston Keys

Buddy's daughter, Kathy. One day Buddy tells Tom they are going to need a piano player. So Tom suggests Preston Keys and arranges a meeting so that Buddy can meet Preston. Now it is difficult to think of two more unlike people —Mike Tyson and Ralph Nader, maybe. Rich flies Preston in for a meeting. Rich looks at Preston and says, 'I've heard a lot about you, Preston.' Preston looks at Rich straight in the eye and says, 'Well, I've heard a lot about you, too.' One night when Rich is in one of his bad moods, he yells out so that everybody in the club can hear, 'Hey Preston, do you think you could light it up a bit?' This really pissed Preston off and he smoked Buddy and the rest of the band with some fiery lines that I don't think Buddy has ever heard."[10]

As well as Preston plays, he carries no affectations and can't stand anyone who does. "I wanted to take a Spanish course at Toledo University and I needed some assistance. I saw this guy who was in a suit standing outside of the front office and I asked him if he was an instructor. He said to me, 'I'm a professor, if that's what you mean.' I left but quick and never turned back."[11] For years, Preston Keys worked at the J and R Lounge playing on a small spinet with a synthesizer, prophetically eight feet from the exit door. On weekends it was noisy, people laughing, shouting. Preston never heard any of it. He just shut it out, getting deeper into the music.

Chapter 25
Horatio Hornblower

One would never imagine, not for a second, that Jerry Sawicki, one of the most successful businessmen in Ohio and a fine baritone saxophonist would grow up without any self-esteem. "I thought I was dumb," said Sawicki, "All through Nathan Hale and my year in DeVilbiss, I figured that I better learn a trade, so I immediately transferred to Macomber High School. I found out later that my IQ was way above average." His musical talent got him a scholarship to Valley Forge Military Academy. The disciplined military life gave Sawicki confidence. He blossomed. He became the drum major, complete with the babushka and baton. In 1949, he led the parade down Pennsylvania Avenue during President Truman's inauguration.[1]

Like the proverbial Horatio Alger, Sawicki started at the bottom, living in near poverty with a wayward mother who married four times. The first marriage was to a man named Sawicki; and during a heated argument one night, Jerry learned that he was not a Sawicki. He wasn't even Polish. His biological father was English and his real name was Foster, Jerry Foster. Like F. Scott Fitzgerald's masterpiece, *The Great Gatsby*, Sawicki met a man, by accident, who completely changed his life. His name was John Whalen who was a real estate man. He said to Sawicki, "Listen, I became a multi-millionaire using a par-

Jerry Sawicki at Mardi Gras Nite Club 1953
Courtesy of Jerry Sawicki

ticular formula. You do the same, follow my advice, and you can be very rich." "Well," said Sawicki, "I followed his advice to the letter and you can see the result of it."[2]

The Sawicki extended family lived on an estate about the size of a nine-hole golf course, with a blacksmith shop, a sawmill and two manmade lakes. Their palace was an impregnable fortress, five floors high, concrete walls three feet thick. Each of the dozens of rooms was color coordinated and filled with imported furnishings. A solid gold chandelier hung above a $20,000 dining room table. The walls of one room were covered with various business awards: Toledo's Realtor of the Year, President of Ohio's Board of Realtors, voted by the Junior Chamber of Commerce one of the ten outstanding men of the year. Calling Jerry Sawicki an entrepreneur was like calling Tiger Woods a golfer. Before his extremely successful business career, he was a tenor saxophonist. His business duties forced him to give that up for 25 years.

Jerry Sawicki and Jimmy Cook
Courtesy of Jerry Sawicki

Before that, he played with Jack Runyan and Jimmy Reemsnyder. In 1949 he was in a spirited group with Arv Garrison, Fred Kopp, and Buzz Selinsky on drums.

He returned to the saxophone, inspired by Gene Parker and wanting to play like Stan Getz. Later he found he could get more work playing the baritone sax. He discovered a record on which tenor saxophonist Stan Getz and baritonist Gerry Mulligan switch horns. Playing the baritone like Stan Getz became Sawicki's goal. The E-Flat, earthy, dark-toned member of the saxophone family was dominated by Duke Ellington's Harry Carney for decades. Then in the 1940s and '50s Serge Chaloff and Gerry Mulligan began transferring Charlie Parker and Lester Young to this brawny, seemingly inflexible instrument. Toledo had some very good baritone saxophonists, Jack Walter with Tony Celeste and Wayne Ruihley with Jack Runyan. Jerry Sawicki is the only Toledoan to make an entire LP on the baritone and the only one of two in the entire body of recorded jazz to make an album of love songs all played on the baritone saxophone. It is called *Second Time Around*. It came out in 1989 on the Sophia Label with an unbeatable rhythm section of Johnny O'Neal on piano, Cliff Murphy on bass, and the late, and much missed, Pistol Adams on drums. One of the selections, Irving Berlin's "Always" is dedicated to Sawicki's wife Lois Ann, the second reason for his astounding success.

The most unforgettable small combo under the leadership of Jerry Sawicki was at the 103 Club on Detroit Avenue. "Phil Greenberg was on electric guitar," said Sawicki. "The bass player committed suicide one night and the psycho drummer, a few rim shots away from the Toledo

State Hospital, carried around a loaded hand gun in his drum kit."[3] Sawicki said that melody was always foremost to him. The first great melody he heard was on a Bing Crosby record. "That really got to me. I think the name of the album was *Please*," said Sawicki. "It was so lyrical. I love melody. That is why I like Stan Getz above all saxophonists, especially on ballads. That is the way I want to play. Controlled, but free."[4]

Chapter 26
Jimmy Cook – Nobody's Better

It used to be that the trumpet was the imperial instrument of jazz. Most of the early bandleaders played trumpet or its almost identical sister, the cornet. Joe Oliver, Louis Armstrong's mentor, was known as King Oliver. The trumpet's great power and flexible range made it the dominant instrument in most of the early ensembles. It took the lungs of a long-distance swimmer and the strength of a weight lifter to play like Maynard Ferguson with Stan Kenton, or Duke Ellington's Cat Anderson, who could hit notes so high that only certain animals can hear them. Richard Sudhalter, the cornet player and author of fine jazz book *Lost Chords* said that "the trumpet is the most physically demanding instrument of them all. It requires unfailing participation of every muscle in the body. It batters the inside of the head with pressure, encountered only by deep sea divers."[1]

Three of the best trumpet players in Toledo in the 1920s according to Russ McGowan were John Nesbitt, Eber Battles, and Bert Dillard. "I was eighteen at Scott High," said McGowan. "And I was playing trumpet and hanging out at Nobles, and listening to all the great ones who were coming through town. Did you ever hear about John Nesbitt? He made a name for himself with the McKinney's Cotton Pickers. He was in Toledo part of 1925 and 1926, best little trumpet player you ever wanted to hear. He and Bix Beiderbecke were close friends. Nesbitt was also a fine arranger who did many of the most popular hits of the McKinney's Cotton Pickers. But Eber Battles is the reason I decided to hang up my horn and decided on the alto saxophone. He could only play in one key—F—but what a blues player. He could have gone with every band that came to town who wanted him to join. He could have gone with Duke Ellington. People would beg him to leave, but he loved Toledo too much. That cat had sharp claws. He could cut anybody in a jam session.[2] For a while I lived on Division Street with a very good trumpet player by the name

Jimmy Cook on flugal horn to the delight of Jerry Sawicki
Courtesy of Jerry Sawicki

of Bert Dillard who, like Louis Armstrong, learned to play in an orphanage. I don't know what became of him. The top trumpet player in Toledo in the 1930s was Francis Williams who was all set to become a piano player until he heard his boyhood chum, Art Tatum, play."[3]

Williams was the only Toledoan to win a membership to the great Duke Ellington Orchestra. Playing with Ellington would not have been possible had he not moved to Cleveland to join the Marion Sears Band. He returned to Toledo a much improved player, apparently because of his association with Cleveland's top trumpeters: Benny Bailey, Emmet Berry, and a fifteen-year-old trumpet phenomenon named Freddy Webster who Miles Davis claimed was his main inspiration growing up.[4] It should also be mentioned that Jabbo Smith, second only to Louis Armstrong, was in Toledo for long periods of time in the late 1930s when he was a member of the Claude Hopkins Band. For forty years until his death in 2008, Jimmy Cook had been the number one trumpet player in Toledo. At a distance, Cook's thick torso and muscular shoulders made him look more like a piano mover than someone who could play the trumpet as soft as a baby's murmur. He started on trumpet when he was nine years old. His dad, a musician, had him listen to Louis Armstrong, Bunny Berigan's "I Can't Get Started," and Chuck Peterson with Tommy Dorsey. Cook had his first lesson from Graham Young, a former lead trumpet player with Henry Mancini. "He showed me lip trills and how to get soft, long tones by pronouncing certain syllables," said Cook.

"The trumpet became my best friend, an extension of my voice. It gave me an identity. When I was working for General Motors as a traveling salesman, I used to keep my horn in the trunk of the car so I could go to the bars after work and ask to sit in.[5] I am one of the few guys in the world to ever play Miles Davis's own trumpet. It happened like this. Before anyone really knew who Miles Davis was, he came to Flint, Michigan, where I was living at the time, to play at the Chicken Shack. It was right in the middle of a snow storm. When he got there, he told the manager that he had driven a long ways and needed to thaw out. The manager points to me. So Miles asks me to fill in for him until he got warm. I told him I didn't even bring my horn because I didn't even think I was playing. So he goes out of the room and comes back with his own trumpet and said, 'Try this.' So I ended up playing for two hours, with Miles Davis standing right there. I was seventeen the next year when I got to play with Charlie Parker. He came to the Chicken Shack and his trumpet player, Benny Harris, got sick on the way, so I got to play with Charlie Parker for a whole evening. Then one night my own little band with Bob Rex on drums and Tom Warrington on bass was playing intermissions for some of these big names. One night my band opened for Billie Holiday at the Chicken Shack. I remember she arrived in a shiny black Cadillac, and as we were getting off the stage, I could hear her complaining about having to use the restroom for a dressing room. As she approached me, she stopped and said to all of us, 'You guys really sound good.'

"I was playing with that same band in Dayton at a place called Gilly's. Stan Kenton was the main attraction that night. Our group just played at intermission. Well after the end of the first set, just before we wanted to get on, Kenton grabs the mike and said, 'Let this group entertain you, I'm going to go out for a Coke and I'll be right back.' Kenton came back and he sat down with his Coke about three feet in front of us. My feet were shaking, so were my hands, like I had palsy or something. When we finished, he comes up to me and said, 'What's your name?' and I told him. He said, 'Did you ever play in a big band like mine?' No. 'Well you sure are good enough. If you need a job, look me up.' In the late '70s, I was playing in town with the Johnny Trudell Band, excellent trumpet player and a good friend. Well, anyway, one day he asked me if I'd like to go to Detroit to see our close friend Tom Warrington who was playing bass with the Buddy Rich Big Band. Well, I sat in the front row through a ten-minute drum solo that just knocked me out. Buddy was as fast as a machine gun and clean. So I told Trudell, sitting next to me, that I just had to talk to him after the end of the show. Trudell said, 'I wouldn't do that. He's tired. See that towel around his head? You see how hard he works.' Well anyway just as he left the stage, I jumped up and told Trudell, 'Man, I got to tell him.' So I went to the back of the backstage just as he was closing the door to his dressing room, towel still wrapped around his head, sweat running down his

nose. I told him I was a trumpet player from Toledo, Ohio, with the Johnny Trudell Band and I just had to tell him what a great solo I thought that was. There was a pause, and he said, 'Do you know what a solo is? You dumb s---.' And then he yells at me, 'Get the f--- out of here, you m----f-----!' I sneaked back to the chair and Trudell said to me, 'I told you so. I told you what would happen. You don't listen to nobody.'" 6

Seymour Rothman, *The Blade*'s peerless columnist, wrote about an even more embarrassing outcome. "Jimmy recalls showing up for an engagement only to find the drummer and all of his instruments parked in the hallway and complaining that the light had been turned off and he didn't want to carry all those drums up a flight of stairs that led to the second floor ballroom without any light. While Jimmy went looking for a light switch and unable to find one that worked. He finally agreed to help the drummer to the second floor. Jimmy said, 'I was really upset that someone would be so inconsiderate not to have a light in such a steep stairway, and I kept expressing my thoughts in some very strong language. All the time the drummer was agreeing with me and I kept getting nastier and nastier and louder and louder,' Jimmy recalled. When we reached the ballroom door and pushed it open, the lights went on and there were 300 people yelling, 'Surprise! Happy birthday, Jimmy.' They had heard every word I'd said all the way up the stairs." 7

Jimmy Cook claimed that most jazz trumpet players, even beboppers, dream of having a sound like Harry James. "Doc Severinsen on the old Johnny Carson show comes close, and so does Ralph Marterie who was in Toledo frequently. But nobody could get it quite like Harry. My own favorites are Miles Davis on *Sketches of Spain* and that six-minute recording that Clifford Brown, Maynard Ferguson and Clark Terry did playing the jazz classic, 'Move.' Clark Terry came here to play with the Toledo Jazz Orchestra and we became friends and he ended up giving me an extra mouth piece he had. It's when I first heard Chet Baker, it might have been on that *Jazz At Ann Arbor* record, that I changed my feeling about the trumpet. I didn't believe it was a trumpet at first, played with two lips just like mine. I wondered how warm lips on cold iron could get a tone like that, and those lines he plays, he breathes so easily and there doesn't seem to be any circular breathing. I went to Baker's Keyboard in Detroit to see him; and at intermission, I asked him if he uses circular breathing to play such long beautiful lines on ballads. 'Don't need to,' Chet said, 'because I take enough breath at the top and get my ideas on the way down.'" 8

Russ Freeman, the piano player on the Ann Arbor recording, said that "some nights Chet would finish his solo and I would just sit there and wonder, now what am I going to play after that." Freeman said that "Chet Baker is the only trumpet player who can

Saxophonist Mary Combattelli
Courtesy of Buzzy Jasinski

Jerry Sawicki, Jimmy Cook and Mahlon Aldrich
Courtesy of Jerry Sawicki

whisper a high C. He never takes a big breath to reach a high note," said Cook, "but POW there it is. I used to go to bed each night listening to him and wondering why I can't play like that. I bought a mouthpiece just like his and tried to work with it but it was like trying to break in a catcher's mitt. When I'm playing, I think I am Chet, like kids do when they are imitating famous sports figures." Cook decided early that no matter who asked him, he would not go on the road. He hated the crowded hotels, the bad food, and always being tired.

"I like raising a family, getting a paycheck, and having the greatest wife in the world waiting for me. There are plenty of world class players in Toledo: Claude Black, he could play like Oscar Peterson; Buddy Sullivan, he could have gone with anyone; Jimmy Riggs left to play with Stan Kenton. Riggs sounded like Sonny Stitt. I used to walk by his house and the window would always be open to his bedroom and music would always be coming out. If you didn't hear his alto saxophone, you knew that he must be sick. And I shouldn't forget saxophonist Mary Combattelli. She could really play."[9] Jimmy Cook always wondered whether he could have made it in New York. He admitted this to Ric Wolkins, lead trumpet for the Toledo Jazz Orchestra. "I've played all over the United States," said Wolkins. "There's nobody better than you."[10]

Chapter 27
Rusty's Jazz Café – She Coulda' Been Mayor

One of the best things about living in Toledo, Ohio, in the last quarter of the 20th Century was Rusty's Jazz Café. It was more than a jazz club; it was a cultural resource, a landmark like the world famous art museum or the zoo. It was on the "don't miss" list of attractions for people visiting Toledo with a disclaimer that read, "If you haven't been to Rusty's, you haven't been to Toledo."[1] Rusty's, one of the oldest jazz clubs in America, was owned and operated by Rusty Monroe, a strong-willed, big-hearted businesswoman in a high-risk field dominated by men. Joan Crawford in *Johnny Guitar* and Jo Van Fleet in *East of Eden* come to mind.

Rusty disclosed her secrets of success at the Red Wells Restaurant in the fall of 2004. She had on high heels, a tight fitting tailored dress from Youngland with tinted nails and

Courtesy of Rusty Monroe

Rusty Monroe
Courtesy of Rusty Monroe

Jean Holden
Courtesy of Lisa Holden

lipstick to match her flaming red hair. It was the middle of the afternoon and she looked like she just got off the plane from Las Vegas. "Present your best self out of respect for your company," she liked to say. Rusty was a country girl with city instincts. "When my friends were playing tag or climbing trees, I was inside winding up the old Victrola or reading."[2]

From her sparkling purse she drew out a list of the jazz luminaries she had hired over the past forty years since beginning in the Westgate Shopping Center next to a strip joint: Cannonball Adderley, Lionel Hampton, Woody Herman, Phil Woods, Thad Jones, and Mel Lewis, just to mention a few. In all those countless nights over forty years, what stood out as the most spectacular? "So many," said Rusty, "but nothing could top Maynard Ferguson and his big band in 1996. The whole band marched up and down the narrow aisles. Maynard was shaking hands with one hand and playing the theme from *Rocky* with the other. And then when they went into 'MacArthur Park,' I thought the roof would come down."3 No recording of that unforgettable night surfaced but there is an album done years earlier called *M.F. Horn* that will give you some idea of the electrifying effect of this band.

Trumpeter Jimmy Cook, who was there that night, said, "Maynard Ferguson liked Rusty's so much that he told everyone from Sweden to San Francisco that Rusty's Jazz Club was his favorite place to play." Cook said that "just as the Maynard Ferguson bus was leaving for their next destination, Rusty appeared with two dozen box lunches for the whole crew. Did you ever hear anything like that? I never did. I think that Maynard Ferguson was responsible for Gerry Mulligan and Cannonball Adderley coming to town."4

Kelly Broadway just getting started
Courtesy of Kelly Broadway

"Well it's not all party," said Rusty. "I married Jazz when I became owner seven days a week for 52 weeks a year, eighty hours a week. I practically slept there and some of the biggest names were kind of difficult to handle. Jimmy Witherspoon, the blues singer, was an hour and a half late. He phoned while the crowd was getting anxious to say that he was in a huge accident and would get there as soon as possible. I learned later that he was in a Motel 6 partying. So I confronted him on the spot when he finally arrived and we had a little talk eyeball to eyeball, and we finally agreed to his taking half of his paycheck."5

Bob Rex, a drummer with the El Myers Quintet, called Rusty's a musical sanctuary where writers, DJs, musicians, and fans could call their second home. "She's very cool to work for; the only thing is, if breaks get too long between sets, Rusty will come up and say, 'Robert, you've got to get up there now.' She is very discreet, never insulting."6 A distinguished pianist in town was insulted when she installed a time clock in back of the bar. He threw the thing across the room and yelled out, "I don't work with a time clock." "Well," said Rusty, "we had to have a chat, a little fireplace chat, where I informed him that customers who come for the music, will leave if the breaks are too long, which costs me money." Then she said, "There are the acts that don't go over, that this artist is in the wrong place at the wrong time. I felt so sorry for Betty Carter. She gave it everything she had, but no applause. She was heartbroken, and yet the dynamic Kelly Broadway, Ramona Collins, and the wonderful Jean Holden could knock 'em dead, and they are from here."7

You get the idea that the people who worked for Rusty thought of it more as a service than

Ramona Collins
Courtesy of Rusty Monroe

as a business, and it's a good bet that not one of them ever stole a dime. It would be like lifting from the offering plate. Scott Potter, a trumpet player with the Toledo Jazz Orchestra and a contributor to the Toledo Jazz Society, said, "Rusty's was like a University where anybody who was learning to play can get up and ply their trade. Not often to you hear that a jazz club is open seven days a week."[8]

Saxophonist Gene Parker, who spent many nights at Rusty's, said, "It's just incredible, the number of musicians who learned at Rusty's. This club did what multi-million-dollar educational institutions couldn't do. I think about all the people who learned to play there. Even Detroit musicians came down to Toledo to play here. Rusty's turned out so many musicians who have spread all over the world." He named some of them: "Jeff Halsey, Larry Fuller, Tom Warrington, Dan Faehnle, and Jim Riggs."[9]

Eddie Abrams
Courtesy of Rusty Monroe

Jimmy Cook, Dave Pope drums, Buddy Sullivan, Jeff Halsey bass, El Myers piano at Rusty's
Courtesy of El Myers

    High school students could sit in the back of the club sipping soft drinks. Candy Johnson gave extra credit to his high school students if they went to a jazz attraction at Rusty's. The great Wynton Marsalis noticed the aspiring young musicians in the back when he played one weekend there in the late 1980s. He was so turned on that he played until 3:00 in the morning when the last student left. Rusty's was in the southwest part of Toledo on Tedrow Road. Later it also became known as "Jazz Avenue." Colored photographs of the local artists who played at Rusty's covered the walls. There was a fireplace where customers could roast marshmallows if they wished and a stage barely big enough for a big band.[10]

    Rusty said there were three reasons for her success. One was her "Sunday night strategy." Sunday was travel time, so bands traveling between Chicago and New York often come through Toledo on a Sunday, so it was easy to book them. The second reason for her success was the experience she had right after the war working in Las Vegas in some of the big casinos and hotels. "I watched the good managers," said Rusty, "the ones who knew how to handle personal relations, the ones who were firm and fair. I learned how to run a kitchen and how to stock a bar. I learned how to book bands and what to listen for, what swings and what doesn't swing. You know there is an excellent piano player in Toledo and I enjoy listening to him, but he couldn't swing from a tree. I was a waitress for awhile at the Miami Fontainebleau. This was the setting for Frank Sinatra's movie *A Hole in the Head*, and I had a cameo appearance. I am sitting around the pool in a bathing suit. I think I am in just one scene. I don't say anything. I just walk into a cocktail party and that's it. Watch closely or you'll miss it." Rusty's would not have happened without her musical director and protector for 23 years, Eddie Abrams. "I owe him everything," said Rusty. "He was the Detroit Funnel and without the Detroit musicians, I couldn't have made it. He got Claude Black, Tommy Flanagan, and the other Detroit heavies to play here including Johnny O'Neal who Toledo adopted as their own."[11]

"Eddie Abrams was the top piano guy when I first moved here in 1960," said Jimmy Cook. "He had a lot of soul in his music, a lot of gospel. Let me tell you something about Abrams. One time Rusty's was being robbed, just as Abrams was arriving for work. He walks right up to the gunman and said, 'to get to that cash register, you're going to have to shoot me.' The guy was so surprised; he dropped his gun and ran. Another time involves me. I was playing one night and this guy from the local musicians union is hassling me about playing with nonunion guys, right in the middle of my solo. I started ignoring him. He shoves the palm of his hand against the bell of my horn and cut my lip badly. Blood is running everywhere. Abrams flies off his piano stool, grabs the union guy by the collar and seat of his pants and proceeds to throw him out on the street with the warning that if he ever saw him again, he would rearrange his face."[12] Rusty remembers that Abrams was a mentor to all the young players. "He encouraged the young," said Rusty. "Not only those who could play but also those who were trying and he never had a harsh word or insulted anybody no matter how challenging. He brought Dan Faehnle and Larry Fuller and so many others along." When Rusty's closed in 2003, it was like the Toledo Mud Hens had left town. "My

Hometown Jazz
Courtesy of El Myers

walls are decorated with lifetime achievement awards," said Rusty, "even one from a national men's magazine naming me as one of the fifty best bars in America. But it finally got to be too much for me to handle."[13] El Myers thought that Rusty could have been mayor or at least a CEO of a blue chip company. He said, "Toledo ought to be grateful that Rusty made a commitment to jazz and never deviated from it over the forty years she was here."[14]

Afterword

Bob Dietsche has produced a fascinating account of jazz in Toledo, my adopted hometown since 1978. I thought I had learned a lot about its jazz heritage in the 36 years I've lived here, but Dietsche has educated me about many people and events that had escaped my notice. One of Bob's most important themes has been the "infrastructure" that allowed jazz to survive, and sometimes, flourish in Toledo—the fans, venues, donors, schools and non-profit organizations that have supported the music. These included the entertainment needs of organized crime but also the incubator for talent and jazz enthusiasm provided by Rusty's Jazz Café during its many years of operation. Rusty Monroe's combination of devotion to the music and astute business practice was a combination seldom encountered in any city. Since the closing of Murphy's Place, Degage Jazz Café is the leading "jazz almost nightly" venue now. It remains to be seen whether it can grow to the standard set by Rusty's, a tall order indeed.

During the last thirty years jazz has been featured at various festivals and special events, including First Night, the Old West End Festival, ToledoFest, the Jazz in the Garden series at the Toledo Botanical Gardens, the Art Tatum Jazz Festival and concerts by the Toledo Jazz Orchestra. Some of these have been continuous and others have come and gone.

The incubator now is largely an academic one. Several universities in the area (Bowling Green State University, University of Toledo, and Wayne State University) offer "jazz studies" as a major. Many of the leading performers in the area (including Jeff Halsey, Gene Parker, Gunnar Mossblad, and Chris Buzzelli) are faculty members at these schools. Bowling Green State University also hosts an annual vocal jazz camp each summer in conjunction with the New York Voices. This intense six-day workshop is open to high school and college students, professional musicians, choral directors and anyone interested in improving and developing their knowledge of vocal jazz.

The Toledo School for the Arts provides a foundation in jazz and other musical arts for high school students. Morgan Stiegler, Ramona Collins, and the Take Six vocal sextet represent the area well as jazz vocalists. The Toledo Arts Council commissioned a statue in honor of Art Tatum in downtown Toledo. Several excellent young players left Toledo in the 1970s, '80s and '90s to seek their fortunes in the wider world. One was Larry Fuller who worked extensively with Ray Brown, Jeff Hamilton, and John Pizzarella. Another was Tom Warrington who was with Buddy Rich, and Dudley Moore. More recent exports to New York are Ron Oswanski and Jacob Sacks.

Two very promising young players who are still here are Josh Silver (piano) and Nelson Overton (drums). There are, of course, many others who will inform me of my incompetence when they read this and don't see their names. I apologize in advance to all of them.

John Cleveland
2014

Endnotes

Introduction
1 Letter from Lucy Riebe to George Presser, August 1, 2008.
2 *Nothing Personal, Just Business*, p. 126
3 *Toledo Blade*, June 1, 1933
4 Harry Gregory, Interview, October 1990
5 *Toledo Topics*, Summer 1930

Chapter 1
1 *Down Beat*, January 25, 1956
2 Liner notes, *Art Tatum*, Time/Life Records
3 Anita O'Day, *Anita*, Verve Records
4 Arlene Tatum, Interview, November 1988
5 Ibid.
6 Russ McGowan, Interview, October 1990
7 *Before Motown*, p. 21.
8 Harry Gregory, Interview, October 1990
9 *The Blade*, January 23, 1989
10 *The Tatum Legacy, Toledo*: WGTE, 1983 DVD
11 *Toledo Magazine*, March 14, 1986
12 Ibid.
13 Steve Allen, *The Tonight Show*, June 1955
14 *Collector's Jazz*, p. 256
15 *Too Marvelous for Words*, pp. 62-64
16 Russ McGowan, Interview, October 1990
17 *Toledo Topics*, November 1929
18 Harry Gregory, Interview, October 1990
19 Bud Osborn, "art tatum," *The Blade*, July 18, 1977
20 Rex Stewart, *Jazz Masters of the Thirties*, pp. 181-182
21 *Jazz Ancedotes*, p. 276
22 Harold Payne, Interview, October 1990
23 Liner Notes, *Capital Jazz Classics, Volume 3, Art Tatum, Solo Piano*,
24 *God is in the House*, Onyx Records
25 *Bird Lives*, pp. 99-100
26 Liner notes, *Smithsonian Collection*
27 Arlene Tatum, Interview, Fall 1988

Chapter 2
1 *Unholy Toledo*, Chapter 2
2 *Blade Magazine*, March 23, 1986
3 *Nothing Personal*, p. 22
4 *Toledo Profile*, p. 65
5 *Unholy Toledo*, Chapter 6
6 Russ McGowan, Interview, October 1990
7 *Nothing Personal*, Chapter 7
8 *Blade Magazine*, March 23, 1986
9 El Myers, Interview, October 2004
10 Joanna Shank, Phone interview, March 2011
11 *Nothing Personal*, Chapter 15
12 *The Blade*, July 14, 2005
13 Angelos Tsipis, Interview, September 2008

Chapter 3
1 *Swing Era*, pp. 770-805
2 Ibid.
3 Ibid.
4 *Big Band Jazz*, pp. 121-123
5 Liner notes, *Swingin' on the Town*, Verve Records
6 *Down Beat*, February 19, 1970
7 *Jazz Makers*, p. 311
8 Ibid., p. 312
9 Jon Hendricks, Interview, October 2004
10 *Jazz Makers*, p. 299
11 Harold Payne, Interview, October 1990
12 Liner notes, *Roy Eldridge (Early Years)*, Columbia Records
13 Liner notes, *Prebop*, Bob Thiel Records
14 Liner notes, *Sing Along*, Roulette Records
15 *Talking Jazz*, Chapter 1
16 Ibid., Chapter 2

17 *Down Beat*, May 2, 1968
18 *The Famous 1938 Carnegie Hall Jazz Concert*, Columbia Records

Chapter 4
1 *Storyville*, August 9, 1969
2 *Jazz Magazine*, April 1956
3 Harold Payne, Interview, October 1990
4 *Storyville*, August 9, 1969
5 Ibid.
6 *Life*, May 30, 1938
7 Ibid.
8 *Big Band Jazz*, p. 165
9 John Chilton, *Who's Who in Jazz*, p. 20
10 *Swing Era*, pp. 342-344
11 *Storyville*, volumes 4 and 5, 1978
12 Harold Payne, Interview, October 1990
13 *Storyville*, volumes 4 and 5, 1978
14 Liner notes, *Pieces of Eight*, Smithsonian Records
15 *Jazz Journal*, January 1988
16 *Storyville*, September 10, 1973
17 *Toledo Times*, October 7, 1934
18 Ibid.
19 *Storyville*, volumes 8 and 9, 1973
20 Thomas Hennesey, "Black Chicago Establishment," *Journal of Jazz Studies*, December 1974

Chapter 5
1 Harold Payne, Interview, October 1990
2 *Reminiscing with Sissle and Blake*, p. 95
3 *The Jazz Age*, p. 89-90
4 *Reminiscing with Sissle and Blake*, p. 148
5 *Harlem Heyday*, pp. 137-139
6 *Toledo Blade*, April 2, 1923
7 *Toledo Blade*, March 23, 1923
8 El Myers, Telephone interview, June 2006
9 *Time/Life Series, 1937-38*, p. 42
10 *Lost Chords*, p. 351
11 *Time/Life Series, 1937-38*, p. 42

12 *Swing Era*, pp. 632-645
13 Ibid.

Chapter 6
1 Jon Hendricks, Interview, October 2004
2 Ibid.
3 Ibid.
4 Ibid.
5 *Toledo Magazine, The Blade*, February 16-22, 1986
6 Ibid.
7 Ibid.
8 Ibid.
9 Ibid.
10 *The Willamette Week*, May 17, 1982
11 *Down Beat*, September 12, 1959
12 Ibid.
13 Liner notes, *Evolution of the Blues Song*, Columbia Records
14 Ibid.
15 Ibid.
16 *Down Beat*, "Record Reviews," volume 6

Chapter 7
1 Julie Runyan, *Jack Runyan's Music Career*, DVD
2 Ibid.
3 *Jack Runyan's Music Career*
4 Ibid.
5 *The Trianon, the Paramount and Kin Wa Low: The Best Nights of Our Lives*, WGTE, 1995
6 Wayne Ruihley, Telephone interview, October 2008
7 Ibid.
8 Julie Runyan, Telephone interview, October 2008
9 Ron Wagner, Telephone interview, November 2006
10 Ibid.
11 Ibid.

Chapter 8

1 Les Brown, Interview, Hilton Hotel, Portland, Oregon, October 1993
2 *Toledo Magazine, The Blade*, August 27-September 2, 1989
3 *The Blade*, June 26, 1992
4 *Down Beat*, February 1, 1953
5 *Down Beat*, December 15, 1952
6 *Toledo Blade*, August 29, 1955
7 Jerry Sawicki, Interview, July 2008
8 *Down Beat*, November 21, 1953
9 Ralph Flanagan Discography, p. 37
10 Ibid.
11 *Cleveland Jazz History*, pp. 168-69
12 *Down Beat*, January 23, 1953
13 *Down Beat*, July 15, 1953
14 Bob White, Telephone interview, April 1970
15 Nick Ceroli, Telephone interview, Summer 1959
16 *Down Beat*, January 14, 1953
17 *Down Beat*, February 20, 1954
18 *Hit Parade*, 1954-55
19 *Life*, December 20, 1954
20 *Confidential File* with Paul Coates, NBC-TV, 1954
21 *Life*, December 20, 1954
22 *Woody Herman Newsletter*, Winter/Spring 2009/2010
23 *Since Yesterday*, p. 268
24 Johnny Knorr, Interview, October 2004
25 Ibid.
26 *The Blade*, January 28, 1968
27 *Big Band Almanac*, Ward Ritchie Press, pp. 100-101
28 Hal Swafford, Interview, September 20, 2000
29 *The Blade*, February 14, 1973
30 Johnny Knorr, Interview, October 2004
31 Buddy Sullivan, Telephone interview, May 2009
32 Jack Walter, Interview, November 2009
33 Mary Ann Russo, Interview, November 2007

Chapter 9

1 *Toledo Blade*, July 31, 1960
2 Bill Cummerow, Interview, May 1985
3 Jimmy William, Interview, May 1985
4 Bill Cummerow, Interview, May 1985
5 Ibid.
6 Vivian Garry, Interview, July 1982
7 Liner notes, *Swing Street*, Columbia Records
8 Vivian Garry, Interview, July 1982
9 OPB Radio Broadcast, Dick Cogan, August 1990
10 Vivian Garry, Interview, July 1982
11 *Metronome Magazine*, circa Spring 1945
12 Liner notes, *Black California*, Savoy Records
13 Vivian Garry, Interview
14 Liner notes, *Central Avenue Breakdown, Volume 1*, Onyx Records
15 Ibid.
16 *Inside Jazz*, Chapter 1
17 *Esquire's 1946 Jazz Book*, pp. 51-52
18 Liner notes, *Five Guitars Plus Four*, Milagro Label
19 *Metronome Magazine*, April 1946
20 Wini Beatty, Telephone interview, June 1987
21 El Myers, Interview, September 1982
22 Ibid.
23 Pat Purcell, Telephone interview, August 1997
24 *Blues in B-Flat*, Chapter 12
25 Ibid.
26 Jim Shepard, Interview, November 1987

Chapter 10

1 Buddy Sullivan, Telephone interview, Fall

2010
2 Ibid.
3 Buddy Sullivan, Private recording
4 Buddy Sullivan, Interview, Fall 2010
5 El Myers, Interview, October 2009
6 Ibid.
7 Ibid.
8 *Another Man's Poison*, pp. 73-77
9 Ibid.
10 El Myers, Interview, Spring 2009
11 Liner notes, *Newport Jazz Festival All Stars*, Impulse Records
12 Ibid.
13 Gordon Goodrow, Telephone interview, March 2010
14 Bob Dorough, Phone interview, March 2, 2009
15 El Myers, Phone interview, October 2000
16 Ibid.
17 El Myers, *Best Damn Songs*, CD

Chapter 11
1 Jack Tongring, Phone interview, June 2009
2 Dee Talmadge, Phone interview, March 2010
3 Howard Bellman, Phone interview, November 2010
4 *Down Beat*, March 7, 1952
5 *Down Beat*, December 15, 1954
6 Howard Bellman, Phone interview, November 2010
7 Ibid.
8 Phil Seligman, Interview, Summer 1970
9 Howard Bellman, Phone interview, November 2010
10 *Metronome 1955 Yearbook*
11 "Back to Bach," *Time* magazine, February 12, 1954
12 Fred Lutz, *Conversations*, December 1956
13 Fred Lutz, Interview, Spring 1988
14 Ibid.

15 Ibid.

Chapter 12
1 *Time* magazine, November 8, 1954
2 *Willamette Week*, March 7, 1978
3 *Down Beat*, June 29, 1955
4 Liner notes, *Piano Perspectives*, Cadence Records
5 *Jumptown*, p. 148
6 Ibid.
7 Mark Kieswetter, Interview, June 2006
8 Nat Hentoff, *Washington Post*, April 18, 1986
9 Liner notes, *Albert Nicolas and Barney Bigard*, RCA Records
10 *A Date with Duke, Volume 12*, Fairmount Records
11 *Toledo Blade*, January 10, 1956
12 *Toledo Blade*, January 14, 1956
13 *Jumptown*, p. 157

Chapter 13
1 *The Jazz Revolution*, Chapter 5
2 Ibid.
3 *Toledo Blade*, January 2, 1926
4 *Jazz Anecdotes*, p. 21
5 *The Jazz Revolution*, p. 157
6 Ibid. p.3
7 Harold Payne, Interview, October 1990
8 Cliff Murphy, Interview, October 2004
9 Leroy Williams, *Black Toledo*, Ph.D. dissertation, University of Toledo, Chapters 2 and 3
10 *The Jazz Revolution*, p. 104
11 *Lawless Decade*, pp. 24-25
12 *Chicago Jazz*, pp. 71-72
13 *Toledo News-Bee*, October 3, 1932
14 Russ McGowan, Interview, October 1990
15 *Chicago Jazz*, pp. 16-17, 65
16 *The Jazz Revolution*, p. 36
17 *Toledo Blade*, August 8, 1904 and *Toledo News-Bee*, August 10, 1904

18 Russ McGowan, Interview, October 1990
19 *Toledo Times*, October 17, 1928
20 Russ McGowan, Interview, October 1990
21 Guided Tour, Kathy Steingraber, October 1998

Chapter 14
1 *Toledo Blade*, July 4, 1919
2 *Toledo Magazine*, March 31, 1957
3 Ibid.
4 Ibid.
5 Russ McGowan, Interview, October 1990
6 *Toledo Blade*, July 4, 1919
7 *Toledo Magazine*, March 31, 1957
8 Ibid.

Chapter 15
1 Yazoo Records and Cards, New York, New York
2 "Forgotten Giants," *Jazz Magazine*, p. 8
3 *Jazz Masters of the Thirties*, pp. 51-59
4 "Forgotten Giants," *Jazz Magazine*, p. 8
5 Ibid.
6 14th Census of the United States, 1900; Toledo, Lucas, Ohio; roll T625 1410, page 11B, line 82.
7 *Jazz City*, pp. 86-87
8 *Jazz Masters of the Thirties*, pp. 51-59
9 *Night People*, pp. 7, 34, 116
10 "Forgotten Giants," *Jazz Magazine*, p. 9
11 Ibid.
12 Russ McGowan, Interview, October 1990
13 *Jazz Information*, November 1940, pp. 11-19
14 *Jazz Magazine Part 2*, "Forgotten Giants"
15 Ibid.
16 *Down Beat*, January 15, 1940
17 *Down Beat*, July 4, 1961

Chapter 16
1 *McKinney's Music*, p. 1
2 Ibid., pp. 1-2

3 Ibid., p. 2
4 Russ McGowan, Interview, October 2004
5 *McKinney's Music*, pp. 5-6
6 Ibid., p. 4
7 Ibid., p. 3
8 *Hear Me Talkin' to Ya*, pp. 188-189
9 *Swing Era*, pp. 301-317
10 Ibid.
11 Ibid.
12 *Toledo Topics*, September 19, 1925
13 *McKinney's Music*, p. 6
14 Ibid.
15 *Before Motown*, pp. 28-29
16 *McKinney's Music*, pp. 7-9
17 *McKinney's Music*, p. 31
18 *Lost Chords*, p. 310
19 Ibid., p. 310, 318
20 Russ McGowan, Interview, October 2004
21 Ibid.
22 *Toledo Blade*, November 22, 1930
23 Ibid.

Chapter 17
1 Information letter, Cakewalkin' Jass Band
2 *Jumptown*, Chapter 2

Chapter 18
1 Liner notes, *Todd Rhodes and His Toddlers Jukebox Lil*
2 Ted Hallock, "AFM Problem," Master's Thesis, University of Oregon, 1946
3 Ibid.
4 *Before Motown*, pp. 179-183
5 Program, Arv Garrison Memorial
6 *Honkers and Shouters*, pp. 170-171
7 *Before Motown*, pp. 186-188
8 Ibid.
9 Buck Clayton, *Hucklebuck Jam Sessions*, Columbia Records
10 *Before Motown*, p. 131
11 Leonard Feather, *Encyclopedia of Jazz*

2 *Jumptown*, pp. 99-100
3 Leonard Feather, *Encyclopedia of Jazz*
4 *Jumptown*, pp. 105-106
5 Liner notes, *Lynn Hope*, Saxograph Records
6 *Honkers and Shouters*, pp. 386-387
7 *Swing Era*, p. 423-425

Chapter 19
1 Candy Johnson, Interview, March 1979
2 Ibid.
3 *Before Motown*, pp. 37-44
4 Ibid., pp. 191-193
5 *Jazz Styles*, pp. 107-109
6 Fred Kopp, Interview, October 2004
7 Bob Pavkovich, Phone interview, June 2009
8 Mark Kieswetter, Interview, June 2006
9 *Coda Magazine*, April 1977, pp. 1-8
10 Seymour Rothman, *The Blade*, August 3, 1977

Chapter 20
1 Claude Black, Interview, October 2004
2 Liner notes, *Tommy Flanagan – It's Magic*, Savoy Records
3 *Before Motown*, pp. 124-125
4 Tape of the Arv Garrison Memorial
5 Claude Black, Interview, October 2004
6 *The Blade*, February 26, 2000
7 *The Blade*, January 18, 2013
8 El Myers, Interview, October 2009
9 Mark Kieswetter, Interview, June 2006
10 Preston Keys, Interview, October 2006
11 Johnny O'Neal, Interview, October 2006
12 Ibid.
13 Cliff Murphy, Interview, October 2004
14 Ibid.
15 Harry Gregory, Interview, October 1990
16 Cliff Murphy, Interview, October 2004
17 Ibid.
18 Ibid.
19 Preston Keys, Interview, October 2006
20 Cliff Murphy, Interview, October 2004
21 Johnny O'Neal, Interview, November 2006
22 Cliff Murphy, Interview, October 2004

Chapter 21
1 John Mast, Interview, October 2006
2 Ibid.
3 Ibid.
4 Ibid.
5 Ibid.
6 *Jazz Loft Project*, pp. 9, 108
7 John Mast, Interview, October 2006
8 Ibid.
9 Ibid.
10 *The Blade*, February 21, 2003
11 *The Blade*, September 22, 2012
12 Don Arnold, Phone Interview, June 2009
13 Gene Parker, Interview, October 2004

Chapter 22
1 *Jumptown*, p. 75
2 *Before Motown*, p. 148
3 Jerry Sawicki, Interview, July 2008
4 Gene Parker, Interview, October 2004
5 Don Arnold, Phone Interview, June 2009

Chapter 23
1 Jack Walter, Interview, October 2009
2 *The Blade*, April 20, 2006
3 Jack Walter, Interview, October 2009
4 Ibid.
5 Ibid.
6 Ibid.
7 Ibid.
8 Ibid.

Chapter 24
1 Fred Kopp, Interview, October 2004
2 Ibid.
3 Ibid.
4 *The Blade*, May 27, 1965; *The Trianon, the*

Paramount and Kin Wa Low: The Best Nights of Our Lives, WGTE, 1995
5 *The Blade*, June 27, 1965
6 Preston Keys, Interview, October 2006
7 *Bill Evans Newsletter*, June 1990
8 Preston Keys, Interview, October 2006
9 Ibid.
10 Mark Kieswetter, Interview, June 2006
11 Preston Keys, Interview, October 2006
12 Jimmy Cook, Interview, October 2004
13 Rusty Monroe, Interview, May 2004
14 El Myers, Interview, October 2004

Chapter 25
1 Jerry Sawicki, Interview, July 2008
2 Ibid.
3 *Second Time Around*, Record, Jerry Sawicki
4 Jerry Sawicki, Interview, July 2008

Chapter 26
1 Liner notes, *Sudwalter, Complete Bunny Berigan, Volume 2*
2 Russ McGowan, Interview, October 2009
3 Ibid.
4 *Cleveland Jazz*, pp. 37, 88, 121
5 Jimmy Cook, Interview, October 2004
6 Ibid.
7 *The Blade*, February 7, 1982
8 Jimmy Cook, Interview, October 2004
9 Ibid.
10 Ibid.

Chapter 27
1 Rusty Monroe, Interview, May 2004
2 Ibid.
3 Ibid.
4 Jimmy Cook, Interview, 2004
5 Rusty Monroe, Interview, May 2004
6 Bob Rex, Phone interview, October 2004
7 Rusty Monroe, Interview, May 2004
8 *The Blade*, October 19, 2003
9 *The Blade*, November 8, 2008
10 *The Blade*, October 19, 2003
11 Rusty Monroe, Interview, May 2004

Bibliography

Allen, Frederick Lewis. *Since Yesterday: The Nineteen-Thirties in America*. New York and London: Harper & Brothers Publishers, 1940.

Allen, Walter C. *Hendersonia: The Music of Fletcher Henderson and His Musician*. Highland Park, N. J.: Allen Publishing Co., 1973.

Barclay, Morgan and Charles Glabb. *Toledo: Gateway to the Great Lakes*. Tulsa, Oklahoma: Continental Heritage Press, 1982.

Bjorn, Lars and Jim Gallert. *Before Motown: A History of Jazz in Detroit, 1920-1960*. Ann Arbor: University of Michigan Press, 2001.

Chilton, John. *McKinney's Music: A Bio-discography of McKinney's Cotton Pickers*. London: Bloomsbury Book Shop, 1978.

Chilton, John, *Who's Who of Jazz: Storyville to Swing Street*. [s.l.]: Time-Life Records Special Edition, 1978

Collier, James Lincoln. *The Making of Jazz: A Comprehensive History*. New York: Delta, 1978.

Crow, Bill, *Jazz Anecdotes*. New York and Oxford: Oxford University Press, 1990.

Dickson, Kenneth R., *...nothing personal, just business*, Fremont, Ohio: Lesher Printing, 2006.

Dietsche, Robert. *Jumptown: The Golden Years of Portland Jazz, 1942-1957*. Corvallis: Oregon State University Press, 2005.

Dupuis, Robert. *Bunny Berigan: Elusive Legend of Jazz*. Baton Rouge: Louisana State University Press, 1993

Esquire's 1946 Jazz Book, Edited by Paul Eduard Miller. New York: A. S. Barnes & Company, 1946.

Feather, Leonard. *The Book of Jazz From Then till Now: A Guide to the Entire Field*. New York: Bonanza Books, 1965.

Feather, Leonard. *Inside Jazz*. New York: Da Capo Press, Inc., 1977.

Feather, Leonard and Ira Gitler. *The Biographical Encyclopedia of Jazz*. Oxford: Oxford University Press, 1999.

Fountain, Charles. *Another Man's Poison: The Life and Writings of Columnist George Frazier*. Chester, Conn.: The Globe Pequot Press, 1984.

Gitler, Ira. *Swing to Bop: An Oral History of the Transition in Jazz in the 1940s.* New York and Oxford: Oxford University Press, 1985.
Gridley, Mark C. *Jazz Styles.* Englewood Cliffs, N.J.: Prentice-Hall, Inc., 1978.

Halliwell, Leslie and John Walker. *Halliwell's Film & Video Guide.* London: Harper Collins Entertainment, 2003.
Hallock, Ted. *American Federation of Music.* Eugene, Oregon: University of Oregon Thesis, 1946.
Hennessey, Thomas J. *From Jazz to Swing: African-American Jazz Musicians and Their Music, 1890-1935.* Detroit: Wayne State University Press, 1994.

Illman, Harry R. *Unholy Toledo.* San Francisco: Polemic Press Publications, 1985.

Jones, Max, *Talking Jazz.* New York & London: W. W. Norton & Co., 1987.

Kenney, William Howland. *Chicago Jazz: A Cultural History, 1904-1930.* New York and Oxford: Oxford University Press, 1993.
Kimball, Robert and William Bolcom. *Reminiscing With Sissle and Blake.* New York: The Viking Press, Inc., 1973.
Knox, J.E. *Ralph Flanagan Discography.* Portland, Oregon: Metolius Music Company, 2004.

Lester, James. *Too Marvelous for Words: The Life and Genius of Art Tatum.* New York & Oxford: Oxford University Press, 1994.
Lord, Tom. *Jazz Discography.* Redwood, N.Y.: Cadence Jazz Books, 2000.

McCarthy, Albert J. *Big Band Jazz.* New York: Exeter, 1974.
Martyn, Vivien. *Blues in "B" Flat.* Tucson: Past Litho, [199?].
Mosbrook, Joe. *Cleveland Jazz History*, 2nd ed., Cleveland: Northeast Ohio Jazz Society, 2003.

Ogren, Kathy J. *Jazz Revolution: Twenties America & the Meaning of Jazz.* New York and Oxford: Oxford University Press, 1989.
Ostransky, Leroy, *Jazz City: The Impact of Our Cities on the Development of Jazz.* Englewood Cliffs, New Jersey: Prentice-Hall, 1978.

Porter, Tana Mosier. *Toledo Profile: A Sesquicentennial History.* Toledo: Toledo Sesquicentennial Commission, 1987.

Russell, Ross. *Bird Lives! The High Life and Hard Times of Charlie (Yardbird) Parker.* New York: Charterhouse, 1973.

Sann, Paul. *Lawless Decade: A Pictorial History of a Great American Transition: From the World War I Armistice and Prohibition to Repeal and the New Deal.* New York: Crown Publishers, 1957.

Schiffman, Jack. *Harlem Heyday: A Pictorial History of Modern Black Show Business and the Apollo Theatre.* Buffalo: Prometheus Books, 1984.

Schuller, Gunther. T*he Swing Era: The Development of Jazz, 1930-1945.* New York & Oxford: Oxford University Press, 1989.

Shapiro, Nat and Nat Hentoff. *The Jazz Makers.* New York: Rinehart & Company, Inc., 1957.

Shapiro, Nat and Nat Hentoff, eds. *Hear Me Talkin' To Ya: The Story of Jazz as Told by the Men Who Made It.* New York: Dover Publications, Inc., 1955.

Shaw, Arnold, *Honkers and Shouters: The Golden Years of Rhythm and Blues.* New York: Collier Books, 1978.

Shaw, Arnold. *The Jazz Age: Popular Music in the 1920s.* New York: Oxford University Press, 1987.

Sklar, Robert. *The Plastic Age (1917-1930).* New York: G. Braziller, 1970.

Stephenson, Sam, *The Jazz Loft Project,* New York: Alfred A. Knopf, 2009.

Stewart, Rex. *Jazz Masters of the Thirties.* New York: Da Capo Press, 1972.

Sudhalter, Richard M. *Lost Chords: White Musicians and Their Contribution to Jazz, 1915-1945.* New York and Oxford: Oxford University Press, 1999.

Tyler, Don. *The Hit Parade: An Encyclopeddia of the Top Songs of the Jazz, Depression, Swing and Sing Eras.* New York: Quill, 1985.

Van Vechten, Carl. *Nigger Heaven.* New York: Knopf, 1926.

Walker, Leo. *Big Band Almanac.* Pasadena: Ward Ritchie Press, 1978.

Wells, Dicky as told to Stanley Dance. *The Night People: Reminiscences of a Jazzman.* Boston: Crescendo Publishing Company, 1971.

Whitlock, Brand. *The Turn of the Balance.* New York: Grosset & Dunlap, 1907.

Wilder, Alec. *American Popular Song: The Great Innovators, 1900-1950.* London and New York: Oxford University Press, 1972.

Wilson, John S., *The Collector's Jazz: Modern.* Philadelphia: Lippincott, 1959.

Wilson, Teddy with Arie Ligthart and Humphrey van Loo. *Teddy Wilson Talks Jazz.* New York: Continuum Press, 1996.

Index

103 Club, 162
3-D Club, 143, 156
"720 In the Books" (song), 75
Abrams, Eddie, xiii, 4, 39, 121, 131, 174, 176
Adams, Pepper, 150, 152, 153, 158
Adams, Pistol, 162
Adderley, Cannonball, 153, 172, 173
"After Hours" (song), 127
"After Midnight" (song), 46
Aku-Aku, xii, xv, 123, 150, 152, 156,
Al Belleto Sextet, 86
Al Cohn, 36, 71
Alabamians, 23
Aladdin Label, 17
Album, Manny, 48
Alcindor, Lou, 158
Aldrich, Mahlon, 169
Alfie's, 124
"All of Me" (song), 71
Allen, Frederick Lewis, 48
Allen, Steve, 4, 56, 82
Allyson, June, 158
"Altitude" (song), 56
"Always" (song), 162
"Amatola" (song), 50
"America the Beautiful" (song), 16
American Federation of Musicians, 113, 114
Ammons, Gene, xvii, 67, 142
Amtrak, 155
Anderson, Cat, 24, 165
Anderson, Marian, 89, 91
Andy Kirk and his Clouds of Joy, 21, 31
Angelina's brothel, 124
Angelo's Northwood Villa, 12, 13
Anthony, Ray, 41
Apollo (Harlem), 32, 189
"Apple Honey" (song), 47
April in Paris, 123
Aragon Ballroom (Chicago), 41
Armory Field, 93
Armory, The, xxi
Armstrong, Louis, 16, 26, 32, 46, 68, 76, 91, 99, 101, 102, 111, 158, 165, 166
Armstrong, Ralph, 129
Arnold, Don, xix, 143, 147, 148, 150, 185
Art Blakey and the Jazz Messengers, 129
Art Tatum Jazz Festival, 179
Arthur Godfrey Time, 86
"Artistry in Rhythm" (song), 88
Arv Garrison Memorial, 61, 122, 127, 141, 184, 185
"As Time Goes By" (song), 19
Associated Negro Press, 80
Atlantic Records, 119
Auditorium Theater, 28
Austin, Cuba, xv, 105, 106, 107
Austin, Harold "Dean," xv, xix, 147, 150
Austin, Will, 132
"Baby Doll" (song), 141
Bach, Johann Sebastian, 6, 8, 82, 157, 183
Badlands, 95
Bailey, Benny, 166
Baker, Chet, xv, 79, 131, 168
Baker, Josephine, 27
Baker, Shorty, 25
Baker's Keyboard Lounge (Detroit), 127, 128
Bakker, Mr., 125
Ball of Fire, 37
Band of Renown, 39
Barber, Pearl, 110
Barefield, Eddie, xv, 23
Barnett, Charlie, 38
Barnett, Cliff, 21, 22
Barrymore, Ethel, 98
Bartok, Bela, 157
Basie, Count, xviii, 6, 15, 17, 21, 32, 33, 99,

100, 102, 117, 122, 123, 124, 127, 131, 133, 138, 152, 153
Battles, Eber, 165
Bauduc, Ray, 56
Baxter, Lee, 101
Bayview Park, 97
Beatty, Warren, 155
Beatty, Wini, 56, 57-59, 182
bebop, 8, 21, 56, 59, 71, 79, 82, 113, 118, 145, 151
"Because of You" (song), 117
Bechet, Sidney, 111
Beginning to See the Light (LP), 71
Beiderbecke, Bix, xvi, 17, 68, 107, 109, 111, 165
Belcher, Frances "Lady B," 80, 116
"Bellboy Boogie" (song), 113
Belleto, Al, 86
Bellman, Howard, 75, 78-81, 183
Belmont Ballroom, 80, 117, 119, 122
Beneke, Tex, 65
Bennett, Tony, 117
Benny Moten Band, 6
Benson, George, 117
Benton, Brook, 50
Berigan, Bunny, 50, 67-69, 76, 166, 186, 187
Berlin, Irving, 162
Berry, Andrae "Fifi," xv, 155
Berry, Chu, 65
Berry, Emmet, 23, 166
"Better Than Anything" (song), 71
Biagini, Henry, 28
big band jazz, 108
Big Break, 137
"Bijou" (song), 47
Bill Doggett Combo, 122
Bill Evans Trio, 134
Billy Berg's (Hollywood), 59
Billy Eckstine bop band, 67, 114
Billy May band, 71, 140
Biographical Encyclopedia of Jazz, 34, 187
Birdland (New York), 79

Birdland Stars of Tomorrow, 131
Bix Beiderbecke Memorial, 111
Bix Beiderbecke Story, The, 68
Black and Blue Records, 24, 124
Black and Tan nightclub, 95
"Black Brown and Beige Suite" (song), 77
Black, Claude, xviii, 4, 33, 63, 66, 114, 121, 127-134, 152, 169, 176, 185
Blade, The, xviii, 3, 6, 12, 92, 97, 98, 124, 128, 138, 140, 156, 168, 180-182, 185, 186
Blake, Eubie, 27
Blakey, Art, 107, 129
Blanton, Jimmy, 132
blind pigs, 5, 93
"Blockbuster" (song), 83
Bloom, Rose, 77
Blue Bird Inn (Detroit), 127, 138
Blue Note, 79
"Blue Velvet" (song), 119
"Blues Back Stage" (song), 33
boogie woogie, 48
Boots Brown and His Blockbusters, 83
Borders, Babe, 78, 117
bossa nova, 48
Bostic, Earl, 117-119
Bowling Green State University, 179
Boyd, Noble, 5, 95
Bradley, Will, 114
Bradshaw, Tiny, 119
Braff, Ruby, 71
Brando, Marlon, 23, 83
Brass Rail (Chicago), 55
"Brazil" (song), 50
Brewer, Teresa, 71, 137
Bridges, Beau, 155
Bridges, Jeff, 155
Briglia, Tony, 29
Brignola, Mike, 47
Brignola, Nick, 152
Broadway, Kelly, 173
Bronze Raven, 80

Brookes, Roy, 129
brothel(s), xii, 5, 91, 95
Broun, Heywood, 27
Brown Buddies, 143
Brown, Clifford, 168
Brown, Joe E., 137
Brown, Les, xi, 37, 39, 41, 47, 51, 81, 137, 182
Brown, Ray, 179
Brown, Ruth, 119
Brubeck, Dave, 76, 79, 85, 122-124, 157
Bruns, Bob, 75
Buckingham Palace, 122
Buckner, Milt, 25, 121, 124, 125, 127
Buckner, Teddy, 124
Bud and Luke's, 154
Budapest String Quartet, 85
Buddy Morrow Band, 73
Buddy Rich Big Band, 134, 167
Bullmoose Jackson and His Buffalo Bearcats, 80
"Bunny Hop" (song), 41
Bunny Plays Bix (LP), 68
Burge, Bob, 41
Burns, Ralph, 36, 52
Burrell, Big Joe, 122
Burrell, Kenny, 78, 133, 147
Busse, Henry, 48, 50
Buzzelli, Chris, 179
Byas, Don, 9
Byrd, Donald, 127, 138
Cabrera, Louis, 147
Cagney, James, 32
Cakewalkin' Babies, 111
Cakewalkin' Jass Band, xii, xvi, 184
California State University, 34
Callaway, Cab, 15
Calvert, Steve, xii, 77, 78
Campbell, Choker, 114
Campus Rumpus (LP), 41
Candoli, Conte, 151
Candy's Mood (LP), 124
Capital records, 114

"Caravan" (song), 46
Carnegie Hall, 19, 129, 181
Carney, Harry, 162
Carroll, Pat, 152, 153
Carson, Jazz, 102
Carson, Johnny, 168
Carter, Benny, 56, 102
Carter, Betty, 173
Caruso, Enrico, 45, 80
Casa Loma Orchestra, xv, 28, 29
"Casa Loma Stomp" (song), 29
Casablanca, 19
Cass Technical High School (Detroit), 127
Cassidys, 105
Catlett, Sid, 101
Cavanaugh, Page, 56
Cecil Harris and his Jazz Jesters, 114
Celeste, Tony, xv, 51, 52, 150, 152, 153, 162
Centennial Jazz Festival, 73
Centennial Quarry, 62
Centennial Terrace, vii, xi, xii 39, 41-53, 82, 86, 87
Central Avenue Breakdown, Volume 1 (LP), 58
Central Catholic High School, 52
Ceroli, Nick, xiii, 45, 46, 182
Chaloff, Serge, 36, 152, 162
Chambers, Paul, 127
Charles, Ray, xviii, 3, 80
"Charleston" (song), 101
Charlie Parker Quintet, 32, 60
Charlie Parker Savoys, 79
Charlie Parker Septet, 59
Chateau La France, xii, xix, xxi, 2, 8, 32
Cheevy, Miniver, 140
"Cherry Pink and Apple Blossom White" (song), 48
Chesterfield cigarettes, 44, 46, 65
Chesterfield Hour (TV program), 41
Chicago Nightingales, xix
Chicken Charlie's, vii, 5, 24, 89, 92, 93, 95
chicken scratch, 95

Chicken Shack (Flint, Michigan), 167
Chilton, John, 16, 108
"China Boy" (song), 1, 19
Chinatown, 68
"Chinook That Melted My Heart, The" (song), 83
Chittison, Herman, 1, 21
Chocolate Beau Brummels, 1, 21
Chocolate Dandies, 102
Chopin, Frederic, 157
Christy, June, 51, 82
Church, Eddie, 35
Civic Auditorium, 63, 73, 88, 117, 118
CKLW radio, xi, xviii, 81
Clam Bake Seven, 150
"Clarinet Marmalade" (song), 111
Clarion Hotel, xv, 147,
Clark, Algeria Junius "June," ix, 101
Clark's Uptown (New York), 8
Clarke, Kenny, 79
Claude Black Trio, 130
Claude Hopkins Band, 17, 166
Clemmons, Chase, 63
Cleveland Orchestra, 65
Cleveland, John, 9, 179
Clovers, The, 119
Club Downbeat (New York), 55
Coast label, 51
Cobb, Bert, 23, 132
Cohn, Al, 36, 71
Cole, June, 5, 132
Cole, Nat King, 19, 46, 55
Coleman, Cy, 131
Coliseum, 22
Collins, Al Jazzbo, 81
Collins, Ramona, 52, 173, 174, 179
Colony Record Store, 76
Colony Shopping Center, 82
Colony Theater, 82
Coltrane, John, 65, 114, 118, 123, 153
Columbia Records, 34, 101, 114, 116, 180-182, 184
Combattelli, Mary, 168, 169
Commodore Perry Hotel, 42, 48
Commodore Perry Lounge, 121, 131
Concert by the Sea (LP), 81
Condoli, Conte, 46
Confer, Gene, xiii, 145
Contemporary Concepts (LP), 87
Cook, Benny, 127
Cook, James Willis "Jimmy," vii, xv, xxi, 48, 66, 67, 73, 149, 153, 162, 165, 166, 168, 169, 173, 175, 176, 186
"Cookin' at Murphy's" (song), 135
Cooper, Gary, 37
Corbett, James Jay, 98
Cotton Club Band, 89
"Cottontail" (song), 63
Count Basie Band 100
Covington, Glen, 134
Coward, Noel, 71
Cowell, Stanley, xv, 3, 4, 31, 134
Coyle, Bill, xv, 69, 87, 159
Crain, Jeanne, 140
Crane, Hart, 98
Craven, Mildred Vivien, xvi
Crawford, Joan, 171
"Crazy Blues" (song), 92
"Crazy Man Crazy" (song), 46
"Crazy Rhythm" (song), 103
Crew Cuts, The, 156
Crosby, Bing, 140, 163
Cuban Fire! (LP), 88
Cummerow, William Otto "Bill," xvi, 3, 54, 55, 182
Cummings, Bernie, 149
Dameron, Tadd, 21
dance marathons, 22
Darin, Bobby, 156
Daughters of the American Revolution, 92
Dave Brubeck Quartet, xi, 85, 86
Dave Poulin Quintet, 156

Davis, Miles, xviii, 39, 46, 56, 60, 61, 62, 131, 153, 157, 158, 166, 167, 168
Davis, Richard, 86
Davis, Will, 127
de Bouchet family, xxi
DeBoe Brothers, 143
DeBoe, Neil, xvi, 117
Debussy, Claude, 141, 157
Debut label, 152
Decca records, 114
"Dee Blues" (song), 102
DeFranco, Buddy, 152
Degage Jazz Café, 179
Dempsey, Jack, 98
Desmond, Paul, 81, 85
Detroit Connection (LP), 127
"Detroit Funnel," xv, 176
Detroit Jazz Tradition, The (LP), 128
Detroit Redwings, 25
"Devil or Angel" (song), 119
DeVilbiss High School, vii, xi, xii, xvi, 54, 66, 67, 75, 76, 77, 78, 82, 161
Deviltries talent show, 67
Devore, Henry "High Note," 23
Dial Records, 59
Diamonds, The, 158
Dickenson, Vic, 15, 59
Dickson, Ken, xiii, 13
"Didn't He Ramble" (song), 111
Dietsche, Bob, xi, xii, 179
Digby's Jazz Club, xviii, 134
"Diggin' for Diz" (song), 59
Dillard, Bert, 165, 166
"Diminuendo and Crescendo" (song), 89
"Dinah-flow" (song), 86
Dixie Villa, xii, 13
"Dixieland One Step" (song), 103
Dixon Hotel, xii, 94, 95
Dixon, Charles, 95
"Dizzy Spells" (song), 19
Django Record Company, xi

Dobbins, Sean, 130
DoKurno family, 14
Dolphy, Eric, 23
Don Shirley duet, 85
"Don't Be That Way" (song), 48
"Don't Get Scared" (song), 32
Donahue, Sam, 71, 140
Donaldson, Lou, 124
Dodds, Johnny, 102
Doors, The, 71
Dorham, Kenny, 32, 151, 152
Dorough, Bob, 71, 183
Dorsey Brothers, 109
Dorsey, Jimmy, 50
Dorsey, Tommy, 50, 103, 145, 166
Douglas, Kirk, 75
Down Beat, 33, 45, 46, 50, 53, 59, 78, 79, 80, 89, 121, 131, 153, 180-184
"Downtown" (song), 50
Dragnet (TV program), 41
Duchin, Eddie, 131
Duke Ellington Orchestra, xix, 132, 166
Duke Ellington's Jungle Band, 101
"Duke, The" (song), 85
Duncan, Hank, 100
Dunham, Sonny, 29
Durham, Hank, 132
Dyers Chop House, 48
Eagle Point Colony, 110
Earl Bostic Fan Club, 116
Earle Spencer orchestra, 59
"Early Autumn" (song), 47, 65
East of Eden, 171
Easterly, Herman, 2
"Ebb Tide" (song), 125
Ebbs Hotel (Louisville, Kentucky), 100
Eberly, Bob, 50
Eckstine, Billy, 67
Eddie Hanf's Dance Studio, 48
Eddy, Nelson, 50
Edgerton, Art J., 3

El Myers Quartet, 63
El Myers Quintet, 52, 65, 173
Eldridge, Joe, 16
Eldridge, Roy, 15, 16, 18, 46, 67, 68, 180
Elephant's Café (Atlantic City), 100
"Eleven 'Til Seven" (song), 118
Ellington, Edward Kennedy "Duke," xi, xvi, 8, 19, 24, 33, 47, 52, 56, 63, 77, 81, 85, 86, 89, 99, 101, 102, 106, 109, 138, 162, 165, 166
Elman, Ziggy, 68
English, "Wop," 12
ESKY trophy, 9
Esquire magazine, 9, 53, 86, 182, 187
Eubanks, Kevin, 71
Evans, Bill, xvii, 153, 154, 157, 186
Evans, Gil, 62
Evans, Herschel, 65
Evening at the Embers (LP), 82
"Every Time We Say Goodbye" (song), 141
"Evil-gal Blues" (song), 117
Evolution of the Blues Song (LP), 33, 34
"Exodus" (song), 127
Fabulous Baker Boys, The, 155
Faehnle, Dan, 147, 174, 176
Fairmont label, 89
Farlow, Tal, 71
Farrell, Joe, 45
"Father of Swing Trombone," 99
Faulkner, Ann, 91
"Fawncy Meeting You" (song), 123
Feather, Leonard, 21, 34, 45, 59, 78, 117, 184, 185
Feldbach, Mrs., 67
Ferguson, Maynard, 158, 165, 168, 173
Fifi's, xii, xv, xvii, 139, 141, 143, 155, 156
Filippi's (Seattle, Washington), 80
Finale Club, (Hollywood), 59
Finkbeiner, Carty, 11, 52
Finston, Lou, 58
Fire House Five, 79
First Night, 179
First Westminster Presbyterian Church, 92

Fitzgerald, Ella, 23, 50, 56, 112, 153, 157
"Five Guitars in Flight" (song), 59
Five Guitars Plus Four, 59, 182
Five Pennies, 17
Five Spot Café (Greenwich Village), 153
"Flamingo" (song), 118
Flanagan Band, 44
Flanagan, Ralph, 42, 44-46, 182, 188
Flanagan, Tommy, 19, 78, 117, 127, 140, 176, 185
Fletcher Henderson Band, 106
Fluckiger, Otto, 125
"Flyin' Home" (song), 124
Fontana, Carl, 88
"Foolish Things" (song), 149
"For All We Know" (song), 154
Ford, Art, 56
Forest Park, 15, 23
"Forgetting You" (song), 109
Foster, Frank, 123
Foster, Herman, 124
Foster, Jerry, 161
"Four Brothers" (song), 32
Four Freshmen, 86
"Four" (song), 34
Fowler, T. J., 121
France Stone Company, 41
Francis, Panama, 25
Franciscan Center, 123, 142
Frank Terry and the Chicago Nightingales, xv, 15, 22, 23
Franklin, Aretha, 127
Frazier, Calvin, 117
Frazier, George, 68, 187
Fred Dale Band, 138
Free, Ronnie, 138
Freeman, Russ, 168
French, Jim, 75
Friendly Bar, 156
Friends of Centennial Terrace, Inc., 41
Frisch's Big Boy, 148

Frishberg, Dave, xiii, 71
Fry, Dan, 2
Fuller, Curtis, 138
Fuller, Gil, 119
Fuller, Larry, 174, 176, 179
Gaillard, Slim, 56
Gaiety Club, 143
gambling, xxi, 11-13, 95, 110
gangster(s), xxi, 13, 32, 92, 108, 112
Garner, Erroll, 56, 81
Garrison, Arvin "Arv," vii, xi, xvi, xix, 3, 17, 48, 53-63, 75, 95, 117, 132, 141, 143, 150, 151, 154, 156, 162
Garroway, Dave, 4
Garry, Vivian, x, xvi, 53-62, 141, 182
Geller, Lorraine, 158
Gene Krupa and his Orchestra, 36
Georgio's Restaurant, 108
Gershwin, George, 73
Gettin' in the Groove (LP), 25
Getz, Stan, xix, 32, 36, 65, 162, 163
Gibson, Althea, 51
Gifford, Gene, 29
Gilbert and Sullivan, 34
Gillespie, Dizzy, 16, 61, 82, 127, 137, 145, 149
Gilly's (Dayton, Ohio), 167
Giuffre, Jimmy, 62, 83
Gleason, Ralph J., 34
Glen Island Casino, 41
Glenn Miller Orchestra, 38
Glenn Miller Story, The, 44, 157
Glover Brothers, 132
God is in the House (LP), 8, 180
Goldkette, Jean, xii, xvi 108, 109
Goldstein, Ben, 93
"Good Lovin'" (song), 119
Goodman, Benny, 1, 19, 28, 30, 48, 50, 109, 116, 145, 152
Goodrow, Gordon, 71, 183
Goody's (New York), 80
Gordon, Dexter, 67

Gottron, James P. "Jim," xvi, 101, 131, 133, 134, 142
Gould, Elizabeth, 137
Governor's Award, Arts in Ohio, 142
Grand Terrace (Chicago), 19
Granz, Norman, 4, 76
Gray, Glen, 29
Gray, Wardell, 32, 73, 79, 121, 149
Great Depression, 5, 13, 22, 31, 42, 189
Green and White Dance Pavilion, 28
"Green Eyes" (song), 50
Green Lite Night Club, 69, 72, 73, 117, 143
Green Mill Gardens, vii, xxi, 105, 107, 108
Green Mill Syncos, 108
Green, Freddy, 124
Greenberg, Phil, 162
Greer, Sonny, 101
Gregory, Harold, "Harry," 2, 4, 5, 6 132, 139, 180, 185
Grey, Al, 128
Grey, Jerry, 145
Greystone Ballroom (Detroit), 108
Griffin, Johnny "The Little Giant," 114
Grinnell's, 82
grizzly bear, 95
"Groovin' High" (song), 32, 137
Guanari, Johnny, 50
Guild Records, 56
Gulf Coast Seven, 102
Gullin, Lars, 32
Gunsmoke (TV program), 41
Haig, Al, 19, 32
Half Note (New York), 71
Hall, Adelaide, 8
Hallberg, Bengt, 19
Halsey, Jeff, 69, 174, 175, 179
Hamilton, Alexander, 156
Hamilton, Jeff, 179
"Hamp's Boogie Woogie" (song), 124, 127
Hampton, Lionel, 19, 118, 124, 127, 172
"Handful of Keys" (song), 17

Handy, George, 58
"Happy Days Are Here Again" (song), 141
Harding, Buster, 123
Harlem Renaissance, 91
Harlem Stride, 101
Harold Jaffe Jewelers, 142
Harris Barry, 3
Harris, Benny, 167
Harris, Eddy, 127
Harrison, James Henry "Jimmy" "Toledo Terror," vii, xii, xvi, xix, xxi, 99-103, 106
Hartwig, Jerry, 49
"Have You Met Miss Jones" (song), 73
Hawes, Hampton, 158
Hawkin, Erskine, 44
Hawkins, Coleman, 6, 55, 65
Hawley Café, xvi, 115, 117
Hayes, Jimmy, 12, 13
Haymes, Dick, xvii, 137, 140
Heard, JC, 128
Heath Brothers, xv, 3
Heath, Ted, 81
"Heebie Jeebies" (song), 102
Heitger, Raymond A. "Ray," xvi, 111
Helen O'Connell Day, 51
Henderson, Fletcher, 102, 106, 109, 187
Hendricks, Jon, vii, xvi, 13, 16, 17, 31-34, 71, 116, 153, 180, 181
Herman, Woodrow Charles "Woody," xi, xvi, 32, 36, 47, 48, 51, 52, 122, 148, 172, 182
Herman's, xii, xxi
"Hi, Beck" (song), 149
Hill, Howard, 50, 156, 157
Hill, Phil, 127
Hines, Earl "Father," 17, 19, 23
Hobbs, Gary, 87
Hoefer, George, 121
Hogan, Ben, 1
Holden, Jean, xvi, 52, 172, 173
Hole in the Head, A, 175
Holiday, Billie, 19, 55, 73, 138, 167

Holland, Eddie, 2
Hollywood Cocktail Lounge, 62
Hollywood Palladium, 41
Holman, Bill, 88
"Honeysuckle Rose" (song), 111
"Honky Tonk" (song), 122
Hoosier Melody Lads, 15
"Hop Off" (song), 102, 103
Hope, Bob, 35, 37
Hope, Lynn, 118, 185
Horace Silver Quintet, 127
Hospitality Inn, 52
"Hot House" (song), 137
"Hot Toddy" (song), 44
House of Israel, 132
Houseparty Hop (LP), 41
"How High the Moon" (song), 9
"How Much Is That Doggie in the Window" (song), 86
Howard Hill Trio, 157
Howard Manor (Palm Springs), 60
Howard Rumsey's Lighthouse All-Stars, 62, 158
Howard, Bart, 2
Hoyt, Elliot, 35
Hubbard, Freddy, 138
Hucklebuck dance, 116
"Hucklebuck, The" (song), 116
Huffman, Max, 72, 73
Hughes, Bill, 123
Hughes, Howard, 59
Hughes, Langston, 91
Huntley, Lucius, 117
Huston, John, 68
Hutchenrider, Clarence, 29
Hygait, Hyman, 79
Hyman, Dick, 1
"I Can't Get Started" (song), 68, 166
"I Got Rhythm" (song), 19, 139
"I Love Being Here with You" (song), 51
"I Thought About You" (song), 147
"I Want to be a Sideman" (song), 71

"I'll Take Romance" (song), 155
"I'm a Ding Dong Daddy" (song), 102
"I'm Gonna Go Fishin'" (song), 71
"If I Had You" (song), 149
"If I Should Lose You" (song), 128
"In the Mood" (song), 68
Indiana Tavern, xvii, 78, 115, 117
Indiana University, 137, 138
"Indiana" (song), 9, 139
Indie record companies, 114, 118
Inkspots, The, 156
Inverness Country Club, xv
"It Might As Well Be Spring" (song), 63, 127, 140
J and R Lounge, 160
Jabar, Kareem Abdul, 158
Jack Frost and his Eskimos, 25
Jack Runyan Big Band, 63
Jack Runyan Orchestra, 86
Jack the Bellboy, 81, 113
Jackson, Bullmoose, 80
Jackson, Michael, 155
Jackson, Milt, 128, 134, 147
Jackson, Ozie "Jack," 2, 117, 125
Jackson, Willis, "Gatortail," 80, 114, 119
Jacquet Street (LP), 25
Jacquet, Illinois, 25, 124, 137
"Jaffe Variations" (song), 142
Jaffe, Harold, 142
Jail, The, 5
James, Harry, 37, 41, 48, 68, 168
Jasinski, Buzzy, 146, 156, 168
Jay Leno Show, The 71
Jay, Bob, 37
Jazz at Ann Arbor (LP), 168
Jazz at Oberlin (LP), 85
Jazz at the Philharmonic (LP), 137
Jazz at the Philharmonic, 15, 73, 76
jazz fans, xi, 19, 76, 119
Jazz Goes to College (LP), 79, 85
Jazz in the Garden, 179

Jazz Journal, 25, 181
Jazz Masters of the Thirties, 6, 180, 184, 189
Jazz: Red Hot and Cool (LP), 85, 157
Jean Goldkette Orchestra, 109
Jefferson, Eddie, 32
Jenkins, Freddy, 89
Jimmy Reemsnyder Band, 52
Jimmy Ryan's (New York), 55
Jimmy Zito Orchestra, 51
Jimmy's Chicken Shack (Harlem), 8
"Jingle Bells Mambo" (song), 47
Johnny Guitar, 171
Johnny O'Neal Trio, 130
Johnny Trudell Band, 167, 168
Johnson, Bass, 132
Johnson, Bob, 49
Johnson, Charlie, 102
Johnson, Floyd "Candy," vii, xii, xvi, 63, 114, 119, 121-125, 138, 156, 175, 185
Johnson, J. J., 99
Johnson, Jack, 98, 110
Johnson, James P., xvi, xxi, 1, 101
Jones Brothers, 133
Jones Junior High School, 48
Jones, Claude, 105, 106, 109
Jones, Hank "The Dean," xvi, 19, 127, 131, 140
Jones, Jimmy, 62
Jones, Jo, 67
Jones, Samuel M. "Golden Rule," xvi, 11, 12
Jones, Spike, 80
Jones, Thad, 123, 138, 153, 172
"Jumpin' at the Woodside" (song), 122
Jungle Band, 89, 101
Junior Chamber of Commerce, 162
Junior-Senior Prom (LP), 42
Justice, John, 156, 158
Juvenile Protection Agencies, 92
Kallao, Alex, 81, 82
Kallile, Sam, 47, 48
kangaroo dip, 95
Ka-See's, 156

Kaye, Ellen, 8
Kaye, Teddy, 55, 56, 60
Kelly, Pete, 111, 112
Kelly, Wynton, 131
Kelly's Stables (New York), 56
Kenton, Stan, xi, xv, xvii, 19, 37, 38, 51, 62, 75, 81, 82, 85-89, 102, 148, 149, 165, 167, 169
Kern, Jerome, 73, 140
Keys, Preston, xvii, 50, 52, 128, 133, 139, 153-154, 157-160, 185, 186
Kiddies Karnival, 52
Kieswetter, Mark, xvii, 87, 124, 128, 158, 183, 185, 186
Kiker, Clyde, 76
Kin Wa Low's, xii, 156, 157, 181, 186
Kincaid, Dean, 38
Kind of Blue (LP), 65, 153
King Oliver's Creole Jazz Band, 101
King Porter Band, 114
"King Porter Stomp" (song), 68, 102
King Records, 114, 119
King, Wayne, 134, 150
Kinney, Brad, xvii, 75
Kinney, Bruce, 83
Kipling, Rudyard, 77
Kirk, Andy, 21, 23, 31
Kirk, Roland, 133
Kismet, 44
KISS, 155
Klines (Detroit), 3
Knights of Syncopation, xvii, 25, 26
Knorr, Johnny, vi, 38, 41, 48-50, 52, 141, 182
Konitz Quartet, 149
Konitz, Lee, 73, 149
Kopp, Fred, xvii, 52, 123, 155, 156, 158, 162, 185
Krall, Diana, 73
Krupa, Gene, 15, 32, 36, 37, 44, 67, 80, 101, 106, 158
Ladies' Home Journal, 91
Laine, Frankie, 56

Lair, Jim, 157
Lambert, Dave, 32, 33
Lambert, Hendricks & Ross, 17, 31-33
Lang, Eddie, 109
Lateef, Yusef, 3
"Lean Baby" (song), 71, 82
Lee Wiley Fan Club, 75
Lee, Delbert C., xvii, 21
Lee, James, 145
Lee, Lewis C. "Swing," xvii, 63, 78, 117, 123, 156
Lee, Peggy, 51, 112
Lee's Sensation, 124
LeFaro, Scott, 134
Lehman, Howdy, 158
Lemmon, Jack, 68
Leroy's, 87
Les Brown and His Band of Renown, 39, 82
"Lester Blows Again" (song), 17
"Let Me See" (song), 17
Let's Go Dancing (LP), 141
Lewis, Mel, 88, 172
Libbey High School, 35, 48, 50, 143, 156
Licavoli, Pete, 11
Licavoli, Thomas "Yonnie," xvii, 11-14
Lichtenwald, Danny, 75
Life magazine, 22, 48
Lightfoot, Frank, 21
Lighthouse Café (Hermosa Beach), 62, 158
Lindsey, Harold, xvii, xix 62, 65, 117, 142, 143
Lindy (dance), 48
"Little Darlin'" (song), 158
"Little Niles" (song), 34
Live at Franklin Park (LP), 52
London House (Chicago), 4
"Long Ago and Far Away" (song), 141
Long, Johnny, 42
Lorraine Hotel, 63, 65, 66, 156
Lost Chords, 165, 181, 184, 189
Louis Herman's, 100
Louis, Joe, 8

"Love for Sale" (song), 86, 117
Love Supreme, A (LP), 65
Love Themes from the Classics (LP), 45
"Love Will Find A Way" (song), 28
Loy, Myrna, 51
Luna Pier, xvi, 12, 15, 21, 30, 67, 89, 109
Lunceford, Jimmie, 15, 21, 28, 31, 71, 127, 145
Lutz, Fred, xi, xiii, 82-84, 183
Lutz, Fred, Sr., 82
Lyons, Jimmy, 33, 81, 158
M and L Rendezvous, 62, 133, 150, 151, 154
M.F. Horn (LP), 173
"Mable's Dream" (song), 101
"MacArthur Park" (song), 173
Machito's Band, 47
Mackenzie, Ed, 113
Macomber High School, 156, 161
Madison Gardens, 35
Magic Flute (San Francisco), 80
Mailer, Norman, 78
Make Mine Music, xi
"Mambo the Utmost" (song), 48
mambo, 47, 48
"Man I Love, The" (song), 82
Mancini, Henry, 166
Manne, Shelly, 62, 83, 150
Mardi Gras Nite Club, 161
Marian McPartland Trio, 71, 79
"Marie" (song), 68
"Marilyn Monroe Mambo" (song), 47
Marion Sears Band, 166
Marks, Chet, xv, 12
Marlboro cigarettes, 46
Marsalis, Wynton, 134, 175
Marsh, Warne, 138
Marterie, Ralph, xvii, 45, 46, 140, 168
Martin, Vern, 63, 127
Mason, Velmar "Fats," 98
Masonic Temple, 51
Mast, Clare, 137
Mast, John, vii, xii, xvii, xix, 4, 46, 50, 73, 132, 133, 137-143, 147, 150, 151, 155, 156, 185
May, Billy, 46, 69, 71, 82
McCall, Mary Ann, 52
McCoy, Clyde, 48, 50
McCrae, Carmen, xvii, 137, 138
McDonald, Jeanette, 50
McEachren, Murray, 29, 65, 71
McGhee, Howard, 59
McGowan, Russ, xvii, 2, 5, 95, 105, 165, 180, 183, 184, 186
McKellar, Phil, xvii, 79, 81
McKinley Elementary School, 82
McKinley, Ray, 38
McKinney, William, 105, 106
McKinney's Cotton Pickers, xv, xvii, xxi, 5, 16, 21, 29, 105-110, 113, 125, 132, 165, 187
McNeeley, Big Jay, 118-119
McSqueely Brothers, 118
Mel Lewis Orchestra, 153
"Melancholy Baby" (song), 22
Melle, David "Dave," xvii, 38, 50, 142
"Memories of You" (song), 29
Memphis Five, 103
Mencken, H. L., 92
Meng, Larry, 82
Mercer, Johnny, 50
Mercury Records, 45, 46
Metronome Magazine, 39, 56, 59, 78, 79, 81, 182, 183
Metropolitan Bopera House, 60
Mewhort, Charles Alan "Charlie" "Chazz," xi, xvii, 75, 87, 88, 151
Miami Fontainebleau, 175
Michigan State University, 87
Midnight Blues (LP), 124
Miff Mole and the Molers, 103
Miles Davis *Birth of the Cool* band, 60
Miles Davis Sextet, 153
Miller, Glenn, xvii, 35, 38, 42, 48, 49, 50, 65, 68, 103, 152, 158
Miller, Mike, 50

Milt Senior Sextet, 17
Milt Senior Small Combo, 110
Mingus, Charlie, 23
"Misty" (song), 81
Mitchell, Billy, 133
"Moanin'" (song), 34
Mobley, Hank, 65
Modern Jazz Quartet, 79
Mole, Irving Milfred "Miff," xiv, xvii, 102, 103
Monitor, 81
Monk, Theolonius, 34, 81, 89
monkey glide, 95
Monroe, Margaret "Rusty," xvii, xviii 4, 9, 72, 77, 115, 139, 145, 146, 171, 172, 174, 179, 186
Monterey Jazz Festival, 33-34
"Montoona Clipper" (song), 82
Moody, James, 32, 145
"Moody's Mood for Love" (song), 32
"Moonglow" (song), 23
"Moonlight Serenade" (song), 75
Moore, Dudley, 179
Moore, Oscar, 53
Morgenstern, Dan, 8
Morocco (Los Angeles), 59
"Morocco" (song), 118
Morrow, Buddy, 46
Morton, Jelly Roll, 2, 6
Mossblad, Gunnar, 179
Moten, Benny, 44
"Move" (song), 168
Mozart, Wolfgang, 38, 48
Mud Hens, xxi, 13, 35, 176
Mulligan, Gerry, 71, 152, 162, 173
Murphy, Cliff, xii, xv, xviii, 66, 69, 92, 114, 123, 128, 130, 132-135, 156, 162, 183, 185
Murphy, Turk, 111
Murphy's Place, xvii, 66, 128-131, 134, 150, 179
"Music, Music, Music" (song), 137
Musicians Union, 44, 52, 176
"Muskrat Ramble" (song), 111

"My Baby Rocks Me With One Steady Roll" (song), 25
"My Buddy" (song), 125
"My Foolish Heart" (song), 157
"My Funny Valentine" (song), 52, 65, 154
"My Old Flame" (song), 51
My Reunion at Murphy's (LP), 135
Myers, Elvin F. "El," xii, 5, 33, 58, 60, 63, 65-68, 70-73, 87, 128, 130, 132-134, 139, 142, 149, 156, 175-177, 180-183, 185, 186
"Nagasaki" (song), 106
Nance, Ray, 24
Nathan Hale Elementary School, 161
Navarro, Fats, 67
NBC Symphony, 89, 103
"Nearness of You, The" (song), 51
Nesbitt, John, xviii, 29, 107, 109, 165
"Never Let Me Go" (song), 128
New York Voices, 179
Newborn, Phineas, 1, 131
Newman, Fathead, 134, 135
Newman, Jerry, 8
Newman, Joe, 124
Newport Jazz Festival All-Stars (LP), 71, 183
Newport Jazz Festival, 89
Newsweek, 27, 33
Nichols, Red, 17
Niehouse, Lennie, 88
Nigger Heaven, 102, 189
"Night in Tunisia, A" (song), 59, 65
"No Name Jive" (song), 29
Nobles, 5, 24, 105, 165
"Nobody's Sweetheart" (song), 107
Nocturne label, 80
Nordstrom, 155
Northern Senior High School (Detroit), 127
Norvo, Red, 109
Not With Empty Hands, 3
Nothing Personal, Just Business, 13, 180
"Now's the Time" (song), 116
"Nutcracker Suite" (song), 25

O'Connell, Helen, xviii, 48, 50, 51, 156
O'Connor, Paul, 38, 50
O'Day, Anita, 1, 52, 73, 180
O'Neal, Johnny, 3, 121, 129, 134, 135, 141, 162, 176, 185
Oh Johnny (CD), 50
"Oh, Baby" (song), 102
Ohio Arts Council, 142
Ohio Bank Building, 13
Ohio Board of Realtors, 162
Oklahoma, 44
Old Ox Road, The (LP), 42
Old West End Festival, 179
Oliver, Joe, 165
Oliver, King, xv, 23, 101-102, 165
Oliver, Sy, 21, 22
"One Mint Julep" (song), 119
"One O'Clock Jump" (song), 122
Only Game in Town, The, 155
Onyx Club (New York), 9, 56
Onyx Records, 58, 180, 182
"Opener, The" (song), 88
"Opus #1" (song), 21
"Opus in Pastels" (song), 37, 86
Orange Blossoms, 29
"Ornithology" (song), 32, 59
Osborn, Bud, 6, 180
Oswanski, Ron, 179
Ottawa Hills, Ohio, 31
Ottawa University, 82
Overton, Nelson, 179
Palace Theater, 145
Paradise Inn, 80, 132
Paradise Theater (Detroit), 127
Paramount Theater, 15, 31, 36, 37, 67, 88, 89, 131, 150
Parker, Charlie "Bird," xvi, 8, 32, 37, 53, 59, 60, 67, 77-79, 86, 116, 121, 127, 131, 137, 138, 151, 162, 167, 188
Parker, Gene, vii, xii, xviii, 49, 143, 145-147, 149, 153, 162, 174, 179, 185

Parrish, Avery, 127
Parrots Lounge (Detroit), 127
Paul Whiteman Band, 65
Paul, Les, 1, 53
Pavkovich, Bob, 123, 185
Payne, Harold F., xviii, 5, 23, 92, 180, 181, 183
"Pearls, The" (song), 2
Pell, Dave, 82
"Pennsylvania 6-5000" (song), 38
Pennsylvania State College, 44
Pepper, Art, 73, 158
Peppermint Sticks, 121
"Perdido" (song), 75
Peristyle, xi, 85, 86, 88, 89, 128, 138
Perkins, Bill, 88
Perkins, Carl, 119
Perry, Mozart, 2, 4, 5, 124
Pete Kelly's Blues, 111
Peterson, Chuck, 166
Peterson, Oscar, 1, 16, 129, 157, 169
Petrillo, James Caesar, 113
Phi Kappa Psi, 83
Phillips, Flip, 137
Piano Starts Here (LP), 101
Pinewood District, 99, 116, 117
Pizzarella, John, 179
Please (LP), 163
Pleasure, King, 32
Plumbers Appliance, 116
Polk, Lucy Ann, 51
Pollack, Sid, 22
Pollard, Terry, 3, 131
"Poor People Bossa Nova, The" (song), 128
Porter, Cole, 1, 73
Porter, King, 121
Potter, Scott, 174
Poulin, Dave, 138, 158
Powell, Bud, 1, 127, 131, 157
Prado, Prez, 48
Prelude Club (Chicago), 138
Premium Records, 118

Presley, Elvis, 36, 53
Prestige Records, 79
"Pretend" (song), 46
Priestly, Brian, 157
Prohibition, 11, 55, 92, 101, 189
Pugh, Jim, 75
Purcell, Pat, 62, 182
Purdy, Aaron, 49
Purple Gang, 14
Quinichette, Paul, 124
Rachmaninoff, Sergei, 45, 138
Radio Room (Los Angeles), 58
Rainey, Overton, 1
Ralph Marterie and His Marlboro Men, 46
Ray Charles Band, 134
Ray, 129
Raymond, Lee "One Putt," xiii, 81, 82
RCA Records, 114, 183
RCA Studio, 83
RCA Victor, 42, 45, 81
Reams, Frazier, 13
"Record Ban Blues" (song), 117
Recreation Ballroom, 23
Recreation Music Box, 23
Red Wells Restaurant, 54, 171
Red, Sonny, 127
Redman, Don, 108
Reemsnyder, Jimmy, 35, 48, 63, 162
Reichman, Joe, 131
Reidley, Jack, 46, 156
Reig, Teddy, 114, 116
Reinhardt, Django, 53, 54
"Relax Jack" (song), 56
rent ps, 5, 8, 17
Rex, Bob, 167, 173, 186
Rhodes, Todd, xviii, 105, 113
Rich, Buddy, 29, 134, 158, 159, 179
Rich, Kathy, 159
Richards, Johnny, 44, 88
"Ricochet Romance" (song), 138
Riggs, James Garland "Jim," xviii, 50, 75, 145, 153, 154, 169, 174
Riverside Label, 153
Rivoli Pit Band, 79
Rivoli Theater, 32, 147
Rizzi, Tony, 59
Roach, Max, 60, 79
Robinson, Prince, 102
"Rock of Ages" (song), 111
"Rockin' Chair" (song), 16
Rocky, 173
Rogers, Richard, 73
Rogers, Shorty, 36, 62, 73, 83
Roland, Gilbert, 48
Rosolino, Frank, 62, 102
Ross, Annie, 32, 33
Ross, Arnold, 73
Rothman, Seymour, xviii, 12, 50, 124, 125, 156, 168, 185
Rouser, Elwood A., 92
Royal Roost (Los Angeles), 56
Royal Roost (New York), 32, 56, 58, 60
Royal Serenaders, 21
Royal, Marshall, 152
Ruben's (New York), 8
Rugolo, Pete, 47
Ruihley, Wayne, 37, 162, 181
Rumsey, Howard, 62
Runyan Band, xix, 36, 39
Runyan, Jack Pearson, vii, xii, xiii, xvii, 35-39, 41, 42, 52, 162, 181
Runyon, Damon, 98
Russ Morgan Orchestra, 49
Russell, Jane, 48
Russell, Joan, xviii, 134
Russell, Peewee, 71
Russin, Babe, 50
Russo, Frank, xviii, 39, 156
Russo, Mary Ann, xviii, 38, 51, 52, 153,
Rusty's Jazz Café, vii, xii, xv, xvii, xviii, xxi, 39, 65, 66, 73, 134, 151, 157, 171, 173, 174, 175, 176, 179

Ruth, Babe, 79, 103
Ryan, Ruth, 75
Sacks, Jacob, 179
Sacred Concert (LP), 52
Sales, Soupy, 79, 82
Salvation Army, 91
San Francisco Chronicle, 34
Sands, Lou, 146
Sarco Label, 58
Saturday Night Swing Session, 56
Save the Tiger, 68
Savoy Records, 114, 182, 185
Savoy Sultans, 24, 25, 119
Sawicki, Henry J. "Jerry," xviii, 42, 87, 88, 147, 152, 156, 159, 161 162, 166, 169, 182, 185, 186
Sawicki, Lois Ann, 162
scat, 32, 52, 59, 153
Schreiber, Cornell, 97
Schuller, Gunther, 23, 107, 189
Scobey, Bob, 111
Scott High Five, xix, 143, 147, 150
Scott High School, 1, 2, 89, 122, 165
Scott, Cecil, 2
Scott, Susanne, 128
Seaman, Dave, xix, 122, 147, 150, 156
Sears, Al, 21
"Second Piano Concerto" (song), 45
Second Thundering Herd, 36
Second Time Around (LP), 147, 162, 186
Secor Hotel, xviii, 25
"Secret Love" (song), 141
Seligman Brothers, xviii, 76, 77, 79, 80
Seligman, Hyman, 80
Seligman, Phil, 80, 183
Seligman's Record Bar, xi, xviii, 79, 81, 82
Selinsky, Buzz, 162
Sellers, Peter, 155
Senior, Milton Penn "Milt," 6, 105, 107-110
Sensation Records, 114, 127, 128
Severinsen, Doc, 50, 168
Seymour, Frederick, 25

"Shadow of Your Smile" (song), 65
Shank, Bud, 62
Shank, Joanna, 13, 180
"Shanty Town" (song), 42
Shavers, Charlie, 124
Shaw, Artie, 15, 109
Shearing, George, 82, 122, 124, 156
Sheppard, Jim, 63
Sherry's, 116
Shipman, Guy, 35
Shirley, Don, xi, 85
Shore, Dinah, 80
Shorter, Wayne, 123, 134
"Shortnin' Bread" (song), 83
Shorty Rogers and His Giants, 83
Shorty Rogers Fan Club, 83
Shuffle Along, 27-28
Silver, Josh, 179
Sims, Zoot, xxi, 36, 131, 137, 138, 147, 148
Sinatra, Frank, 50, 140, 175
Since Yesterday, 48, 182, 187
"Sing, Sing, Sing" (song), 36
Singer, Hal, 114
"Singing the Blues" (song), 17
Sisson, Noble, 27
Siwa, Jim, 63
Skelton, Red, 50
Sketches of Spain (LP), 168
Skylark label, 62
Slapsy Maxie's (Los Angeles), 59
Slenczynska, Ruth, 137
Slingerland Drum Company, 36
Small's Paradise (Harlem), 102
Smith, Bessie, 32, 91, 102, 117
Smith, Jabbo, 16, 19, 23, 166
Smith, Mamie, 92
Smith, Paul, 123
Smith, Tab, 117, 118
Smith, Willie "The Lion," 2, 89, 101, 102
"Smoke Rings" (song), 29
"Smooth Stuff and Funky Dunk" (song), 142

"Snowfall" (song), 141
Snyir, Steve, 65
"Soft" (song), 119
"Some Enchanted Evening" (song), vii, 41, 44
"Somebody Loves Me" (song), 102
Something Cool (LP), 82
"Song Is You, The" (song), 32
"Song of India" (song), 50, 68
"Songs for Our Sister," 52
Sophia Label, 162
"Sophisticated Lady" (song), 124
Sophomore Splash (LP), 42
South Pacific, 44
"South" (song), 44
Spaghetti Warehouse, xxi, 100
Speed Webb Band, 15, 17, 21
Speed Webb Orchestra, 15
Spencer, Earle, 59
Spencer-Sharples High School, 121
Sports Arena, xi, 15, 76, 82, 123
"St. Louis Blues Mambo" (song), 47
"St. Louis Blues March" (song), 158
Stafford, Jo, 117
Stan Kenton Balboa orchestra, 67
Stan Kenton Orchestra, 153
Stanford University, 34
Stanley Cowell Live at the Café des Cobain (LP), 4
Stanley Cup, 25
Stanwyck, Barbara, 37
"Stardust" (song), 85, 155
"Stardust Mambo" (song), 47
State Fair, 140
Stein, Sleepy, 158
Sterns, Marshall, 78
Steve Allen Show, 82
Stevens, Leif, 83
Stewart, Ella P., 8
Stewart, James, 158
Stewart, Rex, 6, 8, 99, 100, 180
Stewart, Sammy, xviii, 25, 26

Stewart, William W. "Doc," xix, 8
Stiegler, Morgan, 179
Stitt, Sonny, 119, 128, 169
"Stop Kidding" (song), 107
Storyville Club (Boston), 149
Storyville label, 80
"Stranger in Paradise" (song), 44
Strawbridge, John E. "Bud," xix, 37, 48, 50, 63
Streetcar Named Desire, A 23
"Stroll, The" (song), 158
Sudhalter, Richard, 165, 189
Sulkin, Jake "Firetop," 11, 12, 13, 14
Sullivan, Buddy, xii, xix, xxi, 52, 63, 65, 66, 70, 72, 73, 133, 142, 169, 175, 182, 183
Sullivan, John L., 98
"Sunny" (song), 50
Supman, Milton, 79
"Sweetheart of Sigmund Freud" (song), 83
Swing Buddies, 31
Swingers, The! (LP), 34
Symphony Sid, 81
Synco Septette, 105
Szor, Samuel "Sam," xix, 63
T. J. Fowler Band, 117
Tabernilla, xii, 12, 17, 110
"Tain't What Ya Do" (song), 21
Takas, John, 157
Takas, William J. "Bill," xii, xix, 68, 69, 71, 72, 73, 139
"Take the A Train" (song), 79
"Take Five" (song), 85
Take Six vocal sextet, 179
Tal Farlow Trio, 71
"Tale of an African Lobster" (song), 83
Talmage, Dee, 75
"Tangerine" (song), 50
Tanner, Paul, 158
Tate, Buddy, 128
Tate's Midway Nite Club, 78, 117, 121
Tatum, Arlene, 9, 180
Tatum, Arthur, Jr. "Art," xii, xv, xvi, xviii, xix,

xxi, 1-9, 11, 17, 19, 21, 23, 24, 32, 56, 71, 78, 92, 101, 124, 129, 131, 133, 152, 166, 179

Tatum, Karl, 1

Tatum Legacy, The, 9

Taylor, Cecil, 89

Taylor, Gene, 127

Taylor, Sam "The Man," 114

"Tea for Two" (song), 6

Teagarden, Weldon Leo "Jack," xix, 55, 100, 102

Ted Heath Band, 78, 81

Ted Heath's 100th London Palladium Sunday Concert (LP), 81

tenderloin district, 92

"Tenderly" (song), 85, 118

territory bands, vii, 15, 21, 65, 98, 101, 121

Terry Gibbs Quartet, 131

Terry, Clark, 168

Terry, J. Frank, xv, 15, 23, 24

Thacher, Addison Q., xix, 97

"Thanks for the Memory" (song), 37, 38

"Theme from the Odd Couple" (song), 152

"These Foolish Things" (song), 58

They Shoot Horses Don't They? 22

Thigpen, Ben, 23, 31

"Things Ain't What They Used To Be" (song), 89

Thomas Hotel, 114

Three Deuces (New York), 55

Tiberi, Frank, 47

"Tiger Rag" (song), 6, 8, 24

"Time Further Out" (song), 85

Time magazine, 82, 85, 89, 183

"Time Out" (song), 85

"Tippin' In" (song), 44

Tivoli, 156

Todd Rhodes and His Toddlers, xviii, 113, 184

Toledo Arts Council, 179

Toledo Ballet Association, 142

Toledo Blade, xi, xii, 8, 27, 80, 82, 89, 91, 110, 180, 181, 182, 183, 184

"Toledo Blues" (song), 8

Toledo Botanical Gardens, 179

Toledo Club, 35, 67

Toledo Jazz Orchestra, xxi, 38, 52, 66, 71, 73, 86, 142, 147, 168, 169, 174, 179

Toledo Jazz Society, 52, 86, 123, 142, 174

Toledo Museum of Art, xi, 3, 85, 142

Toledo News-Bee, 92, 183

Toledo Opera, 142

Toledo Press Club, 82

Toledo School for the Arts, 179

Toledo Script, 80

Toledo Sepia City Press, 80

"Toledo Shuffle" (song), 89

Toledo Symphony Orchestra, 3, 142

Toledo Times, 25, 80, 181, 184

Toledo-Lucas County Public Library, xiii, 9

Tommy Dorsey Bands, 21

Tonal Expressions (LP), 86

Tongring, Jack, 75, 183

"Tonsillectomy" (song), 58

Tony Packo's, vii, xii, 111-112, 147

Toscanini, Arturo, 89, 103

Transition label, 80

Trent, Alphonse, 17

Trianon Ballroom, xii, 30, 31, 35, 36, 67, 69, 86, 108, 181, 185

"Tribute to Two Harolds, A" (song), 142

Tristano, Lennie, 1, 124, 157

Tri-State Festival, 145

Trudell, Johnny, 167

Truman, Harry, 28, 161

Trumbauer, Frankie, 109

Tsipis, Angelo, 13, 14, 180

Tucker, Ben, 138

Turner, BuBu, 127

Turner, Joe, 8

Turner, Lana, 59

"Twisted" (song), 32

Ubelhardt, Jim, 66

Ulanov, Barry, 53, 59

"Uncle Sambo goes Mambo," 48
Underwater, 48
University of Cincinnati, 80
University of Michigan, 49, 187
University of Oregon, xi, xiii, 184, 188
University of Toledo, 32, 34, 41, 46, 65, 71, 84, 85, 86, 88, 89, 179, 183
"Until the Real Thing Comes Along" (song), 121
urban blues, 80, 121
Val's in the Alley (Cleveland), 5
Valley Forge Military Academy, 161
Van Fleet, Jo, 171
Van Vechten, Carl, 102, 189
Variety magazine, 91
Vaughan, Sarah, 52, 131
Village Barn (New York), 50
Village Vanguard (New York), 128
Vinegar, LeRoy "The Walker," 135
Vinton, Bobby, 140
Vivian Garry Trio, xvi, 55, 56, 59, 60
vocalization, 32, 153
Wade, Jimmy, 23
Wagner, Ron, 38, 39, 48, 181
Waite High School, 137
Waiters and Bellman's Club, xii, 5, 16, 31, 56, 67, 117, 127, 149, 156
Waller, Fats, xvi, 1, 3, 17, 31, 32
Waller, Thomas (Rev.), 31
Walter, Jack V., vii, 51, 52, 70, 133, 147, 149, 150, 152, 153, 156, 162, 182, 185
Waltz for Debby (LP), 157
Warehouse District, 95
Warrington, Tom, 158, 167, 174, 179
Washington, Dinah, 50, 117
"Watch What Happens" (song), 52
Waters, Ethel, 8, 27
Waters, Johnny, 2
Watkins, Doug, 132
Watson, Leo, 59
Wayne State University, 179, 188

Wayne, Chuck, 59
"We're Strong for Toledo" (song), 51
Webb, Chick, 102, 106
Webb, Jack, 111
Webb, Lawrence Arthur "Speed," vii, 15, 17, 21
Webster, Ben, 81
Webster, Freddy, 166
Wells, Dicky, 100, 189
Wesley Helvey's Band, 109
West Coast Jazz, 62, 83
Westgate Shopping Center, 172
WGR radio, 113
WGTE TV, 9, 180, 181, 186
Whalen, John, 161
"What's New" (song), 51
"White Negro, The" (essay), 78
White, Bob, xi, xix, 39, 46, 75, 132, 133, 151, 182
White, Skip, 141
Whiteman, Paul, 91
Whittier Grade School, 67
Whyte, Zach, xix, 1, 17, 21, 22
Wilberforce University, 105, 121
Wilborn, Dave, 105
Wilburn, David, 125
"Wild About Harry" (song), 28
Wild One, The, 83
Wildcat Shoot, 92
Wiley, Frank (Judge), 42
Wiley, Lee, 76
Willard, Jess, 98
Willard-Dempsey Fight, vii, xii, 97-99
William, Cootie, 117
Williams, Bert, 99, 100
Williams, Esther, 82
Williams, Francis, xix, 24, 25, 89, 166
Williams, LeRoy, 100
Williams, Martin, 99
Williams, Paul, 114, 116
Willow Beach Park, 15, 23, 28
Willys-Overland, 92, 95
Wilson, Dick, 21

Wilson, Gus, 17
Wilson, John S., 5, 189
Wilson, Juice, 101
Wilson, Theodore Shaw "Teddy," xix, 15, 17, 19, 24, 110, 189
Winters, Jonathan, 17
Witherspoon, Jimmy, 173
WNEW radio, 56
Wolkins, Ric, 49, 169
Women's Christian Temperance Union, 92, 95
Woodbury, Mitch, xxi
Wooding, James D. "Dewey," xix, 2
Woods, Phil, 150, 151, 152, 172
woodshedding, 106, 107
Woodward High School, xix, 38, 69
Woody Herman and his Thundering Herd, 47
Woody Herman Fan Club, 48
Woody Herman Orchestra, 47
Woody Herman Road Band 48 (LP), 36
Woody Herman's Four Brothers Band, 36, 67
World of Henry Orient, The, 155
"Wrap Your Troubles in Dreams" (song), 3
WSPD radio, 8, 31, 52, 113
WSPD TV, 68, 69
WTOD radio, 63, 80, 116
Wynn, Bob, 138
Xavier University, 118
Yammick, Clyde, 49
Yaranowsky, Chalky Red, 95
"Yard Dog Mazurka" (song), 31
"Yardbird Suite" (song), 59
Yonke, David, 3, 128
"You Belong to Me" (song, 117
"You Took Advantage of Me" (song), 3, 4
"You're the Top" (song), 1
Young, Elise, 98
Young, Gig, 22
Young, Graham, 166
Young, Lester, 17, 36, 56, 62, 138, 162
"Yours" (song), 50
Zach Whyte Band, 17, 21, 22

Zentner, Si, 140
Ziegfeld's Follies, 27
Zoot Sims Quartet, 71, 140

www.ingramcontent.com/pod-product-compliance
Lightning Source LLC
Chambersburg PA
CBHW061820290426
44110CB00027B/2923